A Queer Bestiary

A Queer Bestiary

Non/Humans in Contemporary U.S. Literature

Christopher Lloyd

THE UNIVERSITY OF GEORGIA PRESS ‡ ATHENS

Athens, Georgia 30602
www.ugapress.org

Designed by Rebecca A. Norton
Set in Adobe Jenson Pro 11/15

Printed digitally

EU Authorized Representative
Easy Access System Europe—Mustamäe tee 50, 10621
Tallinn, Estonia, gpsr.requests@easproject.com

Library of Congress Cataloging-in-Publication Data

Names: Lloyd, Christopher, 1987– author
Title: A queer bestiary : non/humans in contemporary U.S. literature / Christopher Lloyd.
Description: Athens : The University of Georgia Press, 2026. | Includes bibliographical references.
Identifiers: LCCN 2026018215 (print) | LCCN 2026018216 (ebook) | ISBN 9780820380506 hardback | ISBN 9780820380513 paperback | ISBN 9780820380520 epub | ISBN 9780820380537 pdf
Subjects: LCSH: American literature—21st century—History and criticism | Human ecology in literature | Human-animal relationships in literature | Animals in literature | Ecology in literature | LCGFT: Literary criticism
Classification: LCC PS231.H86 L56 2026 (print) | LCC PS231.H86 (ebook)
LC record available at https://lccn.loc.gov/2026018215
LC ebook record available at https://lccn.loc.gov/2026018216

With love for my companions,
then and now: *Goldie, Honey, Coco, Freddie*

Contents

Preface

I

This bestiary focuses on the ways that contemporary U.S. literature reveals the complex entanglements and interrelations between human and nonhuman worlds, especially as they are shaped by (and, in turn, shape) categories like gender, sexuality, race, disability, and others. These entanglements shed light and operate on the distribution of injustice, vulnerability, and other forms of violence in the name of normativity. I use the term "non/human," as in the book's title, after the work of Noreen Giffney and Myra J. Hird, who theorize the term to describe the enmeshment of human and nonhuman forms.[1] Other terms are used in the fields of animal and posthuman studies (more-than-human, other animals, etc.), but—as I explain more in the introductory chapter—I use "nonhuman" when referring to specific forms and "non/human" when I am talking about the interrelations of humans and others.

The book is an open and unfinished archive, a resistant taxonomy. It is a queer menagerie, in which representations of humans and nonhumans—from groundhogs to taxidermized deer to hunters—are held briefly in focus but soon evade our grasp. The book is an attempt to account for the deeply populous world of nonhumans in U.S. literature today. I began to think through some human-nonhuman connections in my previous monograph (in which I read various forms of life and environment against the backdrop of slavery's aftermaths). This book extends some of those theoretical interventions but in a very different way, though still within the disciplinary frame of American studies.

I focus on contemporary U.S. literature not because I think it offers an exemplary or exceptional model of non/human representation but because it depicts queer entanglements in specifically textured ways: that is, rooted in cultural and historical contexts, like westward expansion, settler colonialism, enslavement, pet keeping, and so on, as well as shaped by particular literary forms and styles. To understand human-nonhuman relations is, on the one hand, to see the human and nonhuman in a broad schema (indeed, lots of the work in animal studies does not limit itself to national or even temporal boundaries); but, on the other hand, it is necessary to track the specific histories and dynamics of non/human production in certain locations and times. For this book, I mean the contiguous United States, but the texts herein inevitably lead us beyond those bordered locations, to other global geographies. Understanding the non/human in this book requires looking at a set of cultural materials in context. I also read literature instead of other cultural forms to 1) limit the corpus, as this study could get *wildly* out of hand (it already did!), and 2), more importantly, to hone in on the literary ways that non/human relations are depicted. I focus on how language and form do queer things at the site of the human-nonhuman interaction. This is not to say film or visual art do not do similar things, but there is a much-needed focus on language's possibility that a multimedia project might have skimmed over. It is also in twenty-first-century U.S. texts that we see, I think, some of the most startling and innovative depictions of non/human worlds. Of course, earlier literatures do related work, but I am most interested in those contemporary works—written in the midst of a climate crisis, the Anthropocene (if we want to call it that), globalization and neoliberalism, and radical upheavals in social and political life—which destabilize the human through careful attention to questions of race, gender, sexuality, and species.

Colleen Glenney Boggs says, "Animals are animals in American literature, and we have not adequately accounted for them as such," and "accounting for them will change how we read that literature." Boggs is suggesting that seeing animals *as* animals (and not merely as symbols) is one way to transform our reading practices in American studies. Indeed, I argue that the nonhumans in this book are both themselves and more than that: often living and breathing organisms and ecologies as well as literary figurations. For Boggs, animal representation in U.S. literature is the "terrain where questions of species—human, animal—get worked out at the intersections with race and gender."[2] This bestiary extends that theoretical work into the contemporary moment and beyond only race and gender.

I do this work, too, via a practice of close reading, framed by cultural and historical context. Close reading is the central practice of literary study, and it has a particular role to play when thinking about representations of the human and other animals. As a method, too, it builds on the ways that medieval bestiaries themselves used a kind of close reading practice when they devoted attention to specific nonhuman forms and the truths that they might illuminate. Derek Ryan, in his introduction to a collection on literary animal studies, similarly argues that "an analysis of 'literature and animals' . . . requires not just close reading but *careful* reading in the two main senses of that word, which is to say being *concerned for* animals as well as *circumspect about* the assumptions we hold regarding them." Thus, careful reading (of metaphor, allegory, narrative devices, syntax, and so on) ensures that close reading does not become "closed reading," not least because of the "centrality of human language" to our literary practices, which by necessity exclude nonhuman lives, forms, and ecologies.[3] The emphasis of my book, moreover, is on the *interrelations* of humans and nonhumans, which enables more reflexivity when it comes to writing with and about nonhuman others.

A brief note on "queer" too (though I'll unpack it more in the introductory chapter): I use the term throughout the book not solely as an identity marker but, in the vein of much queer studies scholarship, as often a querying and undoing of identity. While we will see characters who may or may not go under the banner of LGBTQ+, more often than not we will see queerness as it plays out at the site of human/nonhuman connectivity. That queerness is anti-identitarian and antinormative is to some a given, though of course, in Lauren Berlant's words, "to queer something doesn't mean just to stick an antinormative needle into it, but to open up a vein to unpredicted and nonsovereign infusions."[4] As such, I am not calling all nonhumans queer, nor all humans that engage with nonhumans queer, nor necessarily all the texts I examine queer; rather, I identify the glimmers of the nonsovereign and its wild kin in a range of textual examples.

Non-sovereignty leads me to a small digression on human exceptionalism. Of course, the literary texts I look at are predominantly about—are centered on, are narrated by, and tell us things about—humans. Though they also have things to say about the nonhuman, I want to make clear that this book isn't just about reclaiming "the animal" or "nature" or "ecology" from a humanist focus but rather about showing the human's imbrication in nonhuman worlds (an imbrication I see as queerly inflected). This is a querying—but not a wholesale vanquishing—of humans in contemporary literature. But it's worth stating the obvious: Humans and nonhumans are not so distinct, and indeed are so similar and connected that we usually disavow that fact. As Judith Butler puts it, "human bodies are not distinguished in any absolute way from animal bodies, even though we can easily concede some differences," a statement so simple that we often forget its veracity.[5]

We know—though "know" is obviously a limited word here, given our inability to traverse species boundaries—that nonhumans have a breadth of emotions, have complex inner and outer lives, communicate and engage with one another in and through what we might call languages, and so on. And of course, I am using a specific human language to describe nonhuman qualities that would not be called that (if they would be called anything at all) by those nonhumans, even if they could communicate in ways that we could recognize or acknowledge. The array of nonhumans I have chosen to include in this book is not a way to shore up a kind of anthropocentrism—"look! human traits are so good that nonhumans have them too"—but rather to say quite clearly from the start that there is nothing magical, exceptional, or distinct about humans. When we see so-called human traits in nonhumans, we must simply say that these traits are nothing special after all. And, of course, I am not only interested in this book in nonhumans that are proximate to humans, or that are only meaningful within our frames of reference. But spelling out some of these species overlaps—facts I have gathered along the way of writing this book, largely because they are fascinating and are not, I think, widely known—is one way of staking a claim to an anti-anthropocentrism.

For example, we know that humans and chimpanzees share almost 99 percent of DNA, and thus are more similar than different;[6] we know that elephants are aware of, and are attentive to, other dead elephants, whether kin or not, in ways that we could describe as mourning or grieving;[7] we know horses can play, tease one another, and joke, as well as think "strategically" by planning ahead;[8] we know that ants can recognize suffering or pain;[9] we know that trees can think, communicate, share resources, and help one another;[10] we know that some cannibalistic squid use their skin and bioluminescence to communicate with one another through patterns akin to linguistic syntax;[11] and we know that dogs, horses, goats, and cats can read one's facial expressions, and some prefer those expressions to be happy (not cats, of course).[12] I could build up any number of examples here, but even that apparently "key human trait" of self-reflection has been scrutinized, as scientists think that some nonhuman animals are capable of metacognition.[13] In short, the human and the nonhuman are so alike, so enlaced with one another, so undifferentiable in many ways, that to talk of them separately makes little sense. As such—and I'll explore this more later—I use "non/human" throughout to refer to the interconnectedness and the shared worlds or existences of humans and nonhumans, and use the separate terms where needed for specificity.

II

The first major chunk of thinking and writing time for this book came during the first coronavirus lockdown of 2020 in the UK. I don't want to contribute too much to the "pandemic preface" genre, but a key cultural text that stands out from that moment and that ties together so many of this book's preoccupations is Netflix's *Tiger King* (2020), which even at the time of writing, let alone the time of your reading this, feels both old-hat and cliché. Such are the distortions of time in these pandemic years: As soon as the show finished it felt jejune. But watching *Tiger King*, about caged animals (human and otherwise, in zoos and prisons and ways of life), during a moment when many—though not all—of us were trapped inside our homes, triggered questions of freedom and possibility that are generative to this book. The present study looks solely at literary texts, but this brief diversion through a TV text is hopefully a useful tangential cultural example that will frame my thinking about non/human life in the United States today.

Tiger King: Murder, Mayhem, and Madness, to use its full title, is a true-crime documentary series that focuses on Joe Exotic (the eponymous "tiger king"): "a gay, polygamous zoo owner in Oklahoma who breeds tigers, commissions and stars in his own country-music videos, presides over what he describes as 'my little cult' of drifters and much younger men, and ran for governor. . . . He's also currently serving a 22-year prison sentence for, among other charges, trying to arrange the assassination of his nemesis, an animal-sanctuary owner in Florida," named Carole Baskin.[14]

That summary reveals some of the key threads running through the show: the tying together of nonhumans, queerness, the U.S. South, Americanness, captivity, whiteness, class, gender, and so on. We could talk at length about the ways that Joe Exotic's romantic connections with sexually ambiguous (young) white men complexly overlaps with Joe's relationship to his tigers; we could explore the ways that the documentary itself partakes in stereotypical representations of poor white Americans and their consonance with "mayhem and madness"; or we could discuss the deeply gendered and raced dynamics of nonhuman ownership, captivity, and human exceptionalism. That doesn't even address the show's tangle of politics and ethics.

For the purposes of this preface, though, I want to pinpoint *Tiger King*'s particular brand of Americanness, as defined by J. Wortham and Wesley Morris on their podcast *Still Processing*. On the April 9, 2020, episode, the pair offer a wide-ranging conversation about *Tiger King*'s particular brand of nationalism. They begin by describing Joe's "entitlement" as "so American": "the obsession with freedom" (but only for humans). They also call the show a kind of "poverty porn" and "classploitation" in which *Tiger King* is it itself a zoo, and us the visitors. Yet it's also, for Wortham and Morris, an example of white supremacy, in which white people "get to have fun while committing crimes," which the audience similarly enjoys: "We laugh at someone like Joe Exotic" but "demonize someone like Michael Vick." The racialization in the show is connected to a much longer story of control and entrapment, not just of nonhumans but also of other humans. Morris says, "This entire enterprise . . . struck me as not terribly dissimilar from human enslavement. But it isn't so much that the animals are proxies for enslavement. It's more like the hunger for ownership is really the story."[15]

Central to *Tiger King* is its obsession with captivity, which for Wortham and Morris is a particularly American story (though of course we could read it outward across colonial geographies): "Property ownership, ownership of other creatures, the refusal to acknowledge that there might have to be a limit to how much you can have and land and what you can do on that land because it's yours." Freedom in this show, Wortham concludes—akin to Toni Morrison's summary of whiteness in *Playing in the Dark* (1992)—is dependent on "another being's subjugation," as well as "profit" and "imprisonment."[16] I agree with Wortham that this is a particularly American story. *Tiger King* opens up so many questions about U.S. narratives of captivity and queer entanglements across species lines. Though of course, as Hannah Boast and Nicole Seymour remind us, the show's failure to grapple with issues of race head-on means that we cannot simply praise its potential queer readings.[17] To think sexuality's relation to the non/human while ignoring race is dubious at best (and perhaps indicative of many strains of queer studies that centralize the white cis gay).

I bring this example in here to set up the stall of this book—I have been writing, researching, and teaching for so long about the interconnections of race, gender, sexuality, class, and disability, in ways that constantly fuel not only my intellectual projects but also my ethics. Dedicating attention to the ways that history and memory play out in contemporary U.S. culture requires us to think carefully about the manifold ways that identity is constructed in and through the past. *Tiger King* is but one node in a conversation about what it means to be a human, an American, today. *A Queer Bestiary* does not attempt to account for all contemporary writing about the non/human, but it hopes to offer ways into thinking about multispecies life and ecologies in contemporary U.S. literature.

III

What became clear in my writing process was that putting together an idiosyncratic academic book—based on an idiosyncratic medieval form—had its redirections and changes. I had plans for chapters on nonhumans that did not end up in the final book (bears and were/wolves, for instance), and chapters that I did not foresee (on Tommy Pico's *Nature Poem*, for instance) insisted on their relevance. Even in the planning stage, so many nonhumans had to be left out. I wanted to think about the role of buffalo in Louise Erdrich's *The Round House* (2012); or the insects in Mark Doty's poetry (his dogs do appear, though); or the bees in Jesmyn Ward's *Let Us Descend* (2023); or the arachnids in Tommy Orange's *There There* (2018). In the latter case, one of the main characters, Opal, has spider legs emerge from her own: A bump does not go away, and she thinks, "Were there more legs in there? Was that the spider's body?"[18] Those spider legs both symbolize any number of memories and legacies that refuse to budge from the Indigenous characters' bodyminds, but also simply lodge in the text, unexplained and insistent as nonhuman forces outside of human knowing.

When it came to bears, too, I wanted to think more about those creatures that pop up in numerous U.S. texts. In Andrea Lawlor's *Paul Takes the Form of a Mortal Girl* (2017), for instance, when the eponymous Paul, shape- and gender-shifter, goes to the Michigan Womyn's festival with their love interest Diane, the two are confronted by bears in the forest. A bear rears up at Paul (then in "girl form") as they find themselves caught in between the mother and its cub. But it is Diane who soothes the bear with "gentle bear sounds" and ushers it away.[19] In this moment, it is not just Paul who can seemingly move between sexes and genders, but Diane who opens up thought about trans-species communion and communication.

I also had conversations with people about the elephant story in Torrey Peters's *Detransition, Baby* (2021). The detransitioned Ames—one of the novel's three main characters—has a theory about trans women: that they are juvenile elephants. Ames analogizes trans women via a series of stories about young elephants in Africa who rampage seemingly for fun. Ames narrates how three young elephants had been shot in 2002 in South Africa because they had raped and murdered rhinoceroses; another herd "razed a village" in Sierra Leone; others in Uganda got drunk on "fermenting fruit" and trampled a community in the process. Rather than biological explanations (testosterone, etc.), scientists realized that the young elephants were suffering from "chronic stress, a species-wide trauma" that led to a "breakdown of elephant culture." After moving from "ordered social structures" with clear behavioral norms instilled by elders, the young elephants instead grew up orphaned. The older generations had been poached to extinction, and thus the "familial, social, and emotional skills" required for healthy growth were absent because no elephants were around to pass them on. Trans women, Ames argues, *are* trans elephants—this is metaphor, not simile—because they are a lost generation:

much "stronger and more powerful than we understand," yet deprived of "elders" to help them metabolize pain and trans livability. The older generation of trans women who "died of HIV, poverty, suicide, repression," or were disappeared by medicalization (or even, the book intimates, detransition, in order to simply survive), were not there to support and socialize the young trans women.[20]

I quote at length here to offer another example of the way I am approaching queerness and the non/human in this book. As a cis white queer man, based in the UK, I am aware of my position in relation to much of the literary material I am examining. I want to make sure that my perspective on these texts is clear from the start: I am not trying to itemize or taxonomize, nor to conflate and muddle questions of gender, sexuality, and race. The limitations of my approach are very clear to me, yet I am still interested in the ways that I can think U.S. literature through a queer lens and shed some light on how texts produce questions about human and nonhuman worlds that might be productive for a number of disciplines, not least American studies. Peters's example above is indicative of my project—she is not hierarchizing species difference, nor suggesting that literary metaphor is a way of *using* the nonhuman to simply explain the human. Rather, by putting transness in relation to this particular story of elephants, she is exploring some of the crosscurrents of human exceptionalism that have continually operated via marginalization. The elephants are not a mere figurative gesture: Peters shows how the violences of humanity (poaching, killing, ostracizing, neglecting) move across humans and nonhumans, not *alike* but *in relation*. These are not analogous in an equalized way, but in a complexly layered one. Many more queerly laced stories await us.

NOTES

1. Giffney and Hird, "Introduction."
2. Boggs, *Animalia Americana*, 29, 28.
3. Ryan, "Introduction," 5.
4. Berlant, *On the Inconvenience*, 16.
5. Butler, *Notes Toward*, 132.
6. "DNA: Comparing Humans and Chimps."

7. Goldenberg and Wittemyer, "Elephant Behavior."

8. Slicer, "Joy"; Hearne, *Adam's Task*; Ferguson, "Horses Can Plan."

9. Frank et al., "Wound Treatment."

10. Wohlleben, *The Hidden Life*; Kohn, *How Forests Think*.

11. Burford and Robinson, "Bioluminescent."

12. Müller et al., "Dogs"; Smith et al., "Functionally Relevant"; Nawroth et al., "Goats Prefer."

13. Smith et al., "The Highs."

14. Gilbert, "The Most-Watched."

15. Wortham and Morris, "Frosted Flakes."

16. Wortham and Morris.

17. Boast and Seymour, "Quarantining."

18. Orange, *There*, 165.

19. Lawlor, *Paul*, 89.

20. Peters, *Detransition, Baby*, 99, 100, 101.

Acknowledgments

This book is dedicated to a handful of nonhuman companions that kept me company over the years, even if those creatures can neither read nor understand the words I write here. Looking back, I can perhaps more easily narrate my life story in relation to the "pets" that were around. My list leaves out the gerbils and goldfish (sorry!) and includes a dog, Coco, who was not *my* companion animal per se, but whom I once looked after and love very much. This dedication list is also a story of loss: Goldie ran away before I could form distinct memories of her; Honey I lost contact with because of a romantic breakup, and more recently, I found out, had died; Coco moved to the United States with her lovely humans and canine brother Banjo. Freddie, though, who entered my life with a different ex, is now sharing the sofa as I write this.[1] I foreground this narrative not as a self-centered opening but as a recognition that this project was perhaps always meant to be written: that nonhuman animals have accompanied my development and my thinking, have helped me to understand affective relations in new ways. In other words, where I first saw this book as an offshoot of sorts from my previous monograph, at the time of completion it is a more fundamentally intimate (and yet also capacious) project about non/human relations.

Thanks to the Literature subject group at the University of Hertfordshire, especially Rowland Hughes, for enabling my research leave to get these words down. Thanks also to the History subject group for inviting me to talk about this book's relation to my other scholarship. At Herts, thank you also to Sarah Flynn for always championing me (it means the world); Constantine Sandis, for your research mentorship; Matthew Holman and Kaja Franck for being wonderful friends and interlocutors.

Thank you, Jennifer Aston and Elsa Devienne for inviting me to present some of this book at Northumbria University (and to the participants for their useful questions and comments). Thank you, Kiron Ward for inviting me to present at St Andrews University, and for always supporting my work so wholeheartedly. Thank you to Rebecca Macklin and Nadhia Grewal for pitching a British Association for American Studies panel on the queer nonhuman many years ago, where I first tried out some material on Justin Torres. And thank you to the attendees of the Percival Everett conference in London in 2024, where I presented some work on *Wounded*.

Thank you to the participants of the "post45" workshop gathering at Maynooth University in June 2022, not only for their incredibly helpful feedback ("be wilder" and "[redacted]'s work is giving *late career*" still ring out in my mind) but for inspiring me to think afresh about the book and to trust my queer instincts. In particular, thanks to Catherine Gander for inviting me, to Alix Beeston for being so generous and encouraging when I really needed it, and to Christine Okoth and Arin Keeble (among others) for their comradeship.

Thanks, also, to all those people who responded to my social media calls for examples of texts including nonhumans (some of which appear in these pages): Westley Barnes, Jennifer Cameron, Steve Gronert Ellerhoff, Charlotte Gorham, Tim Groenland, Arin Keeble, Pat Massey, Monica Miller, Katie Noble, Peter Schmidt, Nicole Seymour, Peter Sloane, Alexander Williamson. Thank you, Ethan Mollick, who I don't know, but whose threads on Twitter (I'm not calling it X) about nonhumans have been super useful.

Thank you to everyone who read the book proposal and later chapters: Jacob Breslow, Christopher Clark, Jake Erickson, Daniel Fountain, Stephen Guy-Bray, Daisy Henwood, Paul Johnson, Arin Keeble, and Rebecca Macklin. Thank you, Carl White, for reading so much of this book and giving the funniest track-changes a guy could ask for. Thank you, Seán Hewitt and Geoffrey Maguire, for great reading recommendations.

Thank you to those at the University of Georgia Press, especially Sarah Shermyen and Bethany Snead, for their support and (endless) patience with getting the manuscript from me, and Anjelica Fabro for the last-minute help.

Thank you, Gboyega Odubanjo, for helping me think more clearly about ideas of "the human" and of Black life and joy. You are missed.

Thank you, Danielle Cameron, for your edits, enthusiasm, friendship, support, and rooftop views.

Thank you, Jessica Rapson, for cowriting our article on Barbara Kingsolver's *Flight Behavior*, which makes a brief appearance in the "Butterfly" chapter.

For being gorgeous friends and intellectual sparks, thank you: Loïc Bourdeau, Luís Costa, Hilary Emmett, Monika Loewy, Laura Mee, Jon Ward, Jack Westmore, and Kieran Yates.

Thank you, Barry Carpenter, for helping me in all the ways. If it wasn't for our sessions, I might not have ever finished this book.

Aaron Shaughnessy, thank you for coming into my life at just the right moment and being the most radiant presence. I love you more than I can articulate.

For supporting me always, thank you: Mum, Dad, Andrew, Catherine, Joseph, and Lilly.

NOTES

1. For a devastating glance at cat-sharing after a breakup, see Sam McBean's "Bent Out of Shape."

INTRODUCTION

Introduction

Toward A Queer Bestiary

bestiaries cannot contain what they attempt to

I

The slippery and mutable boundaries between humans and nonhumans are often figured queerly in twenty-first-century U.S. literature. This book examines some of the ways that nonhumans are brought into intimate, estranging contact with humans in contemporary novels, short stories, poems, and nonfiction. Through detailed attention to a selection of real and imagined flora, fauna, and other phenomena in the bestiary form—from horses to taxidermy to dogs and extinction—I probe the ways in which humans and their others (animal, creature, inhuman, nonhuman, unhuman, posthuman, more-than-human) are queerly entangled. Borrowing and extending the figure of the non/human from Noreen Giffney and Myra J. Hird, this book is interested in the blurriness (the slash) between the human and the nonhuman.[1] As such, the book tracks the ways in which the category of *human* has been ossified heteronormatively across time, and also thinks about how contemporary U.S. literature unravels and questions the distinctions between humans and others.

Thus, this book sits in a much larger debate in humanities scholarship about rethinking the humanist focus of our work: that is, bringing animals, things, forces, affect, objects, matter, and ecologies, into the center. *A Queer Bestiary* argues that the human has never been solid, distinct, or singular; that nonhumans of various kinds open up questions of queerness; and that recent literary representations of humans and nonhumans queer the boundaries between these two categories. The human and its normative borders will be unraveled through the following literary investigations. The book sits predominantly in contemporary literary studies and American studies, but it also draws on work from a range of overlapping and interpenetrating disciplines: queer studies, trans studies, Black studies, Indigenous studies, animal studies, posthumanism, ecocriticism, and more.

This introductory chapter unpacks the various terms in my title—"bestiary," "queer," "non/human"—and how they relate to one another. But as noted in this book's preface, I am thinking about contemporary U.S. literature because it seems particularly invested in human-nonhuman relationships that are rendered queerly. That is—and I want to make this point clear from the start—it is not that nonhumans are *innately* queer in these texts, or that *all* the humans are queer (though some are), or that the non/human (i.e., the entangling of the two) is queer, or that *anything* outside of the human is necessarily queer. Rather, queerness, as an anti- or nonnormativity, a dismantling and reorienting of purportedly stable categories like sex, gender, and race (among others), resides in contemporary U.S. literature *at the site of non/human interaction*. The texts relentlessly explore that murky and fluid terrain as queer in some sense—whether explicitly in relation to LGBTQ+ life, culture, and politics, or as a kind of nonnormative frisson: as Sara Ahmed puts it, an orientational disturbance to "the order of things."[2] I will come back to queerness below, but for now: Queer in this book refers not just to nonnormative sexualities and genders but also to other kinds of subject positions cast outside of normativity, as well as a broader turn—with queer studies—away from "the subject" and "the object" as our traditional foci.

II

A bestiary (or a "book of beasts"), produced largely in the twelfth to fourteenth centuries, was a text that offered spiritual and moral lessons to its readers. For those in the Middle Ages, the bestiary was made of "accumulated folklore, legend, pseudoscience, and rudimentary scientific observation of an assortment of real and imaginary animals" organized zoologically, into categories such as beast or fish.[3] There are also examples of nonhuman matter in bestiaries, like stones and leaves and "composite creatures" such as "human-animal forms," like griffins.[4] I continue this historical trend by attending, in this book, to both nonhuman animals and other non/human entanglements, such as oceans, hybrids, and taxidermy. Historically, each of the nonhuman descriptions and images would be used to "illustrate points of Christian dogma and morals."[5] The bestiary's forebear was the Greek *Physiologus* (from around the second century AD), which was often "more theological" or "mystical," but "the bestiary expands the moral-ethical content considerably," becoming more didactic.[6] Important to both forms is not only the cobbled-together nature of the texts—always borrowing from various sources—but also the ways in which nonhumans function symbolically. While the *Physiologus* and the bestiary had a moralistic message—one could learn something spiritual by attending to particular lessons from the nonhuman animal world—they nonetheless entrenched in the popular thought of antiquity and the Middle Ages that creatures could gesture toward something beyond their brute reality.

As the editors of the *Angelaki* special issue "Tranimacies" (which draws together transness, the animal, animacy, and intimacies) put it, "The medieval bestiary is a boundary-making concept and a hierarchy-building instrument, drenched with morality, which continues to influence present interspecies relations."[7] The bestiary form helps produce and uphold certain kinds of normative species hierarchies, inflected as they are by questions of race, gender, sexuality, class, and ability. As Leah DeVun explains, while moral lessons were derived from nonhumans, "aberrant sexuality was a prominent trope" in bestiaries, especially as it was tied to racialized and ethnic embodiments. DeVun tracks hermaphrodites as they appear in works from the European Middle Ages, demonstrating how they were deployed as figures that transgressed and traversed "sexual taxonomies" and geographical locations. Hermaphrodites helped yoke together nonhumans who "expressed deviant or doubled sex" (like bats, rabbits, vultures, and hyenas) with racialized and Othered humans, such as Muslim and Jewish people. The linking of "confused" sexual difference with race, gender, and animality further bolstered a taxonomy of difference for the bestiary's readers.[8] Bestiaries had another wave of popularity in the nineteenth century as empire grew and proliferated. Because the cataloging and ordering of species was so "embedded" in the "discursive landscape of exploration, conquest, and administration," the bestiary helped to reinforce colonial "reach and its enduring knowledge regimes."[9] In all, bestiaries have a long history of enforcing and propagating species hierarchies as well as normative forms of life. As such, why turn to this form now?

Where the editors of *Animalia: An Anti-Imperial Bestiary for Our Times* (2020) see their bestiary collection as "hybrid and unconventional," a "provocation to new ways of seeing and writing about empire," I want *A Queer Bestiary* to pick up that hybridity and provocation but in relation to queerness and literary depictions of the nonhuman.[10] In its organization, presentation, and focus, the present book attempts to query the earlier form, adding more nuance and texture to the way that we think non/humans in contemporary literature. If the historical bestiary is about certainty, fixity, and singular meaning, this one is about uncertainty, unfixity, and capacious meaning. Queering the form and its contents involves reorienting the ways that we talk about life (human and otherwise), as well as critiquing the normativity at the heart of the humanist project. In this sense, taking the bestiary form and putting it to skewered ends not only remakes the medieval model anew but helps to undo its violently taxonomizing history.[11]

Such a project is not without its forebears: Indeed, there seems to be a renaissance of sorts for the bestiary form in the twenty-first century. Reasons for this might, of course, include the planet's precarious position in terms of global warming, rising sea levels, acidification of the oceans, and human population growth, among much else. I see the return to the bestiary as a return to a way of knowing and schematizing, an attempt to grasp some of the complexity of our world as it fades and falls apart in front of our (human) eyes. Rather than a religious mode of sense-making, these contemporary bestiaries are secular, but with a similar attentiveness to the proliferations of life and being on the planet. Gerald Hausman's *Meditations with Animals: A Native American Bestiary* (1986), Richard E. Strassberg's translated *A Chinese Bestiary: Strange Creatures from the Guideways Through Mountains and Seas* (2002),[12] Amy Leach's *Things That Are* (2012), and Rebecca Solnit and Mona Caron's *A California Bestiary* (2010)[13] all use the form.

A companion to this book, Leigh Claire La Berge's *Marx for Cats: A Radical Bestiary* (2023) traces the feline through economic history and thought to liberatory ends. And Antoinette Burton and Renisa Mawani's edited collection *Animalia* is a relation of this book in its gathering together of nonhuman animals in light of race. However, where my focus is on queerness and contemporary U.S. literature, *Animalia* thinks more broadly about the ways that nonhuman animals were implicated in the long histories of colonialism and imperialism. Perhaps the closest model to my own is Tom Tyler's *Ciferae: A Bestiary in Five Fingers* (2012), in which he tracks a number of animals that appear in the work of philosophers such as Kant and Nietzsche, the animals being mere "placeholders" for ideas rather than full beings. Where Tyler uses the bestiary to reanimate those creatures, I want to turn away from the white and heteronormative focus of much posthuman and animal studies work. Where Tyler's project is innovative, it is also, like much in the field, indebted to a white male intellectual (philosophical) tradition. (I will come back to this later.) The bestiary, then, has long been used as a form to make sense of the nonhuman, whether through moralizing and Christian means or through more recent philosophical and historical ones. In each case, the nonhuman is imbued with significance beyond its forms.

The idea of the bestiary lingers too in scholarly work that attempts to gather and "archive" contemporary objects of analysis. Queer studies has turned often to the archive to understand all manner of histories, affects, subjects, and phenomena.[14] For instance, Sianne Ngai calls her 2005 book *Ugly Feelings* "a bestiary of affects . . . filled with rats and possums rather than lions, its categories of feeling generally being, well, weaker and nastier."[15] Ngai uses the bestiary as a formal model for her book and uses animals metaphorically to gesture to the kinds of feelings and affects explored in the book.[16] As with *Ugly Feelings*, *A Queer Bestiary* is as much an archive as it is a bestiary—though it is not an archive aimed at totality and comprehension but rather at partiality and connectivity. It is not an airtight vault of historical documents and artifacts but a particular and partial accumulation of literary examples. The following chapters bring into a focus a selection of literary texts in relation to one another. While Jacques Derrida has noted the dual dynamics inherent in "archive fever" (simultaneous collection and destruction, remembering and forgetting),[17] I am keen to stress the slippery and tangential nature of this book's archive-work. That is, if archive fever runs in two directions at once, coherence and partiality, this archive of texts and non/humans is by its nature incomplete. I have selected contemporary texts that speak to one another, but there are so many more that could be added to this archive. Jack Halberstam writes, in *In a Queer Time and Place* (2005), that his book's "archive is not simply a repository; it is also a theory of cultural relevance, a construction of collective memory, and a complex record of queer activity."[18] Thus, rather than storing and fossilizing examples of non/human representations, I am pointing to their relevance and importance in the present moment. Like the unruly gatherings of objects, artifacts, and matter in the queer archives of Halberstam, Ngai, and others, this archive of non/humans opens up questions and connections.

I am wary of fixing—through the archive, the bestiary—a taxonomic and categorical form as the mode for approaching queerness, not least because these ways of thinking about and classifying the world are rooted in violent histories of colonialism that sought to, among much else, stabilize and fix gender, race, sexuality, and other categorizations. Ann Laura Stoler notes that racialization, for instance, was a "central colonial sorting technique" which distributed physical and psychological markers to particular groupings of people.[19] Classificatory schemes and hierarchies justified slavery, colonialism, and other violent endeavors.[20] Colonial taxonomies of racialization also overlapped of course with categories of sex, sexuality, and gender. Thus, we should be incredibly wary of engaging with historical forms that produced violent normative effects. As Marquis Bey writes, "Much of the normative gesture to taxonomize comes from a sense of identities and knowledges being ownable only by those who occupy certain classifications. Too, it often goes unnoticed that classifications are not self-evident; classifications are in fact constructions."[21] In Bey's framing, taxonomizing (whether self- or other-defined) is not evidence of natural order but of normative construction. As such, while forces of marginalization and domination have figured certain populations outside of the human (lesser-than, dehumanized), those categorizations were and are not totalizing. As Stoler puts it, "Colonial categories were binding but unbound within them, were excessively rigid and exceeded their limits," thus revealing the precarity at the heart of this taxonomic method.[22] Something always escapes and cannot be fully captured. As fugitive subjects, marginalized people everywhere have resisted and reworked the classifications marshaled around them. *A Queer Bestiary* does not want to capture its subjects and objects in some kind of rhetorical zoo, but to hold them temporarily still—catch their fleeting movements—before they break out of sight.

What, then, is a queer bestiary? To clarify, it is not that the humans or nonhumans in this book are necessarily queer, but rather the boundaries between them often are. And, more importantly, it is my bestiary itself that is queer; it is a queering form. It is queer for a number of reasons. First, the bestiary is filled with strangeness, weirdness, otherness, the non- and antinormative.

While earlier bestiaries contained this too, they intended to produce normative schemas out of differentiating kinds of life. Second, the bestiary focuses on literary texts that map gender, race, sexuality, class, ability, and so on in relation to one another and across species lines. Third, the book focuses on those non/human *relations* that might be queer or are touched by queer concerns: It is in the entanglements that queerness is visible. Fourth, as noted, the bestiary is non-containing and non-taxonomic: that is, rather than schematizing nonhumans, they always break free and reveal their multiplicity. Fifth, the book moves between the "real" and the "less real" (dogs and machine-hybrids), sitting in the liminality these designations fail to uphold. Sixth, the book attends to form and language in literary texts in ways that account for form's queerness, the ways it can do things awry. Seventh, finally, the book shows how non/human boundaries are never fixed, and that identity itself is continually queer(ed) by the texts. In all, then, this is a bestiary that queers its precedents, fails to capture the non/humans it looks at, and holds open space for identity's fluidity.

III

At this point it is worth briefly framing what I mean by queer and queerness. I do not want to rehearse the histories of the fields of queer and trans studies, but there are a few traditions within which I see this book operating. Lee Edelman describes queerness as never "defin[ing] an identity; it can only ever disturb one," because the queer disturbs social organization wholesale, as a structural negativity that is irreducible to a subject position.[23] In a related but not identical vein, Cathy J. Cohen's 1997 article "Punks, Bulldaggers, and Welfare Queens: The Radical Potential of Queer Politics?" reminds us that if we continue to think of queerness *only* as referring to those who are not heterosexual, we "misrepresent the distribution of power within and outside of gay, lesbian, bisexual, and transgendered communities, and therefore limit the comprehensive and transformational character of queer politics." A radical queer politics needs to be "inclusive of all those who stand outside of the dominant constructed norm of state-sanctioned white middle- and upper-class heterosexuality"—punks, bulldaggers, welfare queens—thus requiring an "intersectional analysis that recognizes how numerous systems of oppression interact to regulate and police the lives of most people." Queer politics is not about locating a shared identity or history but about articulating a "shared marginal relationship to dominant power which normalizes, legitimizes, and privileges."[24]

After Cohen's article—which queer and trans and other scholars are still grappling with—David L. Eng, Jack Halberstam, and José Esteban Muñoz published "What's Queer About Queer Studies Now?" (2005), a special issue of *Social Text* which thinks about queer studies' relevance for questions of "empire, globalization, neoliberalism, sovereignty, and terrorism" as well as "immigration, citizenship, prisons, welfare, mourning, and human rights," among much else at the start of the twenty-first century.[25] That article and special issue required queer studies to think beyond the neoliberal identitarian subject narrowly defined, to apply queer frameworks to a range of sociopolitical issues. A 2020 article by Eng and Jasbir Puar extends that remit further, arguing for "objectless critique," which unfixes "queer theory's attachment to the sexual object" and all manner of "proper" subjects and objects enshrined by the field. Thinking the "exceptionalisms" inherent to these foci in queer studies (gender, the nation, race, etc.), Eng and Puar's update looks to objectless critique for its more radical interruption of assumptions about the human altogether. Their interest in animacy and human/inhuman destabilizations inflect my argument here.[26]

Yet, as much trans studies scholarship argues, the queer turn away from bodies, from identities, from material understandings of gender can bring its own problems for trans people. As Cáel Keegan suggests, the "dissolution of heteronormativity" has as one aim the eradication of gender/sex binaries that some trans people still value. If trans people might fight for an understanding of gender as "felt" and corporeal, what happens when queer theory wants to bulldoze all norms and figurations of the gendered self?[27] And, of course, the antinormativity at the heart of much queer studies scholarship has had its own critiques and interrogations. As Robyn Wiegman and Elizabeth A. Wilson posit, what is queer theory without the antinormative, especially given "norms are more dynamic" than much theory allows?[28]

I want to honor Keegan's position by seeing transness as a movement toward both fixity and undoing, toward stable categories which one might transition to, as well as a focus on transition itself as a fluid state. Marquis Bey's work on Black trans feminism sees "gender self-determination" as a "movement toward dissolving given gender ontologies," an advocation for the "ethical requisite to say 'No'" or to decline the "imposition of gender." Black trans feminism in Bey's argument rejects "classificatory violences" and thus urges the abolition of "the categories we may love."[29] Similarly, Eva Hayward and Che Gossett argue that "Black feminism and black thought as always already trans have troubled the categories of binary gender and of medically assigned sex for their historical and contemporary violences."[30] As such, there is a wide variety of queer and trans approaches to theorizing identity and the rejection of it; the analyses within the following chapters move between and across them.

I want to work with scholarship such as that by Aliyyah I. Abdur-Rahman, who argues that "the queer subject inhabits social (and sometimes sexual) margins, throwing into crisis and into relief our most precious and pervasive ideations of the normative, along with the ideological, economic, and political apparatuses in which the violences of normativity operate." So while queer may call up issues of sexuality and gender, it also calls up by necessity other figurations of identity that are cast outside of the cis white able-bodied male heteronormative sphere. For, in many ways, we cannot understand contemporary identitarian claims about sexuality without seeing the birth of these claims and designations in tandem with histories of racism and colonialism. As Abdur-Rahman argues, "The development of discrete sexual categories in the late nineteenth century coincided with the discursive and legislative deployment of racial blackness to support coercive regimes of race-based social stratification between citizens." In this sense, both sexuality (particularly homosexuality) and race (particularly Blackness) were tied in a U.S. context: Both associated with aberrant and excessive sexuality, gay and Black people were thought of as committing "inappropriate, maladapted, and underdeveloped (read: primitive) expressions of sexual desire." In short, "ideas about sexuality derive from and contribute to racial ideologies": Race and gender and sexuality are deeply entwined.[31] In this way, rather than rejecting entirely the stakes of identity, the queer and trans studies I am utilizing are in productive dialogue with Black studies, Indigenous studies, and queer of color critique more particularly, for the ways in which these fields see queerness not as identity position or ontological claim but rather as a state of flux, possibility, rejection, negativity, or destabilization.

The texts in this book engage queerness at the site of human-nonhuman overlaps (the ways that the two are engaged and enlaced) in ways that are not singular or mappable onto queer studies precisely. Queerness emerges, in these texts, in fits and starts, without loyalty to the discipline or its theoretical trajectories. I borrow from a range of these scholars to make sense of the non/human worlds that the books explore.

IV

This brings us to the question of the animal and nonhuman in relation to queerness. Again, it is worth stating that the queerness I examine in this book is not simply *in* human or nonhuman figures but rather in the messy overlaps lingering in the forward slash of non/human. To follow Susan Fraiman's article "Pussy Panic versus Liking Animals: Tracking Gender in Animal Studies" (2012), this book will not simply reinstall Jacques Derrida or Cary Wolfe as "founding fathers" of animal studies, nor will it reproduce a version of that field which sits in "opposition to emotionally and politically engaged work on gender, race, and sexuality."[32] Rather, *A Queer Bestiary* follows much scholarship by queer and trans theorists, and queer of color theorists, along with many others in posthuman and animal studies who see the "human/Animal divide" as primarily a "racial and colonial divide."[33] I build on work that thinks about the human and the nonhuman as those categories come into contact with, are shaped by, and determine sexuality, gender, race, class, dis/ability and so on. I think with scholars such as Nicole Seymour, for instance, who describe a "queer environmentalism" that links queerness and the "natural world through an empathetic, ethical imagination," which advocates for the interconnected oppressions of humans and nonhumans through species hierarchy.[34]

In particular, I use Giffney and Hird's concept of the "non/human," which relies on the forward slash that cleaves the two words: "While the slash opens out onto—facilitates even—explorations of literal, figural, metaphorical and material relationships, transmigrations and hybridisations between the Human and the nonhuman . . . , its positioning marks out the impossibility of applying a hermetic seal to the distinction between—however temporary and shifting—what gets to count as Human and nonhuman."[35] For them, the non/human—a term I use throughout this book—holds open the ways that the human and its others have never been quite so separate or separable, and that the messy borders between them are far from definitive.

Giffney and Hird pose the non/human as queer, then, because of queerness' emphasis on the undoing of "normative entanglements" and the "fashion[ing of] alternative imaginaries."[36] For them, the non/human must be queer because of the way that the figure questions and undoes all forms of normativity. I differ from their position slightly in that I do not argue that all non/humans (the imbrication of the two) are queer, or that the non/human position is itself inherently queer, but rather it is the blurry and fluid slash between them that is often queered (made strange, made nonnormative, is a radical dehiscence) by literary texts.

Different terminology is used by the wealth of scholars in the overlapping fields of animal studies and posthuman studies. For instance, Catherine Parry uses the term "other animals" in her 2017 book as a way of avoiding the "negative and hierarchical configuration" of "nonhuman."[37] And Sharon P. Holland uses a variety of terms in her book *An Other* (2023), where she parses the differences between "hum/animal" (which points to the distinctions between "human being and nonhuman animal being"), "hum:animal" (which shows how, like the non/human, the "animal opens to the human" and vice versa), and "animal life" (which encourages us to "incline our heads elsewhere" by blurring the distinctions between kinds of life).[38]

Joseph Pugliese uses terms such as "other-than-human" and "more-than-human" in his work on forensic ecologies in Palestine. Both terms for him refuse the "non" of nonhuman, which he argues marks "tacit or explicit deficits" (no language, no emotion, etc.) that prop up a kind of anthropocentrism.[39] He suggests that the "other-" and "more-than-" terms refuse a hierarchy of forms and imply—through the hyphens—an imbricated and relational set of ecologies. However, one could just as easily argue that "other-than-human" has its own negative alterity attached. I do not want to get into too many semantic debates here, and scholars working in these fields will be debating the language we use to talk about lifeforms, ecologies, and forms that are not human for a long time. But the non/human, as a term, uses that slash to both solder and blister the forms of human and non- or more-than-human together. Indeed, rather than the relational hyphens of Pugliese's book, the slash gestures to an at once singular and ongoing set of ontological and epistemological crises in humanity's relation to the planet.

As fields, animal studies, posthumanism, and new materialism share an investment in rethinking the dominance of the human as the only category of study or importance, a resistance to humanism and its associated Western anthropocentric logics, as well as an interest in the numerous ways that humans and non/humans are deeply interrelated rather than discrete. The sharp dividing line that humans wield to differentiate themselves from other animals is bankrupt. Or, as Claire Colebrook puts it succinctly, "The opposition between human and animal is tenuous; whatever quality we select as definitively human is either found in animal life . . . or is frequently not found in humans."[40] The field of animal studies, which is one area that this book engages with, is by now vast and interdisciplinary. Common to many of its threads—as evidenced by Companion volumes, such as Linda Kalof's *The Oxford Handbook of Animal Studies* or Lynn Turner, Undine Sellbach, and Ron Broglio's *The Edinburgh Companion to Animal Studies*—is an investment in an anti-anthropocentrism as a way of sloughing off the centrality of the human to our dominant scholarly discourses. Animal studies, in its variety, is concerned with law, ethics, language, embodiment, representation, language, ontology, environmentalism, global warming, zoos, captivity, "pet owning," and much more. The wealth of material in that field infuses the following chapters, many of which focus on particular nonhuman animals like horses, mountain lions, and dogs.

In addition, various studies of the nonhuman suggest that, as N. Katherine Hayles argues, "there are no essential differences or absolute demarcations between bodily existence and computer simulation, cybernetic mechanism and biological organism, robot teleology and human goals."[41] This posthuman emphasis on technology owes much to Donna J. Haraway's essay "A Cyborg Manifesto: Science, Technology, and Socialist-Feminism in the Late Twentieth Century" (1985), in which she argues that a radical feminist politics should push beyond traditional conceptions of the human into other machinelike entanglements.[42] Later definitions by Cary Wolfe, Rosi Braidotti, and others have similarly thought the "post" as both *beyond* and *after* the human as a discrete entity.[43] Other work in the field of new materialisms, too, such as Jane Bennett's *Vibrant Matter* (2010), seeks to reimagine "matter" as not merely "passive," "inert" "stuff." Rather than "ignore the vitality *of* matter and the lively powers *of* material formation, such as the way omega-3 fatty acids can alter human moods," Bennett's thesis is that we see the *affective* nature of the nonhuman, matter as an actant, and our own human bodies as not solely our own (or solely human).[44] In the same year, Diana Coole and Samantha Frost published their edited volume *New Materialisms: Ontology, Agency, and Politics* (2010), which further cemented the turn toward all kinds of materialist innovations, especially the idea that nonhuman matter is agentic.

Yet, as I suggest, in line with numerous critics, the world of the non/human is critically neglectful of issues of race (and, for that matter, gender, sexuality, disability, Indigeneity, etc.) As Zakiyyah Iman Jackson writes, "The resounding silence in the posthumanist, object-oriented, and new materialist literatures with respect to race is remarkable."[45] Diana Leong makes a similar point in her essay "The Mattering of Black Lives" (2016), arguing that Coole and Frost's book in particular overlooks how understandings of race are central to thinking through matter and the non/human. Critics such as Mel Y. Chen, however, are interested in queering and complicating the existing narrative of the post- or non/human. In *Animacies* (2012), for instance, Chen "consider[s] how matter that is considered insensate, immobile, deathly, or otherwise 'wrong' animates cultural life." Animacy, as a concept, moves beyond "stubborn binary systems of difference" like "life/death, . . . human/animal, natural/cyborg" to open up more complicated questions about matter and unravels the humanist hierarchies that would separate out the animate from the seemingly inanimate.[46] Work like Chen's thus installs queerness and race into posthuman and new materialist studies in ways that I want to build on.[47] This overlooking of race and racialization is also widespread in animal studies (though that is changing). Robert Reid-Pharr, for instance, asks how critics can, in posthuman/animal studies, "unsettle" the human without "consideration of the protocols of race and gender in the articulation of humanism" in the first place.[48] Jackson's *Becoming Human* (2020), too, undoes "prevailing conceptions of 'the human' found in Western science and philosophy."[49]

So the human as a category is, and has always been, a technology of normalization, hierarchization, and supremacy. A range of scholars in queer studies, trans studies, Black studies, Indigenous studies, and beyond have argued that the human has always been a normative category that casts out of its fold those human others that are rendered less-than, or other-than, or nonhuman. As Jodi A. Byrd incisively puts it, "the nonhuman turn has already been met with indigenous skepticism at its belated and Columbusing arrival." Indeed, for Byrd, the "turn" toward the other-than-human above has been central to Indigenous ways of knowing and being all along.[50] In that way, this book will use theories from a range of scholars who question the presumptive universality of "the human." I list some of these theories in the following paragraphs not to flatten their differences or to gut their respective lines of particular critique but to offer a sense of the range of scholarship from queer scholars and scholars of color who have taken issue with the simplistic turn to the nonhuman mentioned above.

For instance, as Dana Luciano and Mel Y. Chen ask, has the queer ever *been* human?[51] If queers of all kinds have often been excluded from the conception of the normative human, then how are we to centralize nonhumans as the main objects of study? In other words, what happens for the field of study when we cast aside those humans that have already been cast aside? In a different but related vein, Tavia Nyong'o argues, how do we begin to decentralize the human and humanist assumptions if Black people have never *been* (seen as) human?[52] From slavery and race science to segregation and the "war on crime," Black people have consistently been dehumanized: rendered not-quite-human, animal. Other people of color have also been seen as nonhuman throughout time. Sohail Daulatzai and Junaid Rana ask, from an "antioppressive, anticolonial, and anticapitalist" position: "Can the Muslim be human?"[53] What does it mean when Brown people are cast—by the white normative order—to be at once Muslim, terrorist, barbarous, and far from human?

Similarly, Eva Hayward and Che Gossett argue that "trans" does not have to "reify that category of 'the Human,'" as "trans/gender/sexual can break from the line of succession that consolidates species differences (predicated on racialization, as in 'human/Black') with sexual difference."[54] For Sisseton-Wahpeton Oyate scholar Kim TallBear, Indigenous people "have never forgotten that nonhumans are agential beings" or that nonhumans "do not adhere" to normative categories like "the animal." An Indigenous framework on the nonhuman critiques settler colonialism and its attendant speciesism because of the link between "violence against animals" and those "particular humans who have historically been linked to less-than-human or animal status."[55] The field of animal studies and posthuman studies that I could outline for you, without engagement with Indigenous or queer or Black or queer of color thinking, is one that merely reproduces the normative human.

Such analyses hinge upon the construction of what Sylvia Wynter and other theorists call "Man"—a Western, white, heteronormative figuration—which "overrepresents itself as if it were the human itself."[56] Thus, the move *beyond* the human/Man in posthumanism, animal studies, and their correlative theories has been critiqued by Black studies critics such as Jackson, Alexander Weheliye, Nyong'o, and many others, for the way in which it obscures if not ignores questions of race and racialization in the construction of the human in the first place. As Weheliye notes of Wynter and Hortense Spillers's work, we must "disrupt the governing conception of humanity as synonymous with western Man," a conception that seems to have lingered in much posthuman and animal studies criticism.[57] Though as Katherine McKittrick reminds us about Wynter's work, we must not simply look at "Man" as our sole focus, as it "privileges and centers the very human she (and we) seek to challenge by disregarding or marginalizing the perspectives of Man's human others." Such a view of "only-the-human" risks ignoring "Wynter's ongoing insistence on a species perspective that is tied to our ecological worlds (plot-and-plantation, drought, desertification, global warming and climate change, and so on)."[58] Thus, invoking Wynter's theorization of "Man" must not end with that figure but must move beyond and athwart its normative governing force of "overrepresentation."

Briefly, then, let us turn to a few of the theoretical frames that interrupt and nuance animal and nonhuman studies which shape the critical analyses that follow. Luciano and Chen, for instance, argue that queer studies must reckon with "queer *in*humanisms" because much of the work in the field already has sought to investigate what norms get upheld by and through the idea of the human. They chart a range of scholarship from Gloria Anzaldúa to Leo Bersani that propose the "queer/trans body" as not only "unsettl[ing] the human as norm" but also as "generat[ing] other possibilities—multiple, cyborgian, spectral, transcorporeal, transmaterial—for living." As such, Luciano and Chen suggest that the answer to the question—has the queer ever been human?—is both yes and no: "*Yes*, because this sustained interrogation of the unjust dehumanization of queers insistently, if implicitly, posits the human as standard form, and also because many queer theorists have undeniably privileged the human body and human sexuality as the locus of their analysis. But *no* because queer theory has long been suspicious of the politics of rehabilitation and inclusion to which liberal-humanist values lead, and because 'full humanity' has never been the only horizon for queer becoming."[59]

As such, the queer "runs across or athwart the human," rendering both terms consistently relational. The "encounter" they propose between *queer* and *inhuman*—the messy and complex ways in which queer antinormativity or nonnormativity ruptures and questions, or enhances and proliferates humanness; and the way that humanness has often been the frame through which lives are counted as worthy, as recognizable, as grievable—thus keeps in focus "both the promise and the costs of the call to move 'beyond' the human" in scholarship today.[60]

Within trans studies, Eva Hayward and Jami Weinstein's "Tranimalities in the Age of Trans* Life" (2015) is a vital touchpoint. In this article they argue that "humanism seems not to have advanced our understanding of what it means to be 'human,' especially if the humans we are theorizing do not fit neatly into privileged categories." If the human "delineates a normative standard of legibility" against which everything else is adjudicated in "hierarchical social structures," then this "administration of norms is the justificatory axle through which violent practices of exclusion, domination, and oppression are meted." Hayward and Weinstein write that because so many queer and trans people have rarely been considered "fully human," those in numerous minoritized studies have come to "unpack the underlying frameworks that provide for the standardizing force privileging the anthro-ontological humanist human over all others." Trans* studies, they argue, is significant in this regard. Thinking trans* (with the asterisk) rather than simply "trans" means moving away from strict ontologies, bodies, and identities that "trans" might describe, and toward, instead, "the expressive force *between*, *with*, and *of* that enables the asterisk to stick to particular materializations." The asterisk, Hayward and Weinstein posit, is an "astral symbol miming a starfish's limby reach," a "spiky allergenic pollen soliciting immunological mobilizations, a viral latching-on to mebraneous surfaces of words." It is "paratactic," denoting a "database search," and is "fingery," relational and tactile.[61]

The jubilant descriptions that the authors deploy are rich with non/human figures and metaphors, the starfish at the center. I linger here to suggest not only that queer and trans* study illuminates questions of species, of the animal, of the non/human but that the very matter of that study hinges upon bodies and forces outside of humanist frames. Building on Hayward and Weinstein, then, I want to read U.S. literary texts that foreground those forces "between, with and of" that attach to particular bodies and lives and communities, like "allergenic pollen." The non/human forces running through the texts I examine in this book are deeply implicated in normative webs that trans* studies, for one, has done so much to question and unravel. There is a joyousness here, then, as well as seriousness, demonstrating how queering and trans*ing the non/human is not merely a critique of humanist assumptions and the hierarchical logics of dehumanization but also a celebration of life and animacy that points elsewhere.

Working in light of the above article, Kadji Amin has written on the "monkey-gland" sensation of the early twentieth century (the grafting of testicular matter from chimpanzees into human testicles), in order to pose questions about trans*ness, the plasticity of the human body, and species. He thinks about "trans*plasticity," which "describes the capacity of organic matter to transform itself in ways that transgress ontological divides between sex, race, and species."[62] Trans* is a dynamic of trans/formation, and Amin's work (among much else in the field) helps parse the complex interrelations between human and animal, as well as all of the normativities that govern both.

In a connected—though not identical—vein, Jackson's *Becoming Human* is a vital text for understanding the non/human in relation to race, especially Blackness. Arguing that "twentieth-century African diasporic literature and culture generate unruly conceptions of being and materiality" that "disrupt the human-animal distinction and its persistent raciality," Jackson thinks about how these texts transform our understanding of the human and the nonhuman. Rather than interpreting the texts as "a reaction to . . . racialization—a plea for human recognition," the works she explores "move beyond a critique of bestialization to generate new possibilities for rethinking ontology: our being, fleshy materiality, and the nature of what exists." Avoiding the pitfalls of animal studies and posthumanism, as she sees them, Jackson moves away from analysis that simply tries to refold Blackness into the mold of humanism, or to reinstall animal otherness to define the human. Instead, texts by Nalo Hopkinson, Toni Morrison, and others "articulate being (human) in a manner that neither relies on animal abjection nor reestablishes liberal humanism as the authority on being (human)." Rather, they "respond to the animalization of black(ened) being by generating a critical praxis of being, paradigms of relationality, and epistemologies that alternately expose, alter, or reject not only the racialization of the human-animal distinction found in Western science and philosophy but also challenge the epistemic and material terms under which the specter of animal life acquires its authority."[63] Jackson reorients animal studies and posthuman scholarship away from the deracialization of the field *and* a reestablishing of humanist modes of inquiry. Other work since Jackson, like Sharon P. Holland's, similarly emphasizes how her thinking Blackness in relation to the animal and beyond "doesn't always already see animal life as something to descend *into* or as descent itself."[64] This warning—that the nonhuman does not automatically become the "de" in "dehumanized"—is vital to our project here.

This book does not wish to contribute further to a version of animal studies, new materialism, or posthumanism that ignores race, gender, sexuality, and disability. Rather, queerness (as a structural relation to dominant power) is at the heart of this book. In contrast to the ways that discourses like animal studies and biopolitics, Weheliye writes, "misconstrue[e] how profoundly race and racism shape the modern idea of the human,"[65] *A Queer Bestiary* tracks (and disturbs) the outlines of the human and the nonhuman as they come into being through racialization, sexualization, and other forces. In other words, the human is revealed to come apart in contemporary U.S. literature; queerness dismantles normative ideas of what the human is, has been, or can be.

Lingering with the non/human means: opening up categories of fixity to expansiveness and ambiguousness; thinking various kinds of life and matter aslant, awry, or anew; querying the long histories of racism, sexism, ableism, homophobia and transphobia that underwrite and make possible idealizations of the human; enjoying the overlaps, interconnections and entanglements of life and matter for the proliferations of possibility they engender. The following analyses sit alongside what Weheliye calls "genres of the human," which Ronak Kapadia glosses as being those "aesthetic works that cannot be reduced to the lexicon of resistance and agency but instead make possible a deeper interrogation of the forms of critical humanity imagined by those cast outside the domain of 'Man.'"[66] Examining genres of the non/human enables us to see new and alternative life-worlds not tied to the human/nonhuman binary and its inherent normativities.

V

The book moves through chapters about certain nonhumans, as earlier bestiaries have done. The chapters largely proceed through close readings of literary texts—either a single text or a broader selection of them to show a breadth of depictions. While the book is arranged in a particular order, the reader is equally encouraged to dip into sections as they see fit. Chapters do not always follow one from the other, and as such there should be different kinds of affect and reading experiences, as in medieval bestiaries, that drive one from section to section. The chapters, too, are of differing lengths, foci, and approaches, as befits the form. In this way, the book is less interested in making a singular and definitive thesis that is unpacked as the pages progress and more interested in putting into dialogue a range of human and nonhuman forms to tease out some of the dominant threads of exploration that I see in these literary texts. Again, the book does not aim for comprehensiveness or totalizing coverage, not least because that wouldn't be very queer. Rather, by posing questions and individual arguments in each chapter, the reader will hopefully come away with a series of interlocking and outward-looking ideas rather than one clean takeaway.

The opening clutch of chapters are instructive of the book's shape and focus: from the general nonhuman "Animal" to the broad figuration of "Nature" to a type of non/human relation, "Hybrid." From there, the specificity of "Groundhog" and "Horse" opens out to larger chapters on the "Ocean," "Hunting," and finally "Extinction." Also of note is that some literary texts appear a few times across the bestiary entries—especially Ocean Vuong's *On Earth We're Briefly Gorgeous* (2019)—for their capacious interest in non/human worlds. Separating out some of those nonhumans (butterflies, dogs, taxidermy, for instance) helps us see them more clearly.

The first chapter, "Animal," explores Justin Torres's *We the Animals* (2011) for the ways that it depicts the entanglements of animality, race, sexuality, and disability. The book is narrated by an unnamed Latinx boy living in upstate New York with his two brothers, Manny and Joel, and his parents, a white mother and Latino father. The figurations of animalization in this novel are saturated with questions of racialization, sexualization, ableism, and in turn queerness. The queer is, in this book, the commingling of multiple designations of nonnormativity and species difference; the narrator is relegated, through heteronormativity and speciesism, to a position below the rest of the family. Even as his family are themselves cast as Other in various ways (as animal for differential reasons), the narrator sits at the confluence of marginalizations that—sutured by his desire for men—render him beyond human in ways that the rest of the family must cast out and institutionalize. My chapter ends on a long discussion of Torres's final chapter, "Zookeeping," which enlaces the zoo, the prison, and the psychiatric institution, which I argue reveals much about the ways that non/humans of various kinds are differentially confined because of their otherness.

Moving from the generic "animal" to literary figurations of the natural world, "Nature" is a briefer analysis of Kumeyaay writer Tommy Pico's book-length *Nature Poem* (2017) for the ways that it puts "nature" in scare quotes, within queer and Indigenous frameworks. Pico's book is important within this larger bestiary because it relentlessly (re)frames and critiques human constructions of "nature" for their normativity and their deep imbrication in colonizing imaginaries. The queerness of Pico's text lies in its representations of queer Indigeneity as well as the text's complicated orientation toward non/human worlds. The chapter explores the ways that Pico's speaker does and does not want to write a "nature poem," because that is what is expected of an Indigenous writer. Yet I suggest that Pico's use of apophasis allows him to confront the normative and historical weightings of "nature" as a concept.

"Hybrid" explores figures of hybridity as they relate to queer non/human mingling. I begin with Ocean Vuong's *On Earth*, in which the monstrous is reconfigured not simply as something horrific but something hybrid, of multiple origins. Seeing both his mother and himself as monsters (queer, different, multiple), the protagonist Little Dog sets the stage for thinking about hybridity's link to non/human boundaries in relation to queerness. The chapter traces a brief history of "hybrid" through postcolonial and feminist theory, in order to show how the term itself struggles to contain the multiplicities within. I then explore Franny Choi's poetry collection *Soft Science* (2019) as an example of non/human mingling in relation to the cyborg—not Donna Haraway's conception, which hinges upon the binary, but Choi's more radical reimagining of the human and the machine as already containing multitudes and not so separate. From there, I look at two books titled *Bestiary*—Donika Kelly's poetry collection from 2016 and K-Ming Chang's novel from 2020—which are interested in the ways that hybridity is central to queer identity. Both texts use hybrid figures to pose questions of species exceptionalism and identitarian certainty. Kelly's poems use numerous hybrid figures—from nature, from Greek myth, and beyond—to substantiate questions of love and loss in and through race, gender, and sexuality. Turning finally to Chang's novel, in which a Taiwanese American girl is inhabited by a tiger spirit, Hu Go Po, this chapter posits the inherently queer nature of hybridity, which puts pressure on the myth of identity and being's singular forms. Daughter, the protagonist of Chang's novel, grows a tiger tail, which becomes both an extension of her queerness and a shaper of it. The book queries all kinds of non/human boundaries.

In the short chapter "Groundhog," I look at Ellen Bryant Voigt's poem "Groundhog" (2011), which thinks about the power of naming, of how we put nonhumans into human language that may or may not interrupt the way we understand them. The queerness of this poem is less overt than some of the other texts in this book, but its power comes from the ways in which the text sets itself up—through the title—to grasp the groundhog, but from the very start fails to do so. Getting to a specific groundhoggy-ness is, I would suggest, exactly the poem's undoing; holding the creature still, as in a textbook or zoo or diorama, proves impossible. This is partly because of language's failings but also because of the nonhuman's resistance to human mastery and understanding. The ostensibly taxonomizing impulse of the poem—*this is a groundhog*—is a ruse. Voigt's poem mocks any normative and singular way of knowing, not least because of language's instability.

In "Horse" I use the doubleness of horses—the ways they have been figured as embodying duality (body/mind, flesh/soul)—to explore the equine worlds in two of Ada Limón's poems, Kristiana Kahakauwila's short story "The Old Paniolo Way" (2021), Mary Gaitskill's *The Mare* (2015), and, more extensively, Percival Everett's *Wounded* (2005). I read those texts as bringing humans and nonhumans together because and in spite of their embodied differences (racialized, gendered, sexualized). This chapter reads horses as *mediating* creatures who act as bridges or contact points between kinds and forms of life, and varying species. In the longer reading of Everett's post-Western novel, I discuss how that book explores the West in a queer non/human framework. The novel, at its core, concerns itself with various kinds of wounds: bodily, psychic, social, cultural. Dead cows, a legless coyote, a traumatized horse, a stupid horse, a murdered white gay man, a dying Black man, and much else litter this novel's pages. The horse's mediating work gestures to a larger non/human world that is scarred by vulnerability.

"Taxidermy" explores the titular practice of skinning, stuffing, and mounting nonhuman animal forms through several literary texts that see such work as queer. Opening on two brief examples of taxidermy—from Jeff VanderMeer's *Hummingbird Salamander* (2021) and Vuong's *On Earth*—the chapter begins by positing that taxidermy is as much about valuing the nonhuman form as it is about encoding death in life. Both texts see taxidermized forms as troubling the distinctions between life/death, subject/object, and presence/absence. After historicizing taxidermy, particularly its colonial moment of popularity, I turn to two novels that place gender and sexuality at the heart of taxidermic endeavors. Reading Matthew Griffin's *Hide* (2016), I take its title as instructive: The book is about both human and nonhuman skins but also the secrets that those skins hide. The novel follows two gay men who have hidden their relationship and sexuality from the world all their lives. Between present-day flashbacks, the novel shows us how the act of taxidermy—getting beneath a nonhuman animal's skin—is a way of enabling the men to literally find a way to each other. In Kristen Arnett's *Mostly Dead Things* (2019), similarly, taxidermy is a mode of queer connection. For the protagonist, taxidermy is a way of carrying on her father's legacy; for her mother, taxidermy is a form of queer art that enables her to reimagine her own sexual and gendered identity. The interplay between humans and nonhumans in taxidermy is enabled and materialized through taxidermy's forms, functions, and indexicality.

"Mountain Lion" analyzes Henry Hoke's novella *Open Throat* (2023) and (briefly) Lucy Ellmann's *Ducks, Newburyport* (2019) for their depictions of mountain lions through divergent formal experiments. Hoke's short novel is written in poetic fragments using the mountain lion's "I" voice; Ellmann's book is an epic book written in a near-continuous sentence. In both novels, the inner lives of mountain lions are depicted—in ways that many of the texts in this bestiary do not attempt—as a way of thinking about non/human concerns like identity and place. In *Open Throat*, a mountain lion roams the Hollywood Hills, looking down over Los Angeles, contemplating the wild, human-nonhuman relations, family and upbringing, and a changing planet. Hoke's novel places non/human queerness within a much broader context of ecological destruction. It ultimately puts emphasis on the connections between nonhumans, the potency of language, and the possibilities of queer sexuality and gender—we will think about the possibilities of queer and trans nonhumans, as Hoke's mountain lion asks us to scramble everything we know about identity and language.

In "Dog" I think about the capaciousness of the category "dog" (its definitional instability skewering any kind of easy taxonomy), while also trying to home in on the specificities of canine representations in the United States. This chapter will thus think about that feedback loop in relation to the social, cultural, and imaginative worlds of humans and dogs, especially as those worlds are striated by race, gender, and sexuality. "Dog" posits that because canines are intimately braided into human life—in homes, workplaces, even our language—they also have the capacity to queer human identities as well as notions of connectivity and intimacy. Rather than see the dog as "man's best friend," we think with the construction of "Man" and the ways that not all dogs, and not all dog-human relations, are equal. More than other chapters in this bestiary, in this chapter we survey a wide variety of literary texts (as if to echo the complex and multifarious relations and connections between humans and dogs). Through brief readings of Matthew Griffin's *Hide* (2016), Danzy Senna's story "The Land of Beulah" (2011), Phil Klay's story "Redeployment" (2014), Ocean Vuong's *On Earth* (2019), Garth Greenwell's *Cleanness* (2020), Mark Doty's *Dog Years* (2007), and then Danez Smith's poem "dogs!" (2020), the chapter figures the dog's richness and variety. In cycling through questions of intimacy (by revisiting *Hide* and its relation to taxidermy); and racialization (Senna, Klay); we then move to gender and sexuality (Vuong, Greenwell, Doty), before seeing in Smith's poem a threading together of all the above.

Like the life of its namesake, the chapter "Butterfly" is brief. As we see elsewhere in this book, Ocean Vuong's *On Earth* is dense with nonhuman figures. The narrative, though, is bookended by monarch butterflies beginning their migration south from the northern United States to Mexico. Their migration is initiated both by small changes and, as in Barbara Kingsolver's *Flight Behavior* (2012), by destroyed habitats. Vuong frames this novel about transnational migration and queer relationships with the monarch's literal and symbolic relation to temporality and travel. The chapter looks at a final scene of butterflies morphing into other creatures, as well as the butterflies that crop up in his poem "My Father Writes from Prison" in his debut poetry collection (2016).

As with the previous chapter, "Ocean" is short, perhaps counterintuitively, given the ocean's vastness. Rather than attending to its extensiveness, I want to explore two texts that think about the ocean and creatures within it from very specific vantages. In *My Life in Sea Creatures* (2022) by Sabrina Imbler and *Undrowned: Black Feminist Lessons from Marine Mammals* (2020) by Alexis Pauline Gumbs, we see two ways of thinking the ocean from trans and queer of color perspectives. In both, the authors turn to sea creatures and the waters they move in to paint possibilities of queer living for humans and nonhumans alike. The books question what the ocean's breadth and depth, its shifting fluctuations, its ubiquity across the planet and the bodies on it, and its movability mean for non/humans. The ocean is everywhere, within and without us, yet cannot be pinned down.

"Hunting" is a longer exploration of four texts that depict hunting in various U.S. settings and contexts. Placing these texts in a larger history of national hunting narratives, the chapter shows how each reveals the precarious interrelation of hunter and hunted, rather than the ostensible power dynamic. Reading Blackfeet author Stephen Graham Jones's *The Only Good Indians* (2020), David Vann's *Goat Mountain* (2013), Tom Franklin's *Poachers* (1999), and Ocean Vuong's *On Earth* (2019) for the ways that they imagine the hunter/hunted dynamic—via elk, bucks, possums, macaques, deer, and more—this chapter suggests that hunting traverses and queers species lines rather than simply upholds them. Indeed, hunter and hunted are bound so tightly together in these texts that they are near impossible to separate. The texts under scrutiny here are far more interested in the psychic and somatic resonances of the hunt, the way that certain kinds of hunting are made permissible or understandable via culture and history. The texts ask why killing some animals is legitimate, but killing others is not. What are the boundaries, these texts ask, of hunting and killing? If the normative equation is *hunted = nonhuman* (and vice versa), what happens when humans are rendered nonhuman and are suddenly available to be killed?

The final chapter, "Extinction," is different from the others in that it poses a series of questions and problems. Given the bestiary's inevitable openness—its inability to be closed, finalized, or totalized—this final chapter takes that generativity seriously. Using a range of theories of extinction and a couple of short literary analyses, the chapter asks what the concept of extinction does for our understanding of imbricated non/human worlds. It asks, if queerness has been thought of as both *in* the future and the rejection *of* futurity, how do we think a queer ecology for a planet under the weight of species collapse? This chapter does not offer a conclusion to the book but rather shares a set of fragments that gesture to our fragmented world.

NOTES

1. Giffney and Hird, "Introduction," 3.

2. Ahmed, *Queer Phenomenology*, 161.

3. Flores, "Introduction," x.

4. McCulloch, *Medieval*, 15; Flores, "Introduction," xiii.

5. McCulloch, *Medieval*, 15.

6. Clark and McMunn, "Introduction," 3.

7. Steinbock et al., "Thinking Linking," 6.

8. DeVun, "Animal Appetites," 473, 464. For more, see: DeVun, *The Shape of Sex* (2020).

9. Burton and Mawani, "Introduction," 4.

10. Burton and Mawani, 6.

11. Like the medieval bestiaries, too, this book is "illustrated"; each section is accompanied by a collage made by me, which gestures to the messy and layered nature of the non/human encounters. While they're in black and white here, you can find color versions (depending on when you're reading this) on my personal website and socials.

12. He calls the book a "Chinese bestiary," which was produced sometime during the fourth to the first centuries BCE.

13. Solnit writes elsewhere that "A bestiary is buried in our language," because of the innumerable concepts that are named after the nonhuman world (like *arctic* from *bear*, or *hippocampus* from *seahorse*). *The Faraway Nearby*, 173.

14. See, for instance, Cvetkovich, *An Archive of Feelings*; Muñoz, *Disidentifications*; Gopinath, *Unruly Visions*.

15. Ngai, *Ugly Feelings*, 7.

16. In some ways, we might even see those animal metaphors as normative (rats are nasty, lions are not) which feeds into the speciesist logic that I want to unpack.

17. Derrida, *Archive Fever*.

18. Halberstam, *In a Queer*, 169–70.

19. Stoler, "Intimidations of Empire," 2.

20. Patricia Fara, too, shows how gender and sexuality were also entangled in the colonial enterprise, especially as it intersected with botany. See: Fara, *Sex, Botany, and Empire* (2004).

21. Bey, *Black*, 142.

22. Stoler, *Carnal Knowledge*, 8–9.

23. Edelman, *No Future*, 17.

24. Cohen, "Punks," 441, 458.

25. Eng et al., "What's Queer," 2.

26. Eng and Puar, "Introduction," 16.

27. Keegan, "Getting Disciplined," 391.

28. Wiegman and Wilson, "Introduction," 2.

29. Bey, *Black*, 24, 4.

30. Hayward and Gossett, "Impossibility," 18.

31. Abdur-Rahman, *Against*, 6, 7, 10, 24.

32. Fraiman, "Pussy Panic," 93. Fraiman—along with Black studies critics mentioned later—takes particular issue with Jacques Derrida's essay "The Animal That Therefore I Am (More to Follow)" (2002) and Cary Wolfe's *Animal Rites: American Culture, The Discourse of Species, and Posthumanist Theory* (2003) and the ways these texts are often hailed as the groundwork upon which animal studies begins. Fraiman charts a much longer (and more inclusive) genealogy.

33. Hayward and Gossett, "Impossibility," 19.

34. Seymour, *Strange*, 1.

35. Giffney and Hird, "Introduction," 3.

36. Giffney and Hird, 4.

37. Parry, *Other Animals*, viii.

38. Holland, *An Other*, xiii.

39. Pugliese, *Biopolitics*, 3.

40. Colebrook, "What is it Like," 227.

41. Hayles, *How We*, 3.

42. We might note here, though, Haraway's own complicated and sometimes problematic engagement with racialization and the nonhuman.

43. There are, of course, issues with the idea of the "post" that I don't have the space to at length. With postcolonialism, for example, as theorists like Ania Loomba have pointed out, the post implies an *after* that implicitly/explicitly renders colonialism *finished* and in the past, rather than an ongoing history. Similarly, the post in posthuman suggests that the human has already been moved beyond, when in fact we still have not fully considered the human in its variety and complexity (not least in the ways that human has always mean synonymous with white Western Man). See Wolfe, *What Is Posthumanism?*; and Braidotti, *Posthuman*.

44. Bennett, *Vibrant Matter*, vii, 112.

45. Jackson, "Outer Worlds," 216.

46. Chen, *Animacies*, 2, 3.

47. Other work in this more race- and queer-attuned posthumanism includes Singh, *Unthinking Mastery*; Lillvis, *Posthuman Blackness and the Black Female Imagination*; Ellis, *Antebellum Posthuman*.

48. Reid-Pharr, *Archives of Flesh*, 6.

49. Jackson, *Becoming Human*, 1

50. Byrd, "Beast," 602.

51. Luciano and Chen, "Has the Queer."

52. Nyong'o, "Little Monsters," 266.

53. Daulatzai and Rana, "Writing the Muslim," xi.

54. Hayward and Gossett, "Impossibility," 18.

55. TallBear, "An Indigenous," 234, 235.

56. Wynter, "Unsettling," 260.

57. Weheliye, *Habeas Viscus*, 5.

58. McKittrick, *Dear Science*, 42.

59. Luciano and Chen, "Has the Queer," 187, 188.

60. Butler, *Frames of War*; Luciano and Chen, "Has the Queer," 189.

61. Hayward and Weinstein, "Introduction," 195, 195–6, 197, 198.

62. Amin, "Trans* Plasticity," 51.

63. Jackson, *Becoming*, 1, 2.

64. Holland, *An Other*, 12.

65. Weheliye, *Habeas Viscus*, 4.

66. Kapadia, *Insurgent Aesthetics*, 34.

ANIMAL

Animal

queer worlds are wild

I

In "Theory in the Wild" (2018), Jack Halberstam and Tavia Nyong'o argue that the wild has functioned "as a foil to civilization, as the dumping ground for all that white settler colonialism has wanted to declare expired, unmanageable, undomesticated, and politically unruly." Wildness clings to ideas of primitivity and "virgin" territories and thus cannot leave those colonial imaginaries behind. Indeed, like "queer"—a kindred conception —"the wild" names "while rendering partially opaque, what hegemonic systems would interdict or push to the margins." Thus, wildness is not one thing but manifests in many nonnormative ways. "Wild are the worlds," Halberstam and Nyong'o go on, "that anarrange gender, sexuality, ability, and other modernist paradigms of normalization into unstable vocabularies and idiolects."[1] Unstable discourses, disarray, colonial histories, the undomesticated, and nonhuman animals provide an entry point to Justin Torres's 2011 novel *We the Animals*.

We the Animals explores how wildness (animality, the marginal, the unstable) and queerness intersect. The book is narrated by an unnamed Latinx boy living in upstate New York with his two brothers, Manny and Joel, and his parents, a white mother and Latino father. Much of the book is narrated in first-person plural (the "we" of the title), but a steady revelation of the singular "I" comes into focus as the book progresses and the narrator's sexuality is made clear. The novel traces the boys' development—their wild domestic world of strange temporalities, relationalities, and identities—from a collective unit (albeit with the narrator as an outlier from the start) to a brotherly split. The final sections of the novel detail the family's finding out that the narrator is gay (or is at least having sex with men) and his subsequent violent lashing out against them. The last chapter of the book sees the narrator in an institution, put there by his family because of his outburst and his queerness.

I use "queer" here not as a sign of his sexual behavior (though it partly informs this designation), nor as simply a marker of otherness. Rather, the figurations of animalization in this novel are saturated with questions of racialization, sexualization, ableism, and in turn queerness. The queer is, in this book, the commingling of multiple designations of nonnormativity and species difference—the unnamed narrator (denied, we might say, the fixity of such nomenclature) is relegated, through heteronormativity and speciesism, to a position below the rest of the family. Even while his family are themselves cast as Other in various ways (as animal for differential reasons), the narrator sits at the confluence of marginalizations that—sutured by his desire for men—render him beyond human in ways that the rest of the family have to cast out and institutionalize. Ricardo Ortiz describes Torres's writing on the Pulse shooting in Orlando as invested in the "intersection of queerness with a particularly 'latinx' brownness," and this chapter argues that *We the Animals* is concerned with similar overlaps.[2] Much of this chapter will focus on the final moments in the book and the entangling of the zoo, the prison, and the psychiatric institution, for the ways that they incarcerate (but cannot define) the queer.

The book begins with the demands of the "we," that Caren Irr glosses as the "collective animal body": "We wanted more. We knocked the butt ends of our forks against the table, tapped our spoons against our empty bowls; we were hungry. We wanted more volume, more riots. . . . We had bird bones, hollow and light, and we wanted more density, more weight. We were six snatching hands, six stomping feet; we were brothers, boys, three little kings locked in a feud for more."[3]

The boys are driven by precarity and lack, both corporeal and psychic. The anaphoric "we" solidifies the boys into a hoard, "kings" fighting for a sovereign power that—in the frame of wildness—is precluded. Their bones are like birds, one of the first references to animality that the book introduces, but this collective other-than-human status is related largely to their wildness as children, their chaotic demands and "riots." As I have suggested, animality is not a singular position in a species hierarchy but a shifting designation that overlaps with, informs, and reframes other markers of identity (or identity's rejection).

In thinking through the novel's links between animality, race, gender, and sexuality, we must ask, as José Esteban Muñoz does, what it means, "in the face of" the consistent animalization of brownness and queerness in the past and present, "to take on an animality that is often projected onto one."[4] While I would add to Muñoz's list the animalization of disabled people (picked up later in this chapter), the question remains: How does Torres rescript the tropes of animality—as they stick to things like race and gender—without enabling dubious tropes to reassert themselves? If "the wild," too, requires us to remember its roots in colonial fantasies of exploitation and capture, it also forces us to think beyond those epistemes to question what wildness means "for those who have been forcibly gathered under its sign." As a "loud and disruptive" form, wildness "interrupts the neat narratives of freedom and escape."[5] It is this loud and disruptive wildness—a wildness linked to queerness but not conflatable with it—that *We the Animals* opens on. The boys' plural demands for "density" is a claim for substance in a world that denies their humanity, primarily because of their Latinx-ness but also, in the case of the narrator, because of his queer difference.

We see the animalizing of the characters both from the family themselves and from outsiders. This latter designation might suggest, of course, that the external world's animalizing of the boys is the reason for their own self-description. The non/human references in this book (via metaphor, simile) sit uneasily between both resisting and amplifying hierarchies of life.[6] The narrator throughout sees the family as animalized: The boys follow Paps around the kitchen "like baby geese" (9; and Ma, too is a "confused goose of a woman," 3); Manny and Joel "swim like a couple of goldfish" (20); the boys, playing as a three, figure themselves as "monsters," as the "three bears," as the Stooges, and as "chipmunks" (25); Paps is "like an animal" (45), who has a "dog growl" (52), and Ma has a "tiny bird neck" (45); even their truck has mirrors that jut out "like elephant ears" (63). I list these few examples of the book's many to show how Torres embeds a language of animality into the novella in ways that reveal this entire family as linked to the nonhuman. Early in the novel, Paps calls the boys "mutts" because they are mixed race: "You ain't white and you ain't Puerto Rican," he tells them, whereas he's a "purebred"

(10). Paps's enjoining of racial and species "purity" underscores one of the reasons why the boys see themselves as complexly animalized, not one thing or another, but something more mixed;[7] I pick this idea up in "Hybrid."

Similarly, an old man in their street calls the boys "animals" and "locusts" when they steal food from his garden. In part, this is because they have taken his produce, but it's also because the man sees their brownness as akin to locusts, which are "invaders, marauders, scavengers" (33). The man uses racist and xenophobic language, particularly attached to migrants of color in the United States, that links the nonhuman and racialized others. There are various ways to read the above examples, including a kind of internalized devaluation of racialized and queered life; "colonial notions of the wild," as Halberstam tells us, "are all too familiar" and linger in various representations of human and nonhuman wildness. Yet they also tell us that these colonized inscriptions of the wild and the non/human "do not exhaust" its meanings, and that attending to the wild "questions the hierarchies of being that have been designed to mark and patrol the boundaries between the human and everything else."[8] The animalization within the book—the murky and queer territory of both metaphor and simile, where humans *are* and *are like* animals—both conforms to and resists the dominant narratives of dehumanization.

We see non/human blurring throughout the text, from the opening chapter onward. The narrator says that they "hunted animals . . . , chasing down bullfrogs and water snakes," and they also "plucked baby robins from their nest" to "feel the beat of tiny hearts" (2). Their oscillation from animal to hunter to carer suggests that the boys are not simply animalized others but rather walk a line between non/human positions (see also "Hunter" later in this book). This dynamic is mirrored late in the novella, just before the narrator's sexuality is revealed; the brothers, drinking at the docks in the snow, find a stray cat with a litter and buy her some milk: "The kittens clawed and pushed in the suckling pile; some seemed to be asleep at the tit; they were ugly, desperate things" (107). Manny and Joel question how long it is before the kittens "forget they're kin, start fighting," and "jump the runt"; they look at the narrator as they say this, "the fay, the runt of our litter; we were once those kittens—three thick, three warm" (107). At this point in the narrative, the boys are about to separate for good, and the narrator's difference (not entirely marked as "queerness" though his difference is haunted by it: effeminacy, strangeness, otherness) makes him the runt. Though it is not just that queerness or nonnormativity that renders the narrator as an animal, because the brothers are too. While Manny and Joel want to Other their brother, to see him as different, they still all share the same creaturely existence: hungry kittens grasping for sustenance. As both human and nonhuman, drawing lines between *kinds* of humans and nonhumans, the boys perhaps partake in a kind of speciesism, or at least play into the logic of hierarchizing life.

The boys' inhabitation of the non/human middle ground might also be seen as a kind of amalgam or assemblage of life forms. Read alongside Muñoz's conception of a queer brown bestiary (in relation to Carmelita Tropicana, the persona of performance artist Alina Troyano), we might think of the boys' non/humanness as something of a "queer assemblage." As Muñoz argues of Tropicana, the assuming of animal roles (horse, pig, bear, cockroach) in her performances is a kind of queer becoming, a "deterritorialization of the body itself" where fixedness—of the body, of identity—is eschewed. Moreover, where "systematic state violence" against people of color in the United States and beyond is often enmeshed with the "animalization of minoritarian populations," Tropicana's work provides a different kind of animalized figure, one that is "nonmimetic" (i.e., not a direct representation), and thus disrupts the capture and subjugation of certain queer lives.[9] The becoming-animal of Tropicana—and we might say, the boys of *We the Animals*—is not a simple transformation into *this* or *that* specific creature (indeed, "animal" is the usual vague designation in Torres's book) but rather a middle space of becoming non/human. If humans need the figure of the nonhuman animal to justify violence against it (and, by necessity, other humans), then the *becoming* position ruptures the binary of human/animal. Muñoz calls this, in light of his earlier work, "disidentification's blueprint,"[10] where speciesist logics of devaluing life are resisted, and where "becoming" is a queerly "brown" endeavor: "not being a foreclosed and often disposed identity, . . . instead participating in new and potentially emancipatory lines of flight."[11] I want to think about the boys' becoming non/human in *We the Animals* in this frame, though perhaps as less liberatory. I see it as a kind of simultaneous doing and undoing of the logics of speciesism, and the violences enabled against non/humans of all kinds. (Such violence might include the novel's depictions of ostracization and racism, or the broader kinds of emotional and physical violence done to queer and racialized humans, as well as nonhuman animals).

II

The novel moves through nineteen short fragments that build a picture of this young family in the process of coming together and apart. While the final sections of the novel—"The Night I am Made" and "Zookeeping"—seem to be the telos of the novel, the sections preceding are not always obviously moving toward that conclusion. It is not clear that each section moves us forward in time; rather they paint childhood as an expansive terrain that is open. The boys fuse together so often as an animalized unit that we cannot always differentiate their ages or maturity. In one section, "The Lake," even the telling of that event is narratively looped: We learn that the family goes swimming in a lake and that the narrator and his mother almost drown, but we only find that out at the end of the section. The narrator circles back to what actually happens, as though the memory is difficult to face, but there is also the sense here of time moving elliptically, rather than in a straight line (with all of those normative connotations).

The sections move outwards, horizontally, rather than upward or linearly, in line with Kathryn Bond Stockton's famous conception of the "queer child." In her book of the same name, Stockton poses that "if you scratch a child, you will find a queer, in the sense of someone 'gay' or just plain strange." Thinking about queer children in twentieth-century culture enables her "to outline, in shadowy form, the pain, closets, emotional labors, sexual motives, and sideways movements that attend all children"; in other words, "a gay child illuminates the darkness of the child" more broadly. Stockton is insistent too on the heteronormativity of traditional conceptions of childhood and a child's growth. Children, she argues, grow and develop slowly, their transition into adulthood (and "experience") a delay, but that movement has "been relentlessly figured as vertical movement upward (hence, 'growing up') toward full stature, marriage, work, reproduction, and the loss of childishness." Instead, Stockton suggests, we might think about "notions of the horizontal—what spreads sideways—or sideways and backward—more than a simple thrust toward height and forward time."[12] *We the Animals* moves sideways and loops back around in an elliptical fashion to grasp the particular queerness of its narrator.

One of the main ways in which the family is made queer by the narrator is through the identifications and overlaps between the boys and their parents; their familial and gendered roles are swapped, performed, reworked. For instance, in the book's second chapter, the boys play at the kitchen table, smashing tomatoes with a mallet. Their depressed mother, thinking they should be in school (it's a Sunday) emerges from her bed with smudged mascara, "like a raccoon . . . : surprised, dangerous" (5). Ma says she hates her life, but seeing the tomatoes everywhere evokes a wild "dreamtime" world to play in with the boys: "That's what you looked like when you slid out of me" (6), she says. This birthing imagery is then reversed as the mother asks the boys to "make" or birth her (6).[13] She puts her chin on the table next to a ketchup bottle, Joel swings the mallet, and she slides to the floor, sauce everywhere, "looking like she had been shot" (6). The entwining of life and death, birth and violence, are telling in this child-birthing-the-mother scene. The boys shout, "It's a mom! . . . Congratulations! . . . Happy Birthday! . . . It's never-never time! . . . It's the time of your life!" (7). This strange dreamworld—a time that is no time and all time—is one where familial roles are upended and we see an estrangement (perhaps queering) of birth itself.

A later scene, when their father has left the family, sees Joel and the narrator inhabit their parents' roles. Desperate for food and attention, the boys listen to the phone ring; Ma knows it is Paps and ignores it. As Manny shuts himself in the bedroom, Joel and the narrator escape to a crawlspace and use an old phone to act out their parents' (imagined) conversations. Joel says, "How come you don't answer the phone," playing the role of Paps. They try again: "The next time Joel called me, I made my voice sexy," and they "both [hung] up, blushing" (43). It is as if the narrator's effeminacy, or his becoming-queer, shows through in the adoption of the mother's role. The subsequent conversation sees them blur roles—"I was confused about who he was pretending to be," the narrator says—and ask, "What are we gonna do?" (43). Ending on uncertainty, this intermingling of roles and genders, the two younger brothers enact a family dynamic where they are both mother and father, parent and child, desirous and desired. This escape is a way to hold the ambiguity of the world at bay but also bring it (somewhat) within their control.

As Marion Rohrleitner puts it, "While Paps' machismo determines the traditional gender roles in the family early on, his absences and temporary abandonment of the family force Ma into the role of provider, and her breakdowns and mental frailty cast her sons in the role of nurturing caretakers." As such, "the lived experiences of 'the pack' thus begin to deconstruct any preconceived notion of normative family life long before the narrator is violently outed," further complicating this family's nonnormativity.[14] While we might not call the whole family queer in terms of sexuality—especially given their outing of the son—they do occupy nonnormative positions due to the entanglements of gender, race, ethnicity, all of which surface within images of the non/human.

The boys' mother is also depicted as potentially queer in the book (and I say "queer" rather than "bisexual" given the narrator's refusal to "fix" anyone's sexuality through particular language). When Paps leave her, Ma takes to her bed in depression and stops eating and working. After a few missed shifts, Ma's supervisor Lina calls at the house. This Chinese American woman is "tall and thick, with high cheekbones that stuck out like handlebars below her eyes" (31). Immediately, her otherness stands out to the boys—her physicality, her (potential) female masculinity, to borrow Halberstam's phase—and they say, "You're huge. . . . There's no room for you" (31), shutting the door. Lina's "bigness" is in some ways a reminder of their own father, and there being "no room" seems to suggest that Lina is not able to take his place. But Lina "muscles" (31) into the house and tells the boys that other women from China were similar to her, "like Cadillacs" with "big hands" (32). Lina's butchness indexes a gendered, sexualized, and racialized nonnormativity that is then connected to their mother. She hands the boys a bag of groceries and they tear into the food all over the carpet, "drinking the milk out of the carton, looking straight into Lina's eyes, the three of us, daring her"; they want to see if they can get away with this "wild" behavior in the house, whether Lina will discipline them. In response, she "flashed her long, wide horse teeth at us" and said they might choke (32). Again, the metaphor of horse teeth joins a litany of images in this book that tie together non/humans.

When Ma hears Lina's voice ("*Comrade!*"), she comes out of the bedroom, "throwing herself into Lina's big arms, burying her face in Lina's silky black hair, and crying" (32). Lina's "comrade" evokes a kind of (gendered and classed) solidarity that then transforms into something more intimate. Lina kisses Ma "all over . . . , even her nose and eyebrows," but then "puts her lips on Ma's lips and held them there, soft and still, and nobody . . . said a word. There wasn't a word to say" (32). Here, the novel comes closest to suggesting that Ma has a sexual identity that is potentially like her son's; while at first Lina seems to be just a boss, and then a friend, it is obvious that she is more than that. That the boys have no response conjures the kind of unspeakability of queer love generally and perhaps lesbianism or bisexuality more specifically. Rohrleitner says that Lina "becomes the protective and gentle lover Paps has never been able to be," yet the elliptical nature of the novel means that we don't get further access to this relationship or Ma's sexuality outside of her relation to Paps.[15] In short, I am suggesting that the narrator's queerness is framed in this novella by the rest of his family's uneven and unequal nonnormativity, which runs across racialized and gendered lines and is tied to questions of animality and the non/human.

III

The book's interest in queerness as it is produced and queried at the boundary of the non/human escalates in the book's penultimate section, "The Night I Am Made." Again, I am locating this book as interested in queerness and the non/human in light of Giffney and Hird's work (outlined in the book's introduction). As they write, their theorizations "consider the status conferred on the Human as a proper object by probing the desire for the Human, the desire for recognition *as* Human and how desire itself becomes prefigured in the pit of heteronormativity as an extension of the Human subject narrowly conceived, that is, the Human subject as analogous to heterosexuality."[16]

Here we can see the manifold ways that those who do not fit into the category of "human" help us to trouble and problematize both that category's foundational importance in violence against all kinds of animals (human and nonhuman) *and* the ways that it can be destabilized. If the Human is singularly white, heterosexual, cis, and able-bodied—the normative Man of Sylvia Wynter's theorizing—everyone that falls outside of those designations becomes caught in net of nonhuman figuration. We see this play out in complex ways at the end of *We the Animals*.

Before this moment of being "made"—made into something gay, something queer, something different—there are numerous precursors in the novel where the family see the narrator as Other to them. The brothers often call him a "baby" (73, 81) and always gesture toward his difference from them; they separate him slowly from the "we." Later, that babyishness takes on a queerer luster, as in the scene where Paps takes the narrator to Niagara Falls. Left alone in a museum, the narrator dances in front of a projection of the falls, pretending to be a "mer-boy prince" who tries "to catch all the men in barrels and save them from their deaths" (100). Paps watches him dancing and twirling: "I was thinking how pretty you were." Paps says, "Now isn't that an odd thing for a father to think about his son? . . . I was thinking to myself, *Goddamn, I got me a pretty one*" (102). Here, "pretty" connotes something like queer difference, which Paps almost venerates even as it confuses him. The narrator as mer-boy captivates by transcending non/human gender roles. All of this frames the scenes in which the narrator has sex with a man for the first time, his family finds out about his desires, and he lashes out at them.

Across five parts (through "midnight" to "dawn"), "The Night I Am Made" both breaks apart the brothers for good and "outs" the narrator in ways that turn him, fully, we might say, into a queer non/human.[17] The brothers, this night, are drinking by the docks, where they find a stray cat. The narrative shifts here more than we have seen previously: The tense, and first-person voice, move from "they grew up wiry" (rather than "we") to "one of them will smash his face into a locker-room mirror over a girl" and "they'll flunk. . . . Later they'll truck in all manner of pornography" (103). This movement from past to future, from *we* to *they*, indicates the kind of sudden (sideways) growth that has happened between the last section at Niagara and this night of revelations. It is a moment that Irr notes is the shift from an inclusive "we" to an exclusive one ("us not you"). This "clusivity," she outlines, is the grammatical deviation in *we* that exists in different languages. Who or what gets included in the "we" is central to what Irr calls the making of democracy (in some languages, the "we" is nonhuman as well as human). The novel, she suggests, "counts down from the family of five to the four-against-one of mother and sons versus the father and the fraternal threesome and erotic twosome, until it reaches the solitary unit of the domesticated narrator lost in the bad animality of the zoo. According to this narrative arithmetic, extracting one from the *we* creates a depressive 'prince' rather than the actively engaged member of an implicitly more democratic animal body."[18] I will come back to the zoo and the "depressive prince," but here we can note that the collectivity of the family (*we the animals*) gradually fractures so that the narrator is on his own, outside of the group, outside of the (hetero) norms that they hold up even as their racialization and class render them Other too.

The "we" of the book, though, also links to Juana María Rodríguez's *Sexual Futures, Queer Gestures, and Other Latina Longings* (2014). In this book about sexuality, gender, and race, Rodríguez often invokes the first-person plural as a "rhetorical gesture of future possibilities" where, "rather than define itself through the exclusion of its others, this 'we' is continually coming together and coming undone, a precarious bond that performs its own disarticulation of desire and discontent."[19] This could be a slightly different description of Torres's narrator, shifting from "we" to "I," from collective to individual, across the undoing and remaking of a queer Latinx identity. As the "we" moves and dis/articulates a sense of selfhood and otherness, so too does the narrator's understanding of his own identity become both clearer and more opaque. In both Irr and Rodríguez's framing, the "we" contains a plurality that refuses to be fixed or finalized, holding open possibility and futurity for this marginalized narrator.

As they are separating, in these penultimate scenes, Manny and Joel, like nonhuman predators now "smel[l]" the narrator's "difference—my sharp, sad, pansy scent"; they also hate his "good grades" and "white ways" (105), all of which acknowledges the entanglements of gender, sexuality, and race as central to his alterity. In "Late Night," the narrator walks alone to the bus station, where he has been "sleazing around the bus station's men's room. This was the scent they'd picked up" (113). He has spent time spying "through the cracks" of the bathroom cubicles, never quite ready to join the other men there. But this night, a truck driver talks to him and invites him into his cab. At this galvanizing moment, the driver says, "You want me to make you"—not quite a question—"I'll make you. I'll make you." At this, the narrator writes: "And I was made" (113). "Made" here points to the way the narrator is ushered into a sexuality he does not name; the act is offstage, as it were, but proves to be "constitutive." He is transformed—constructed (made) in a sense—from watcher to participant, yet of course the power dynamic in this moment cannot go unnoted (the narrator's age remains unclear here).

Following this scene, in "Deep Night," the narrator returns home to find the family gathered in the living room. The "air reeked of grief" (116) because they now know about his sexuality. Ma—animalized with "mascara tiger-striped down her face" (116)—has found his journal, which contains fantasies in "bold and explicit language," of "what I wanted done to me": "a catalog of imagined perversions, a violent pornography with me at the center, with myself obliterated" (116). The narrator's written cartography of sex revolves around the erasure of his body, or at least a masochistic drive toward pain. It is an example of what Leo Bersani, following Sigmund Freud, calls "self-shattering," that dissolution of psychic and somatic integrity, the fixity of the ego and the body's walls.[20] When, during sex, a "certain threshold of intensity is reached," Bersani elaborates, "the self is momentarily disturbed" by affects beyond one's borders (crudely put, the presence of the other).[21] This shattering of coherence in the sexual scene is tied, elsewhere in Bersani, to masochism too. Important to us here, though, is the *shattering* of the narrator that is twinned with *making*—both creation and destruction entwined. Again, in a kind of middle ground, the narrator hovers between states (made/unmade, human/nonhuman, self/other).

The transformation that occurs through sex(uality) quickly morphs into intense anger, aimed at Ma: "I'll kill you," the narrator says (116). In the next sentence, the narrative voice shifts in time and tense: "Two hours later, I am packed into the car and taken to the psych ward . . . where I will be turned over to the state and institutionalized" (117). This small shift in temporality is indicative of the whole section, where the first person moves as the narrator's identity undergoes alteration. We move back in time, before he is "strapped to a gurney, before the sedation." The narrator acknowledges that "I could have risen" from the floor to the family's embrace but instead "behaved like an animal" (118). The simile codes the narrator's actions as nonhuman: "I bucked and spat and screamed," he says. "I cursed them: we were, all of us, sons of whores, mongrels, our father fucked a beast" (118). This "animalistic" behavior is directed at Ma, because she finds the journal, but it is notable that she is in turn made non/human, a beast; moreover, the boys' "mongrel" status is because of the white Ma, rather than the Latinx Paps, as we saw earlier.

The narrator's "animality" is met with kind resistance from the family. They pin the narrator down, and the "wilder" he becomes, the more the family "retreated into their love" (118). Instead of yielding to them, the narrator lashes out: "You sick fucks, I bet you liked reading [the journal]. . . . I let the spit fly, nostrils wide" (118). This unleashing of non/humanness, a kind of border zone freighted by anger and shame, leads the narrator to say and do "animal, unforgivable things," as though his humanness (humanity) has waned now that his queerness is more fully revealed. "What else," he concludes, "but take me to the zoo?" (118). Non/human boundaries are made most visible and malleable in this book at the site of identity's overlaps. And in this fraught moment the construction—or "making"—of the narrator's identity through sex (and then through the revelation of that sex, via a forced "coming out") is twinned with the unleashing of a nonhuman animality that was, in effect, there all along.

But that wildness—disorder, scattering, inhumanness—becomes the very trigger for violence and the subsequent institutionalization. I think in the next section about the final "zoo" section of the novella, but we might say here that queerness and wildness have complex overlaps, un/productive constitution. Glossed in other language, as Michel Foucault writes about the invention of homosexuality as a medicalized category, "the sodomite had been a temporary aberration; the homosexual was now a species."[22] We could say the narrator was once a temporary aberration in the family, but now—through speciesism and its languages of exclusion and hierarchy—has become fully nonhuman, a species all on his own outside of the family unit.[23]

IV

A close reading of the end of the novel, "Zookeeping" (barely half a page), ties together and also opens up many of the questions we have been tracking. The present-tense verb of "zookeeping" draws us into the *now*, a site of enclosure, and to a process of ongoingness (or becoming, in Muñoz's words). Rather than "zoo," for instance, the title gestures toward the *act* of keeping non/humans captive. In thinking about zoos, the book links together various forms of carcerality and containment—the zoo, the prison, the asylum. As Chris Chapman, Allison Carey, and Liat Ben-Moshe argue, the long history of institutionalization in the United States has always been an enmeshed one. Various populations (the poor, the sick, people of color) have been relegated to jails, poorhouses, hospitals, and other locations. These institutions were made to "classify, control and treat danger, and to safeguard the rest of the population from the dangerous individual."[24] The narrator's confinement at the end of *We the Animals* is one such example of control of purported dangerousness.

Torres's novel also, though, links this carceral history—an "institutional archipelago" of sites and systems of containment[25]—to nonhuman detention too. Lori Gruen argues that spaces of human captivity like prisons and jails are ubiquitous but are not often seen or made visible. Yet zoos, on the other hand, often display their means of captivity (of nonhumans) explicitly. In both cases, Gruen argues, while there are many differences between the enclosure of humans and nonhumans, "there are common ethical themes that imprisonment raises, for example, the value of liberty, the nature of autonomy, the meaning of dignity, and the impact of routine confinement on well-being."[26] With these conceptions of the zoo in mind, Torres's final chapter suggests an end for the narrator whereby he is rendered non/human.

"These days" in the zoo/institution, the narrator says, "I sleep with peacocks, lions, on a bed of leaves" (125).[27] If zoos and prisons are intimately linked in their technologies of incarceration, the other kinds of medicalized (psychiatric) institutions are part of the same landscape of containment and scrutiny. In this long present ("these days"), the narrator sleeps with—sexually and/or fraternally—peacocks and lions on a decorous, soft "bed of leaves." These species are culturally tied to ideas of regality, power, and beauty, which fleshes out this vaguely romantic tableau and suggests a distinct difference from nonhumans the narrator was previously tied to (e.g., locusts). Though he lies with these creatures, he notes, "I've lost my pack." His family, an animal "pack" (loyal, like dogs or wolves), are non/human because they are cast outside of normativity, though it is notable that they have not abandoned him to the zoo, but rather he has lost them, and is himself implicated in their separation.

The narrator's life in the zoo is rendered ambiguous, not least because his animality, his sexuality, and his mental health are entwined. As Sunaura Taylor argues, ableism and speciesism are entangled concepts because both use hierarchies of life that rest upon the normative human (whether in terms of race, for instance, or in this case ability). Disability activism and scholarship, Taylor notes, ignores the nonhuman at their peril, not only because disabled people have often been cast as less than human but because the logic of ableism is so linked to a normative anthropocentrism that is central to all systems of domination.[28]

The narrator, in his non/human form, "dream[s] of standing upright, of uncurled knuckles, of a simpler life—no hot muzzles, no fangs, no claws, no obscene plumage—strolling gaily, with an upright air." The good life, as it were, is one of verticality: in Stockton's terms, a heteronormative growth as upward movement. Casting aside his status as a queer non/human, the narrator imagines a world of straightness, free from animality and gayness. Rohrleitner suggests that in this final section, "the narrator . . . places himself outside of the norm, and embraces a world of outcasts and mongrels, where he strives, for the first time, to walk 'upright,'" in itself a "politics of queer refusal" and "active dissent," which Rohrleitner ties to a larger sociohistorical Puerto Rican resistance.[29] However, I want to temper that reading slightly, not least because I would refute the idea that the narrator "places himself" in the zoo or chooses the institution over his family; they are the ones who take him there after his lashing out. Instead, I think that this dream of uprightness also gives way to different futures. For instance, "muzzles" connotes both institutional restraints for patients as well as, perhaps, a fetishistic "hot" leather; "no fangs, no claws" indexes a physical kind of creatureliness principally related to harm and violence; and "obscene plumage" opens up images of a bird's feathers in what we might see as a gay ostentatious display. And even that hetero world of uprightness is one where the narrator can stroll "gaily," a linguistic tell that might point us back to queerness everywhere he looks.

We are then returned to the narrator's sleeping with "other animals in cages and in dens, down rabbit holes, on tufts of hay. They adorn me, these animals—lay me down, paw me, own me—crown me prince of their rank jungles." The language here is alternately constricting (cages, holes, rank) and comforting (tufts, adorn, paw), pointing to the simultaneous captivity and freedom the narrator must feel surrounded by "other animals" like him. He is even "prince of their rank jungles," a muddle of images that gesture back to regality (like the lion/peacock) and deviance (rank jungles). While Irr quoted previously calls him a "depressive 'prince'" rather than an "engaged member" of the democratic "we," I think the picture is more nuanced.

The zoo, we might say, is a space to lock up those on the outside of the normative human. As with the carceral nature of zoos for nonhumans, so too are queers frequently put in prisons, cages, and more generally detained by the state; indeed, as Chapman and colleagues argue, citizens get rights in "exchange for conformity, normalization, self-support, . . . erasing differences," and so on, the complete abnegation of otherness, of queerness writ large.[30] Stephen Dillon similarly argues that "race, gender, sexuality, and class are central processes that determine what bodies are captured and immobilized. . . . Within just four decades the prison emerged as a technology for the capture and management of racialized and gendered populations considered waste under the logics of twentieth-century racial capitalism."[31] Hovering at the border of a zoo and psychiatric institution, the final section of *We the Animals* puts the narrator behind the bars of normativity.

Even though the narrator and the other animals are caged, they make a home within its bars, a quasi-sanctuary within captivity. The narrator's final words, "'upright, upright,' I say, I slur, I vow," finds him caught in a repetition, an urging for something like normalcy or at least normativity. Rohrleitner writes that "the narrator moves from a drug-induced 'I slur' to a proudly affirming 'I vow'—ending his coming of age narrative with a promise to himself to not bend to anyone else's rule," which is, I think, more optimistic than the novel indicates.[32] At the intersection of various identities cast outside of the figuration of Man, the narrator is left yearning toward the normative category of human from which he will forever be excluded. But there seems to be queer potential here in this ending, even amid the narrator's internment. This final section of the book moves us from the past tense to the present, and from the idea of the zoo to zoo*keeping*. That shift into the present-day activity makes us think, among other things, Who is the zookeeper, and for how long are these people locked up? I suggest that it is the narrator and his "other animals" who do the keeping. We see no doctors, no medics, no zookeepers per se, but instead a model of collectivity (a new, differentiated "we"), a group of outsiders looking after one another. Approximating a kind of queer kinship—what Kath Weston famously termed "families we choose"[33]: those rearrangements of heteronormative sociality—the animals of this zoo tend themselves and look toward a framework of care outside of heteronormativity's strictures, even while those strictures de facto enforce this entrapment. Within normativity's binds, queer spaces can nonetheless flourish.

This scene of zookeeping might just be a form of what Muñoz calls "the brown commons." In his words, "brown people, places, feelings, sounds, animals, minerals, flora, and other objects" are brown because they at once "suffer" and are devalued but also because they "flourish under duress" and "smolder with a life and persistence." This "sense" of Brown, for Muñoz, refers to both those who have been racialized as Brown, as well as an orientation toward a kind of Brownness as ontology. The Brown commons are central to articulations of identity and agency, but they also register the structural positions of alterity and outsideness. Yet the commons are not merely human but, in my terms, queerly non/human. As both human and nonhuman, the Brown commons move between the singular and the plural, the individual and the assemblage, shuttling back and forth, not neglecting the particular subject nor their "coterminous[ness] with plurality."[34]

Muñoz is helpful for thinking the end of *We the Animals* because his theorization throws into relief much of what we have seen so far: that zookeeping is a mutual process, a form of collective care and group organizing; that those non/humans in the zoo are put there because of the so-called inhuman things that they have done, or are, or might be; that a psychiatric facility cast *as* a zoo links both the pathologizing of queer, ill, sick, and racialized others with the captivity of nonhuman animals; and that this particular zoo ends with the narrator both in a state of suffering and persistence. As in Muñoz's theorizing, the Latinx narrator of Torres's novella is Brown, "flourish[ing] under duress." If "brownness is a kind of uncanny presence in the face of distressed conditions of possibility," then the narrator of Torres's novel—locked up as, or like, an animal, "prince" of a "rank jungle"—is an example of this persistent presence.[35]

While his final say-slur-vow is not a full articulation of sovereignty, it is nonetheless a sideways exclamation of non/human agency. His upright movements might underscore certain forms of heteronormative growth, but they simultaneously articulate a Brown blossoming, a way of being in the commons both singularly and multiply non/human. Queer captivity or fugitivity? To return to Dillon: "The fugitive is a queer figure who is the site of a dramatic reimagining of freedom that points the way out even as life is increasingly surrounded."[36] The entanglements of sexuality, race, and non/human boundaries, then, are fuzzy at the book's conclusion. But in moving, on the final page, to the present moment (out of the memories that made up the rest of the book), *We the Animals* is temporarily grounded. In the *now*, the narrator is protected, at least safe from the ravages of the past. Though vowing to be upright, to leave the category of nonhuman animal behind, the narrator can, for now, merely inhabit his wild queerness, or queer wildness.

NOTES

1. Halberstam and Nyong'o, "Introduction," 453, 454, 456.

2. Ortiz, "Queer Latinx Studies," 52.

3. Irr, "The Multispecies," 281; Torres, *We the Animals*, 1. Torres cited hereafter in text.

4. Muñoz, *The Sense*, 82.

5. Halberstam and Nyong'o, 455.

6. To borrow Judith Butler's phrase.

7. The boys are "half as ugly, half as dark, half as wild" (54), in relation to their father's Latino-ness/brownness, which is itself tied to a "wild" non/human condition.

8. Halberstam, *Wild Things*, 9, 4. In this book, as noted in the introduction, Halberstam extends their argument with Nyong'o into a broader territory of wild scenes, genres, and figures. I use both here to think about the queerness/wildness link.

9. Muñoz, *The Sense*, 78, 79.

10. Disidentification is the way that minoritized populations (queer and raced, in particular) relate to mainstream culture and discourse. Rather than simply resisting or aligning with the mainstream, minoritized people transform and reimagine the mainstream through culture, music, performance, art and so on. Disidentification refuses the binary of reject/assimilate, instead queerly transforming the very fabric of the normative world.

11. Muñoz, *The Sense*, 85.

12. Stockton, *The Queer Child*, 2, 3, 4.

13. There are other complicated scenes around motherhood in the novella; such as when Ma learns she is pregnant with Manny at age fourteen, "heart ticking like a bomb" (26), leading the boys to ask a pregnant woman on the street if she has a bomb in her belly (28). Or when Ma more generally can't face the boys growing older, she says "When you boys turned seven, you left me" (14), and is not ready for the narrator to leave too.

14. Rohrleitner, "Refusing," 4, 5.

15. Rohrleitner, 5.

16. Giffney and Hird, "Introduction," 9.

17. Though I should note, in a previous chapter, a neighborhood boy, a "white trash" "headbanger" takes the boys into his basement and shows them a video of gay porn which, the narrator tells us, "tore us open, thinned what was thick." The video and the sexuality it ushers into the brothers' world begins to fissure their relationship, even though they already call the narrator a "faggot, a pest" (90).

18. Irr, "The Multispecies," 282.

19. Rodríguez, *Sexual Futures*, 7.

20. We will see this again in "Hunter."

21. Bersani, "Is the Rectum," 24.

22. Foucault, *Will to Knowledge*, 43.

23. The narrative voice shifts one more time in this section, "Dawn," to the third person: "Look, a father gently lowers his son, fully clothed, into a tub filling with bathwater" (119). Paps washes his son, who is dirty and smells (fully other now), and cares for him one final time. This scene, too painful perhaps for the narrator, becomes distanced through this third-person voice; the aftermath of violence too tender to face.

24. Chapman et al., "Reconsidering Confinement," 10.

25. Chapman et al., 14. They adapt this term from Foucault's "carceral archipelago."

26. Gruen, "Introduction," 2.

27. All quotes from this section are from the same page.

28. Taylor, *Beasts of Burden*.

29. Rohrleitner, "Refusing," 3.

30. Chapman et al., "Reconsidering Confinement," 12.

31. Dillon, *Fugitive Life*, 7.

32. Rohrleitner, "Refusing," 6.

33. Weston, *Families We Choose*.

34. Muñoz, *The Sense*, 2, 4.

35. Muñoz.

36. Dillon, *Fugitive Life*, 5.

NA
TU
RE

Nature

there is nothing natural about nature

I

This chapter is a brief analysis of Kumeyaay writer Tommy Pico's book-length *Nature Poem* (2017) for the ways that it puts "nature" in scare quotes, within queer and Indigenous frameworks. Pico's book is important within this larger bestiary because it relentlessly (re)frames and critiques human constructions of "nature" for their normativity and deep imbrication in colonizing imaginaries. The queerness of Pico's text lies in its representations of queer Indigeneity as well as the text's complicated orientation toward non/human imaginaries.

As in his other contemporary "epic poems," *IRL* (2016), *Junk* (2018), and *Feed* (2019), Pico uses the semi-fictionalized character Teebs (one of Pico's actual, and textual, nicknames) as the poem's speaker to ecstatically discourse on all manner of cultural phenomena.[1] *Nature Poem* is irregular (in form and layout), full of text-speak and contractions, and urges from the personal to the historical to the cultural and back again. Its speaker roves over white constructions of Indigenous life in the Americas, being a queer Native person while dating, as well as riffs on Aretha Franklin, histories of settler colonialism, and the historical freighting of poetry itself, all in "vignettes" that "refuse narrative cohesion."[2] At the heart of the book, as its title suggests, is a grappling with what it means to write a "nature poem" as an Indigenous person.

Nature Poem is a relentless act of apophasis, wherein one denies something that is nonetheless enacted in its refusal: "You can't be an NDN person in today's world // and write a nature poem,"[3] Pico writes, both making and not making the nature poem simultaneously. Such disavowal starts, in *Nature Poem*, from its very title, announcing the form that will summarily be rejected (even while embodying it). These lines, too, highlight what Teebs sees as an impossible position as an Indigenous person in contemporary America. The stanza break before "and write" yokes Nativeness and the poetic form together, so that it is impossible to both *be* Native and write poems as a Native person. In this way, as Will Clark argues using Gerald Vizenor's concept of the "fugitive pose," Pico's poetry engages this "Indigenous strategy for hiding in plain sight to combat either outright erasure or the tokenization of Indigenous life." Such Native fugitivity is in turn connected to queerness in Pico's work, which continually asks "where the expectations of a nature poem, queerness, or indigeneity originate."[4] *Nature Poem* scrutinizes the eponymous literary form through a queer Indigenous lens for its normative violences.

Pico's primary concern in this poem is that his speaker "can't write a nature poem / bc it's fodder for the noble savage / narrative" (2). He refuses to write about "feather imagery or booze," or to write a nature poem that "describes a slow pocket of dew in a SoCal Feb AM" (62). While the digital-speak of that line's ending contrasts the evocation of the dew in a way that distracts us from the language's potential beauty, Pico repeatedly wrestles with what it means to think about nature, because to do so is to automatically reproduce stereotype. As Teebs says, "Let's be clear, I hate nature—hate its *guts* / I say to my audience" (67), Colleen Eils notes that this refusal of the nature poem is also a stance against the "expectations placed on the poem's speaker."[5] Pico grapples with the ways that he (and Teebs) must *perform* nature negativity to his readership in order to prove his distance from the form, even while he notes that "*I don't hate nature at all*"—though even then his speaker quickly turns: "Fuck that. I recant" (67). Pico's speaker can only say he enjoys nature by simultaneously rejecting it, and performing that rejection in (a white U.S.) public.

An Indigenous appreciation of nature, in Pico's poem, is a near-impossibility because of the deep history linking them. As Chickasaw scholar Jodi A. Byrd writes, "The concept of the wild"—and, in relation, nature—"is so endemic to the production of the Indian that the two are entangled within the racial and colonial nostalgias that imagine freedom beyond the domestications, cultivations, and laws of settlement."[6] If the wild and nature are so entangled in the U.S. colonial imaginary, how is a Native poet able to write into, with, and through the natural world or other ecologies? In this bestiary's introduction, I note that Kim TallBear argues that Indigenous ways of thinking the non/human and the natural world do not conform to white Eurocentric ones. If "nonhuman others may not be understood even in critical Western frameworks as *living*," but "stones, thunder, or stars" ("objects" or "forces" in the new materialist parlance), "are known within our ontologies to be sentient and knowing persons," Pico's interrogation of the "natural" takes on a more particular Indigenous critique.[7] For instance, his speaker writes how "places have thoughts—hills have backs that love being stroked," and that "some see objects in the Earth, where I see lungs" (67). Even as Teebs rejects these images immediately, such an Indigenous perspective on the planet queries not simply how nature and the Native are tied but how there is such paucity in the word "nature" for describing phenomena beyond the human in a white framework.

In this light, Pico unpacks all kinds of *naturalness* in the book. The speaker notes that he's a "natural introvert" and questions the "natural" in the American Museum of Natural History (56). He describes, in an online dialogue with Angel Nafis, Aretha Franklin's voice as being from "THE CORE OF THE EARTH": that "gaia is alive in those pipes" (34). He asks, too, what "*does an NDN person look like exactly?*" (14). In each of these examples, Pico's speaker deploys "nature" in its manifold meanings—an essence, a version of history, an elemental quality, a set of norms—to scrutinize the term and the ways it has been conscripted normatively. Nature is presented as far from *natural*: It is not organically and universally *there* to be picked up and written about. Rather, as Nicole Seymour argues, nature is constructed in so many ways in the popular cultural imagination. While she notes, for example, queer theory's frequent anxiety about nature (for instance, how norms posit heterosexuality as natural, queerness as unnatural), Seymour is clear in pointing out that we should scrutinize the *constructions* of nature rather than "nature" itself. Indeed, she looks to texts—much like Pico's—that ask "'What counts as "natural"—and why?' in regard to *both* gender/sexuality and environment," in ways that illuminate the "imbrication" of those categories.[8]

Pico's poem, as well as thinking about Indigenous forms of writing nature, also enlaces the natural with queerness and gay male sexuality in particular. In reflecting on dating, the speaker Teebs often critiques the white male gaze (gays) for its framing of his Native identity. When a man asks, "WHAT'S YR NATIONALITY!?!?" while waiting in line at a bar, Teebs turns to the natural world to think about the question's im/possibility. "In order to talk about a hurricane," Pico writes, "you first have to talk about a preexisting disturbance over the ocean, so you have to talk about mean ocean temperature, so you have to talk about human industry and sun rays" (9) and so on. This unspooling of nested questions—you cannot talk about one thing without many others—leads the speaker to ask, "How far back do you have to go to answer any question about race?" (9). As we will see shortly, this linking of queries is part of Pico's ethics of non/human entanglement, but for now it is worth noting how Pico's resistance to nature is also connected to the broader ways in which his Indigeneity is seen by white America.

As in many of this bestiary's chapters, Pico's speaker ties human sexuality to animality in ways that sometimes upholds and sometimes destabilizes species hierarchy: The poem is ambivalent at times about how different kinds of life are made valuable. In other words, the poem holds multiple ideas in tension: Its queer Indigenous critique confronts the difficulty of valuing nonhuman lives when they are so often valued above the lives of people of color. The poem refuses to reconcile these speciesist questions. Teebs says that he "literally hate[s] all men bc literally men are animals— // This is a kind of nature I could write a poem about" (2). While the poem suggests that humans are animals too, Teebs is also playing on the trope of "men are animals" that, in a speciesist logic, dehumanizes men for their "bad" behavior. Again, Pico has it both ways. His speaker says that gay men "are the worst" because you are "nothing to them" if "they don't want to fuck you"; however, "they love dogs" (18), which in Teebs's framing suggests that the (white) human desire for dogs trumps the desire for men who are "unfuckable."[9] Early on, too, the speaker notes how "OKCupid asks what's worse—a starving child or a starving dog, and I'm like *is this a fucking joke?*" (7). While we can see speciesist logic here that runs counter to ecological critique—how and why are human lives often seen as more important, more valuable, than nonhuman ones?—Pico's speaker locates this query within the dating framework of OkCupid. There is a sense, along with the other examples above, that gay dating for Teebs is a constant assault on the worth of Indigenous life. As such, this question becomes a way for Teebs to lash out at a gay world that would prioritize a dog's life over an Indigenous person's, because of their identity. It is a replay of white heteronormativity (and homonormativity) that would prioritize nonhuman pets over the lives of people of color, including Indigenous people; Teebs is asking how normative values as such are apportioned to humans and nonhumans alike, even in ways that feel problematic for a queer animal studies frame.

Indeed, the poem gets queerer, stranger, when one of Teebs's lovers "nuzzles his forehead" and "growls" in an "animalistic" way, but to get back at the men who dehumanize him, Teebs "bite[s] [them] on the cheek" to "reify savage lust" (15). Conforming to the animalistic stereotypes foisted on him, Pico's speaker acts out against social scripts by fully embodying them.

II

Throughout *Nature Poem*, Pico offers a highly ambivalent yet caustic relation to the natural because of its normative underpinnings, yet he nonetheless shows how important to our ethics the concept is. His queer Indigenous take on the nature poem is akin to those texts read by Seymour as proffering a "queer environmentalism," wherein the queer is linked "to the natural world through an empathetic, ethical imagination" that "understand[s] oppressed humans . . . and oppressed non-humans . . . to be deeply connected." Where Pico's environmental ethics is perhaps more ambiguous than some of Seymour's examples, his writing attempts—through avowal and disavowal—to "combat the kinds of naturalizations and denaturalizations that enable exploitation and discrimination."[10] Seymour's conception of queer environmentalism hinges on the active entangling of queerness (in all its variety) and the nonhuman (in all is variety). We see this throughout *Nature Poem*, as Pico details not only the linking of Indigenous, queer, and non/human worlds but also the way that "you become a little bit of everything you brush / against" (30). This worldly *stickiness* is Pico's way of articulating what we see throughout this bestiary: the osmosis between the human and the nonhuman (via that membranous slash, *non/human*).

Pico's speaker argues that "it seems foolish to discuss nature w/o talking about endemic poverty," and runs with this idea for a few lines, to think about "colonialism which seems foolish to talk about w/o talking about misogyny" (12). The text-speak, rather than undermining the seriousness of the topic, actually bridges and links—via the slash in "w/o"—each of the concepts, so that formally and thematically they are joined. Relatedly, when talking about romance, Teebs says that all dates feel like "the final date" because gays cannot help but be "rude" to each other, in ways akin to "deforestation" (22). Pico is both raising dating experiences as a queer Native person to ecological catastrophe—putting them in dialogue—as well as highlighting Teebs's melodrama. Dating feels like the end of the world, in this poem, even as it is not that; the destruction of forests is not the same as being ghosted, but the psychic material between those experiences feels relative. By putting such phenomena into dialogue, Pico is highlighting how enmeshed non/human worlds are in this queer cosmology, for better and worse.

Ultimately, though, this queer Indigenous entanglement is complicated for Pico by the English in which he writes. His speaker struggles with the nature poem form,

> bc English is some Stockholm shit, makes me complicit in my tribe's erasure—why shd I give a fuck abt "poetry"? It's a container for words like *whilst and hither* . . . (50)

For Teebs, "poetry" and its English form delimits (as "a container") all decolonial voices because the language is so saturated by white supremacist history. Language, his speaker says, "is engineered so naturally like it doesn't even happen" (53). Here, *natural* signals something like the invisibilizing forces of normativity; how language can hide (an) empire, to bastardize a recent book title.[11] By questioning how poetic language often "tells the story of its own conquests" (53), Pico—in Clark's words—

questions "for whom poetry is universal," and thus "rejects what the poem is supposed to afford because he knows those affordances do not accommodate him."[12] Pico's writing, through apophasis, enables a simultaneity of using and rejecting dominant modes of poetics to queer them from within.

To write a nature poem as a queer Indigenous person, then, is to confront both historical and cultural freighting of "nature" and "poem." Pico's speaker oscillates between wanting and not wanting to play into either normative framework and as such keeps each term suspended. *Nature Poem* is a queer ecological work that thinks, as Seymour puts it in relation to other texts, an "environmental politics even while remaining . . . skeptical, ironic, and self-reflexive."[13] As such, at the end of the poem, the speaker sits on a porch in a tranquil pastoral scene ("lavender in the air," "sun . . . over the hill," "Roy knows the names of all the plants in his front yard" [74]). Lest we think Teebs is finally relating in an uncomplicated way to the "beauty" of the natural world, the punchily alliterative line after this again skewers the moment: "the air is clear, and all across Instagram—peeps are posting pics of the sunset" (74). Clark writes that the poem's final line, the "digitization of the natural world," trivializes and flattens anything we might call nature through its "shared consumption" by humans on social media.[14] In the way that nature is tied to Nativeness, so too is it drained of meaning when endlessly circulated as mere aesthetic.

Elsewhere in the poem, Pico writes that "people r so concerned abt 'the Earth' / in the sense of kale salad and bruised / gin" (47), in a critique not unlike that of Timothy Morton when they write that the "sadistic admiration" of nature instead of attention to *ecology* deliberately obfuscates real environmental concerns.[15] The mythic and romantic valorizing of n/Nature serves to short-circuit engagement and attentiveness with real ecologies and environments. Nature does not get us closer to the natural, Morton argues, but rather distorts and obfuscates it through attention to image over complex materiality. Pico's final move, then, is to both embrace fleeting moments of nature (light, smell, affect) while simultaneously critiquing our/his easy ingestion and recycling of it through aesthetic forms, like Instagram or, indeed, poetry. To be concerned about the earth, about ecologies, about the human's place on the planet (when "human" is doing so much normativizing work that overlooks sexual and racial differences, among much else), is—in the end—the material of a nature poem. Pico's queer Indigenous take on environmentalism forces us to consider the messiness of the non/human as that term's slash *contains multitudes*: of culture, sexuality, gender, race, Indigeneity, place, and identity, in ways that the transcendentalists and their kin would not quite recognize.

NOTES

1. Amin, Musser, and Pérez write that this form can "mess with metrics of scale and taste": Pico "uses the affordances of the long-form poem" (most typically linked to a white poetic tradition), "to invoke the sensual proximity of disparate vectors of experience and thought." On *IRL*, the writers note that Pico uses the long form to "activate a queer, Indigenous interpretation of empire by exhaustively sequencing sex, history, gossip," and so on. In *Nature Poem*, he does much the same, using both the form of "nature poem" and "epic" to scramble and queer our senses of both ("Queer Form," 238).

2. Clark, "Tommy Pico's Fugitive," 526.

3. Pico, *Nature*, 67. Cited hereafter in text.

4. Clark, "Tommy Pico's Fugitive," 524, 532.

5. Eils, "Deborah Miranda," 94.

6. Byrd, "Beast," 600.

7. TallBear, "An Indigenous," 234.

8. Seymour, *Strange*, 5, 2.

9. See "Dog" herein for more on the uneven relations between humans and canines as they intersect with race and gender.

10. Seymour, *Strange*, 1, 5.

11. Daniel Immerwahr, *How to Hide an Empire: A History of the Greater United States* (2019).

12. Clark, "Tommy Pico's Fugitive," 532.

13. Seymour, *Strange*, 2.

14. Clark, "Tommy Pico's Fugitive," 534.

15. Morton, *Ecology*, 5.

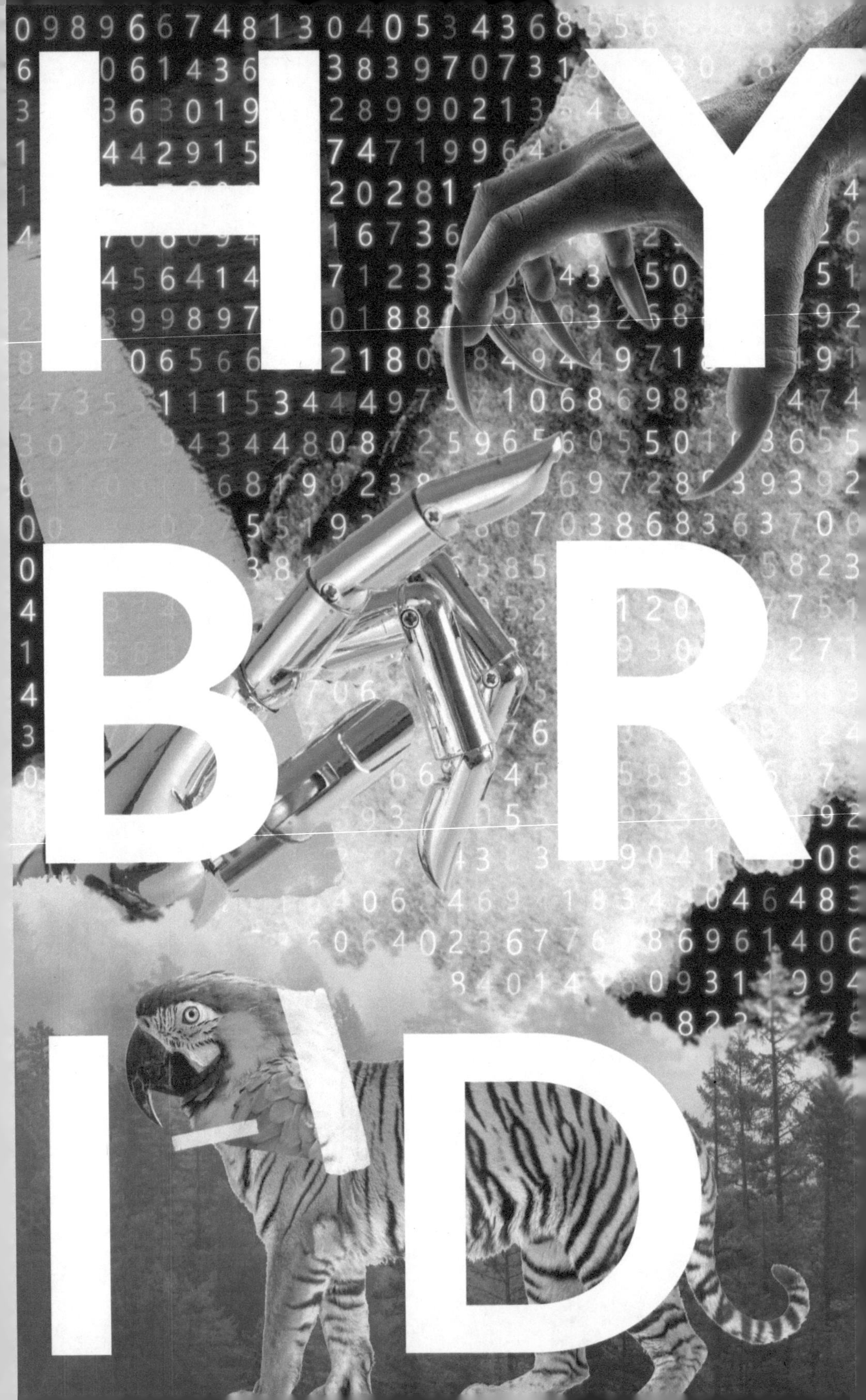
HYBRID

Hybrid

the one is always many

I

"Hybrid," in its first use as noun and adjective (in the early 1600s and late 1700s, respectively), referred principally to the offsprings of two plants or of two nonhuman animals: the outcome of mixing two breeds, species, types, varieties. Only later did "hybrid" get taken up as a marker of human mingling, where the term refers to someone who is a "blend" of two cultures, traditions, or ethnicities; even then, whiteness gets normalized as before or outside hybridity, which is saved for people of color, for Indigenous people, those who are "mixed." As poet Will Harris writes, "To be mixed race is to exist in a state of paradox," for race "is an illusion that depends on purity and singleness." To be mixed race is to destabilize, for Harris, all kinds of narratives about identity and belonging, not least because "with too many heritages or too few, . . . the mixed-race person grows up to see the self as something strange and shifting."[1] "Hybrid" in this racialized sense, then, is freighted with colonial history and sedimented with notions of essence and fixity even in its gesture toward complexity. Yet there is always an emphasis on the pair that makes the "new" singular identity: the blending of two discrete phenomena to make the one. Hybridity is the outcome, the endpoint.

Yet, for postcolonial critics like Homi K. Bhabha, hybridity marks not "a third term that resolves the tension between two cultures" but rather an ambivalent space that ruptures both the colonizer and colonized, such that those designations become less fixed.[2] Scholars have further critiqued the use of hybridity for the ways that the term obscures the innate messiness of all identity, not just that within colonial interaction. The term crops up in feminist posthuman discourse too, onward from Donna Haraway, whose "cyborg" is a "hybrid of machine and organism." We are all, in Haraway's vision, "chimeras," fusions of the human and the technological, queer creatures in a "postgender world."[3] Yet, where Haraway sees the cyborg as a new hybrid state, as breaking apart binaries of human/nonhuman, human/machine, it arguably, as Jasbir Puar points out, just "inhabits the intersection of body and technology."[4] In Puar's and other critics' minds, Haraway's cyborg merely reinforces a binary mode of thinking rather than an entangled one.

I linger in this theoretical muddle because it epitomizes, I suggest, the hybrid's messiness: the term's gesturing backward to two discrete origins, as well as toward new and unimagined states of being. Hybridity seems to be both essentialist and not, queer and not, normative and not. These ideas are probed by so many of the texts in my bestiary, whether under the nomenclature of hybrid or something related. As such, this brief chapter glosses some of the hybrid borderlands between and across the non/human to frame or prefigure some of the chapters that follow.

II

In his novel *On Earth We're Briefly Gorgeous* (2019), Ocean Vuong uses numerous non/human figures to tell a story of queer love, family, and migration; a number of those figures (taxidermy, dogs, butterflies, hunters) recur in this bestiary. Vuong's novel is narrated by Little Dog, a queer Vietnamese American man writing a letter to his mother, Rose, whose lack of English means she will likely not understand any of it. He writes about her abusiveness—perhaps symptomatic of her traumatic years in Vietnam during the war—and their migration to the United States, as well as his growing sense of difference, as a feminized and queer boy who falls in love with a fellow tobacco picker who later overdoses.[5] Early in the book, Rose, who recognizes her abusiveness (even as the behavior continues), says that she is not a monster but simply a mother.[6] Little Dog ostensibly agrees with her, but thinks (and writes): "What I really wanted to say was that a monster is not such a terrible thing to be. From the Latin root *monstrum*, a divine messenger of catastrophe, then adapted by the Old French to mean an animal of myriad origins: centaur, griffin, satyr. To be a monster is to be a hybrid signal, both shelter and warning at once."[7]

Little Dog lays claim to multiple origins, to mixing, to the duality of hybridity and its ambivalences. Taking back the monster is a way both of normalizing and queering his mother's role in his life, as a figure of care and of terror. *Monster* also becomes synonymous with terms like "*freak, fairy, fag*" (14), words that Little Dog dodges yet internalizes. This scene cannot but recall, for me, Susan Stryker's canonical essay "My Words to Victor Frankenstein About the Village of Chamounix: Performing Transgender Rage" (1994), in which she uses the *Frankenstein* story to think sex, gender, and the body. "Like the monster, I am too often perceived as less than fully human due to the means of my embodiment," she writes. Claiming the moniker of monster (and a monstrous identity), Stryker argues that in the way "'dyke,' 'fag,' 'queer'" and so on have been reclaimed by lesbians and gays in particular, so too can transgender people reclaim the "monster." Vuong cites the same definitions of monstrum that Stryker does in this article (his indebtedness to queer and trans theory clearly is on show here), yet Stryker goes further in warning the cis reader that the "Nature you bedevil [her] with" (transness as unnatural, aberrant), is a "lie" and "fabrication." Everyone, trans and non-trans alike, are "constructed" beings, far from normative or singular in corporeality or identity.[8] Little Dog, while not trans, is embracing the monstrous as a marker of his sexuality and his racial identity: as mixed, layered, hybrid. And as Jeffrey Jerome Cohen explains, the monstrous body is always "pure culture": a product that is both "construct and projection," that signifies "something other than itself." Monsters also, as this chapter shows, "refus[e] easy categorization" and are "disturbing hybrids" that destroy binaries and existing forms.[9] In this way, Little Dog's calling attention to the plurality and ambiguity of the monster—rather than a simplified horror—provides one way of reading the queer cultural work hybrid figures.

As becomes clear in the novel, indeterminacy, monstrosity, and multiplicity are at the heart of each of Vuong's characters. Everyone is connected to figures of animality and hybridity as they wrestle with the complexities of identity and the pressures of the past. Each character bears the imprint of, and works through, memory—both personal and national, spanning the timeline and geographies of the Vietnam War and its aftermath. This chapter uses Little Dog's insights to unpack hybridity's centrality to thinking the non/human. The other texts I briefly survey here use hybrids to substantiate a queer mingling and relationality, though the machine-animal, the nonhuman within the human, and non/humans joined together. These states of entanglement—non/human—help unravel stable and heteronormative categories like "human" or "nonhuman."

III

Franny Choi's poetry collection *Soft Science* (2019) links the human and nonhuman in relation to the cyborg, inflected by feminist and queer of color framings of the technological. Rather than see the human and machine as initially separate and then conjoined through the cyborg, Choi's poems emphasize the messy relationality of these already mingled categories.

In a set of prose-poems scattered throughout the book, titled "Turing Test" (and its variations, like "Turing Test_Love"), Choi stages mathematician and computer scientist Alan Turing's "imitation game" on the page. Turing's 1950 test examines a machine's ability to show cognition in a *human* way (itself a complex idea). In Choi's hands, the dialogue between the poem's (we assume) human speaker and machine is a queering of boundaries between so-called subject and object. Indeed, when the speaker asks "*so, how do you like working with humans*" the machine responds with "tips" including "remember / all humans / are cyborgs / all cyborgs / are sharp shards of sky / wrapped in meat."[10] Here, the machine sibilantly turns the query around, positing the inseparability of human and machine, a common cyborg nature that is disavowed: "remember / they love their blood / even as they retch / at the smell of it."[11] The machine pinpoints the human ambivalence about its status as embodied flesh, an articulation that the speaker never questions or critiques.

Choi's Turing tests point to a world of intersubjectivity where the cyborg is "alien turned bricolage beast" as much as the human is.[12] This is not, as Puar describes Haraway, an exceptionalizing and overdetermining of technological progress, but rather an assemblage or agencement.[13] For Puar, thinking agencement (which, in the original French, prioritizes *relation* over the *content of "assemblage"*) is a way of unbounding our conceptions of identity. Critiquing both intersectionality's spatial limits and the cyborg's binary ones, Puar connects agencement and intersectionality to develop feminist theorizing. Here, the matter of relationality is more important than the matter of machine, and Choi's poems—in their dialogic nature—resist the simple binaries that Haraway's cyborg inadvertently ushers in. Instead, the differentiations between machine and human are unfixed to begin with; thus, their coming together is less a joining of two types, but a mingling of the already mingled.

The queer world of *Soft Science*—queer because unstable and anti-identitarian, as well as de-/re-/un-gendered—is linked to Choi's larger body of work in which race, sexuality, gender, class, and nationhood are all entwined through corporeality's vicissitudes. As Choi notes in an interview about the collection, "Blurring the confines of my own identity is a way of embodying a kind of queerness."[14] The cyborg is but one node in that identity-questioning poetry and links back to the imaginative work that Vuong does in his novel where blurred non/human boundaries substantiate a queer embodiment.

IV

In related ways, two queer texts that have *Bestiary* as their titles (Donika Kelly's 2016 poetry collection and K-Ming Chang's 2020 novel) also see hybridity as central to non/human identity. Both texts use the bestiary title because they present so many hybrids—hybrid in the sense of two discrete forms joined together *and* in the sense of pluralized and non-essentialized categories blurring together. Both texts play with mythic imbrications of life forms, referencing Greek and Taiwanese stories of non/human dialogue. And both use the hybrid figure to crack open questions of species, as they are flanked by race, gender, and sexuality.

Poet Nikky Finney describes Kelly's collection as penned "by an all Black girl who teaches us nothing is all black, or all female, or all male, or all belonging to humans, or all tidy."[15] Building on the earlier bestiary tradition, Finney writes, the book is a "Hybrid of longing and lust," occupying a space of in-between-ness, or multiplicity both in the individual poems and the whole collection.[16] This hybridity, too, is partly rooted in U.S. soil. In the opening poem "Out West," the speaker says: "Refuse the old means of measurement. / Rely instead on the thrumming / wilderness of self." As a space of "bison" and "river[s]" and "black bear winters," the speaker's identity is tied to the landscape, an American vision of the frontier that, as the collection progresses, is far from a colonial project but an expansive vision of intersubjectivity and hybrid being.[17] That is, the multispecies archive of poems that make the collection tap into wild spaces, as per Jack Halberstam and Tavia Nyong'o's understanding, by dragging historical associations of the frontier into new and queer arrangements. The wild, in the hands of Black and Indigenous and queer writers can "interrupt[] the neat narratives of freedom and escape" that attended the colonial imagination.[18] As Kelly's speaker writes, this "west-ness" is an internal landscape, a psychic terrain as confined as it is expansive. The poem ends:

> If you could bear
> being a person, you would no longer be
> an iron bluff.
> Do not wander. We are all apportioned
> a certain measure of stillness.[19]

Kelly's speaker cannot "bear" their humanness and is a stationary bluff, a feature of the land. Unable to "wander" in a kind of westward expansion, the speaker remains still and fixed, a hybrid identity that is haunted by the wild, both in its colonial and anticolonial tenor.

In light of that poem, the rest of *Bestiary* unfolds as a multispecies archive, much like its medieval forebears, filled with non/human hybrids. There are some "Self-Portrait" poems ("Self-Portrait as a Block of Ice" or "as a Wooden Flower"), pointing to human identity understood through the nonhuman; as well as poems about bodies coming apart (he "hollows her like a gourd,"[20] and, "I am reeling, spooling / away from what holds muscle to bone"[21]); or beings in states of flux ("To be, always, a waxing / a waning, and, in waxing / again, not ever the same."[22]) But the collection is fleshed out most extensively with hybrid devotional poems, like "Love Poem: Centaur." These poems litter the book like medieval bestiary entries, but are all textured by the overlaps between gender, sexuality, and race in the contemporary. In "Love Poem: Chimera," for example, the speaker "thought myself lion and serpent. Thought / myself body enough for two, for we."[23] Identity is always double-or-more for Kelly. There are poems of Pegasus's birth, of a satyr's call to their lover, of a mermaid's cry, and so on. Kelly's bestiary is a collection of non/human voices, all articulating the same self: this is identity as multiple, as riven from within by the nonhuman, both animate and not, in Mel Chen's words,[24] as always on the threshold of something other than itself, queer.

In a late "Love Poem," the speaker moves through five parts that link them to their beloved through the non/human. They are first "fish" who "flop and gasp and rub our scales"; and then the speaker "pine[s]," as longing and as tree, "bark and needle"; they then imagine the lover as "the sun and water"; and when the lover returns, the speaker (who we assume does not identify as a man) is "the strongest / man in the world"; finally, at night, "the bed is covered with pollen / and scales."[25] That it is love poetry through which Kelly keenly articulates hybridity is striking; she seems to articulate what Dominic Pettman calls "creaturely love." Combating ideas of love as something that nonhuman animals have been said not to experience (because of its complexity, its humanness), Pettman argues that "what we love in the beloved precedes and exceeds that abstract element we call the human. Love thus makes us both more and less than human," an idea that seems central to Kelly's work. When Kelly's lovers end up covered in fish scales and pollen, the poem gestures to the ways that what is loved about the other is a kind of creatureliness, in Pettman's terms, but one that is intimately queer. Where Pettman's book sees love in broader social terms, Kelly's poems situate hybridity at the heart of queer love: Her poems often trace ambiguously gendered figures and their loved ones. Pettman asks, wryly, quoting *Othello* and others, "how do we remain human while making the hybrid beast-with-two-backs? Indeed, *should* we remain human at such a moment?"[26] For Pettman and Kelly, love and sex are seen most clearly in the hybrid inseparability of human and nonhuman forms.

In K-Ming Chang's *Bestiary*, hybrid forms are similarly concerned with the limits of the human as they relate to sex and gender but also race and ethnicity. All of those are framed, moreover, by transcultural memories. The Taiwanese American protagonist, Daughter, one day hears the story of Hu Go Po—a tiger spirit who inhabits a woman's body and consumes children—and the next day she grows a tiger's tail.[27] The tail becomes a sign of Daughter's difference, though it is both separate from and central to her identity. If Hu Go Po is a monstrous figure (like the monster invoked by Vuong's novel), it does not make Daughter wholly monstrous too, but rather an inhabited figure of hybrid identities.

At the same time, handwritten notes start to spring from holes in the ground that Daughter digs. These notes turn out to be from Ama, her grandmother, which Daughter and her girlfriend Ben translate (both literally, in terms of language, and metaphorically, in terms of their symbolic content). As Daughter learns about her family's past in Taiwan and their migration to the United States, she bears the weight of that memory; at the same time, she grapples with her queerness (in terms of sexuality and her new animality). As such, hybridity takes on queer meaning as it relates to both history and identity. The novel, as the title suggests, is filled with nonhumans and, more than anything, corporeality in extremity—from the very start, Chang foregrounds sweat, blood, vomit, feces, urine, and other bodily fluids. The novel is saturated with the body's very fleshiness, especially across and within species lines: Characters are constantly coming apart. As in Vuong's novel, the nonhuman animal links queer Asian American youth to past generations across geographies; like Choi and Kelly's poems, Chang paints non/human relations as intimately queer, especially as that queerness is inflected by gender, sexuality, and race.

Before Daughter even grows a tail, we know that the family is rendered in similar non/human terms. For instance, her father is "embroidered with bits of bullets" from war and is "scaled into some hybrid species."[28] Ba is literally changed by violence as the metal becomes part of his skin;[29] war transforms both body and mind (as we see also in Vuong's novel). Such bodily hybridity is also connected to Ma's past in Taiwan where her life is marked by language shifts that are worn "like a collar": "Tayal and Yilan Creole in the indigo fields . . . , Japanese during the war, Mandarin in the Nationalist-eaten city" (5). As if animalistically on a leash, Ma's relation to Asia and history is one of geographical and cultural mixing, which is also a "life in slashes, everything a choice: Leave/Stay. Mother/Daughter. Love/Life" (16). These options leave Ma both in and on the binary. She is a hybrid between and beyond categories, a liminality that is passed down to Daughter, which is then literalized (via myth) into her human-tiger state.

In the myth, Hu Go Po remains in women so long as they hunt, and in the novel Daughter's tiger-ness is tied to both protecting her family and exploring her queer sexuality. A "sapling" emerges from a hole in Daughter's back one day that, in this first simile, is "stiff as my brother's morning wood, a kind of kindling" (48). As two kinds of *wood*, the tail is both phallic and un/natural, a link that Chang extends throughout the novel. Daughter's tail is relentlessly sexualized, even in the way it seems to take over her body; she says, "The tail must be breeding with my bones, seeding what would breach my skin next, claws or canines" (49). "Breeding" and "seeding" figure the tail as penile and procreative, but not in any heteronormative way (this is no reproductive futurism). Indeed, Hu Go Po is the "governor" of Daughter's body, but it is an ambiguous hybridity, for is the tail under her control or something autonomous? Is she a girl with a tiger inside her, or is she something more mixed, a girl-tiger?

As Daughter learns more about her family's past and gets closer to her (masc-named) girlfriend Ben, her tail becomes more agential, embodying her unconscious. When she sees Ben, the tail "moved like a compass hand and tautened in her direction" (73), a rigidity that she tries to hide. When they finally have sex, Ben grabs the tail, which is "tensed" (107) like a penis, something that Daughter is fraught by (but Ben seems to enjoy). The tail is not only this sexual object, though; it is also a weapon Daughter uses against her father. On a day out, he terrifies Daughter's brother into peeing himself, pertinently calling him "an animal, a beast that couldn't behave its bladder" (95). Daughter attacks her father with the tail, protecting her and her brother, vanquishing the literal and metaphoric father figure (she sends Ba away).

The tail is a phallus in all its psychoanalytic resonance. As Judith Butler writes in *Bodies That Matter* (1993), "The phallus functions as a synecdoche, for insofar as it is a figure of the penis, it constitutes an idealization and isolation of a body part and, further, the investment of that part with the force of symbolic law." Yet, as Butler goes on, the "integrity" of the normative sexed body is "paradoxically achieved through an identification with its reduction into idealized synecdoche." That is, binary sex is held up through the phallus's inherent impotency. But bodies like Daughter's—queer ones that, in their hybridity, escape the heteronormative binary—are those that "fail[] to submit to the law" or contract "its dictate," and as such appear as "imaginary" or "fictional" bodies that rupture the norms "that govern the intelligibility of sex."[30] In other words, Daughter's girl-tiger hybridity is defined by this tail-cum-phallus, which both articulates queer desire and topples the law of the father.

Later in the book, when Ben and Daughter try to translate grandmother's letters that appear from the ground, Ben speculates in a footnote that the tail might be an umbilical cord: "What if you're being fed through it? I know cords don't usually grow out of the ass, but if I were an umbilical cord, I'd want to come back and avenge being cut" (156).[31] Where the cord is severed to separate parent and child, Ben sees the tail as a queerly anal regrafting, an awry way to re- or self-feed the body. In seeking revenge for being cut—for dismantling the parent-child bond—the tail reforms itself as a weapon, a "lesbian phallus" (to twist Butler's term), and a queer partner in and of itself. Chang's girl-tiger is a hybrid that substantiates the messiness of familial, gendered, racial, and cultural identity—forever resisting and revisiting the myth of origins, and the stability of selfhood.

At the end of the novel, Daughter asks Ben to "cleave" the tail from her. Ben's reply is a perfect epigraph for the queer hybrid texts we have been looking at in this chapter: "Ben said there were two definitions of *cleave*. I said she knew which one I meant" (246). As a contranym, cleave contains dual and opposite meanings (to separate *and* to bring together), central to queer hybridity. Ben notes that "*Having a body is a liability*" (246) and that it is not something to reject (or cut off). Indeed, corporeality's messiness, its hybridity, is part of *Bestiary*'s point. When Daughter tells her teacher that there are not plural forms of Chinese words, she replies, "*Then how do you know if it's one thing or many?*" Daughter's answer, "*One thing is always many*" (80), defines the hybrid tout court.

To think hybridity is—for these queer writers of color—to think the messy interrelations of the non/human as they intersect with sexuality, gender, and race (among other markers). For Vuong, Choi, Kelly, and Chang, the hybrid figure is a way to conceive of identity's multiplicity, not in the dominant sense of hybrid as two things welded together, but rather as the always plural anoriginality of the self. There are no separate breeds or types, as in the dictionary definition, that then create a hybrid third, as those primary types were already riven from within by the multiple. Each of these writers paint hybridity as intimately queer because of queerness' proximity to destabilization and the rejection of the categorical. These texts put it directly: The hybrid is queer.

NOTES

1. Harris, *Mixed-Race Superman*, 15, 14.
2. Bhabha, *The Location*, 162.
3. Haraway, "A Cyborg," 5, 7, 8.
4. Puar, "'I would rather,'" 56.

5. For more on the feminization of Asian American men in general, see Eng's *Racial Castration* (2001).

6. It is worth noting, as an aside, the linguistic closeness of mother/monster.

7. Vuong, *On Earth*, 13. Cited hereafter in text.

8. Stryker, "My Words," 238, 240, 241. A reappraisal of her article more recently has Stryker identify this move as a critique of the "unstated cisnormative bias in queer theory" (40).

9. Cohen, "Monster Culture," 38, 40.

10. The slashes here appear as in the original; they do not indicate end-lines.

11. Choi, "Turing Test_Love," 69.

12. Choi, "Turing Test_Boundaries," 37.

13. Puar, "'I would rather,'" 57.

14. Quong, "Queerness."

15. The capitalization and non-capitalization are Finney's.

16. Finney, "Introduction," x.

17. Kelly, "Out West," 3.

18. Halberstam and Nyong'o, "Theory," 455.

19. Kelly, "Out West,"

20. Kelly, "Where," 9.

21. Kelly, "Love letter," 47.

22. Kelly, "Self-Portrait," 14.

23. Kelly. "Love Poem: Chimera," 10.

24. Chen, *Animacies*, 11.

25. Kelly, "Love Poem," 64.

26. Pettman, *Creaturely*, xi, 13.

27. We might also think about the ways that tigers litter C. Pam Zhang's *How Much of These Hills Is Gold* (2020). In this queer Asian American telling of the U.S. West (in which neither the American setting nor century are defined), Zhang's Chinese immigrant family are forever seeing traces of tigers in this new country: paw-prints, bones. The tigers that haunt the story seemingly trouble the idea that the narrative is in the American West and help to substantiate Zhang's queer perspective on this moment of history. Like Chang's book, also, Zhang is interested in how racialized hybridity is also tied to sexual and gender nonnormativity. There is much to glean from linking these two texts, not least through the tiger image.

28. Chang, *Bestiary*, 10. Cited hereafter in text.

29. We could say that metals, too, are already changed by virtue of their being transformed from ores. Ba becomes doubly mixed.

30. Butler, *Bodies*, 139.

31. These lines are all in capitals in the novel.

GRO
UND
HOG

Groundhog

can the animal be written?

Groundhog Day, celebrated on February 2 in the United States and Canada, derives from a Pennsylvania Dutch superstition, brought from Europe to the Americas in the seventeenth and eighteenth centuries. German colonists believed that if the groundhog emerged from its burrow on this day and saw its shadow, winter would continue for another six weeks; if it did not, spring would arrive early. Interestingly, there is already creaturely slippage here, as the colonists were talking about badgers originally, not groundhogs. But the groundhog's iconicity in the United States was further cemented by the 1993 release of *Groundhog Day*, starring Bill Murray and Andie MacDowell, in which a TV weatherman is stuck on a loop, reliving Groundhog Day over and over again. If there is anything to be gleaned here, it is that the symbolic function of the groundhog (itself overlaying a badger) is connected both to changing seasons and providence, as well as a sense of repetition, of reliving the superstition.

Each of these feature in Ellen Bryant Voigt's poem "Groundhog" (2011), which thinks about the power of naming, of how we put nonhumans into human language that may or may not interrupt the way we understand them. The queerness of this poem is less overt than some of the other texts in this book, but its power comes from the ways in which the text sets itself up—through the title—to grasp the groundhog, but from the very start fails to do so. Kaveh Akbar and Kevin Young, in conversation on *The New Yorker Poetry Podcast*, gloss the poem as not simply *describing* the groundhog but instead trying to *get at* the creature itself: it's "so groundhoggy," Akbar notes.[1] Yet that groundhoggy-ness is, I would suggest, exactly the poem's undoing; holding the creature still, as in a scientific textbook or zoo, proves impossible. This is partly because of language's failings, but also the nonhuman's resistance to human mastery and understanding. As the speaker of "Groundhog" says in the final lines (all of which run on, punctuationless), "it matters / what we're called words shape the thought."[2] We cannot know a thing outside of the ways in which we describe it, or so the poem seems to suggest. As Ferdinand de Saussure might put it: "Nothing is distinct before the appearance of language."[3] But that process of description is not so easy.

Closely reading the poem will tease out some of these complexities. What does it mean to talk about the animal, the nonhuman—in simply neutral or even ethical ways—if that subject cannot partake in the discussion, let alone understand it? Timothy Baker argues that "the presence of animals in fiction presents a continual challenge to questions of linguistic representation," because the nonhuman animal "cannot be anything other than represented, seen through a linguistic prism that it does not share."[4] Extended to other kinds of literature, Baker notes how nonhumans will forever be simply the represented, rather than the ones representing. Or, as Kari Weil puts it, "Those who constitute the objects of animal studies cannot speak for themselves, or at least they cannot speak any of the languages that the academy recognizes as necessary for such self-representation. Must they then be forever condemned to the status of objects?"[5] We will pick up this objecthood in "Taxidermy," but for now Voigt's poem suggests questions about the bind that Weil identifies.

The poem opens on a double-negative, a semi-comparison that is in medias res, or at least in the middle of a thought:

> not unlike otters which we love frolicking
> floating on their backs like truant boys unwrapping lunch

The "frolicking" ends this first line and then begins the first of the second stanza five lines later, and describes the playful movement of the poem itself, running from line to line without any punctuation: its looseness attempting to capture formally what is being registered linguistically. The otters are "like truant boys," a comparison that takes us a little further away from the titular groundhog itself. Running then on sibilance—the otter and groundhog have the "same sleek brown pelt some overtones of gray and rust"—the description of the otter's color and texture is one of Voigt's ways of reaching for the tactility of the animal.

The poem then leads us back to groundhogs which *unlike* otters "have no swimming hole" but eat from the ground "beneath short legs small feet / like a fat man's odd diminutive loafers." Thus another simile joins the litany of comparisons and anti-comparisons, and even this line ends on "not" before the next stanza, emphasizing an unlikeness: "a fat man's odd diminutive loafers not // frolicking but scurrying." Within six lines, Voigt's poem is layering ways to describe and make sense of the groundhog through inversion and talking around it. While neither are queer per se, there is a subversion to the poem that becomes more antinormative as it goes along.

The speaker makes a comparison in the poem which becomes its central question: the groundhog's

> triangular face like the hog-nosed skunk another delicate
> nose and not a snout doesn't it matter what they're called I like swine.

Like a skunk, the groundhog's nose (not snout) draws a link to pigs through association, but "doesn't it matter what they're called" becomes a rhetorical question that isn't just about accurately naming things (a categorical impulse) but rather about our failures to grasp things as they really are. The end of the line and stanza, "I like swine," runs over to the next stanza: "which are smart and prefer to be clean using their snouts" to move their feces away. The speaker of the poem, suddenly emerging in that "I," interrupts the flow of non/human associations to reclaim, perhaps, the pig from its cultural associations with dirt and stupidity. The pig has "hairy skin not fur his fur / shimmers"; the two creatures' boundaries overlap through these words rubbing together. But the "swine" also references the *hog* in groundhog, as well as the term "whistle pig," which is often given to the groundhog because of the high-pitched noises it omits when under attack. The poem is working associatively, linguistically, and corporeally through ways to grasp the groundhog's singularity (or perhaps its multiplicity).

The groundhog's teeth, the poem goes on via another simile, "are blunt squared off like a sheep's," but the speaker asks,

. . . if cornered does he
cower like sheep or bite like a sow with a litter is he ever

attacked.

The speaker gathers the previous similes to question how the groundhog reacts when under attack: ostensibly this refers to predatory threat, but we might also ask if that danger comes from the speaker/poem too. Here, almost at the center of the poem, is its only single line—"attacked he looks to me inedible he shares his acreage." As elsewhere in the poem, the line is connected to those that precede and follow it. The groundhog's inedibility, its unavailability to be eaten (perhaps even its resistance to being consumed by humans, both literally and symbolically) is central to the poem and the creature itself. His "acreage" opens out into the page as the line stands out alone, giving the groundhog breathing room as it were. It lives alongside, assonantly and rhymingly, "moles voles ravenous crows," but more important than this connective sound-play is that "someone / thought up the names." The process of naming, of humans giving shape to nonhumans through language, is central here, but so are the normative and colonial underpinnings of that language. The groundhog's "other name is botched Algonquin," a reference to the fact that it can also be called a woodchuck (there is no real difference between them), which in turn is a mispronunciation of the Algonquin word *wejack* or *wuchak*. From the Indigenous *wuchak* to the English *woodchuck* to the *groundhog* (via, of course, the original badger of *Groundhog Day*), this creature's ability to be named is a process of substitutions and mistranslations. Such name-blurring is echoed by the poem itself, a slippery and circuitous exchange of one metaphor and simile for another.

Here the poem lifts into a different register and links the groundhog to humans. First, it "burrows" beneath a farmer's barn that "once" was part of an agricultural life that we assume is gone. Apprehending a "lawnmower swollen brook high wind"—the human-made mingling with the elemental—the creature "lifts his head / as Gandhi did," standing "erect / like a prairie dog," except that "dogs don't waddle like Mao." The figures of Gandhi and Mao open the poem to a much broader and global history (beyond the "fat man" and the farmer), with two seemingly unalike reference points.

But the speaker goes further:

> with a tiny tail he seems asexual like Gandhi like Jesus if Jesus
> came back would he be vegetarian also pinko freako homo
>
> in Vermont.

Why the "tiny tail" gives way to "asexual" is unclear, but "asexual like Gandhi like Jesus" also perhaps confuses celibacy with asexuality. Yet "if Jesus / came back would he be vegetarian" seems a way for the poem's speaker to contemplate these figures as somehow nonnormative, associated with the explicitly queer "pinko freako homo": that is, communist, outsider, gay. The line spills over into a new stanza, "in Vermont natives scornful of greyhounds from the city" which yields further connections to the idea of the population rejecting outsiders (coming in on Greyhound buses) as well as the racing dog, both of which reference two kinds of outsiders. And then the image of a "homo" Jesus "in Vermont" plays with figurations of Christ as a queer liberal in New England. That the groundhog links to Mao, Gandhi, and Christ near the poem's end suggests both a queerer reading of the text (and creature) than at the text's opening, as well as a strangely logical extension of the comparative, substitutive logic of the poem. If groundhogs are "not unlike otters" they might also move unlike Mao or seem asexual like Jesus. Voigt's expansiveness here evidences one way that the poem moves through association and playfully mocks the referentiality of language itself. By offering one substitution after another, Voigt's poem makes queer the idea of accounting for a nonhuman in any fixed or taxonomic way.

The final stanza gestures toward a further understanding of both language's power and its inadequacies, the ways it can be used to precisely name and yet also to misidentify. The speaker asks, "who would shoot on sight an actual fatso shy mild marmot radiant," addressing both the hunting of wild creatures (see the later chapter, "Hunter"), and the anthropomorphizing of the groundhog: "fatso shy mild marmot." The creature is, via comparisons again, as "radiant / as the hog-nosed skunk," "cleaner than sheep" and "fluffy." However, that "fluffy" is

> . . . like a girl's maybe he is a she it matters
> what we're called words shape the thought don't say
> rodent and ruin everything.

Much depends upon the power of words in particular arrangements: It matters what humans or nonhumans are called. If words "shape the thought," then language is the system through which we understand the world. "Maybe he is a she it matters" clumsily gestures to a more open or queerer understanding of gender and pronouns (if still in a binary). But "it matters" also spills into the next line, as "it matters / what we're called"; words, whether gendered pronouns or a creature's Indigenous or anglicized name, are significant. "Don't say / rodent and ruin everything" warns both of a taxonomic failure (do not group groundhogs with rodents) and also of taxonomy's power (call this thing what is is). Like the novels Timothy Baker examines, this poem might just "demonstrate the ways in which an essentially human, language-based form can be used not to elevate the human, but to open a space for the exploration of species and linguistic boundaries."[6] Rather than completely foregrounding the human, the poem's language makes room for understandings of non/human thresholds, of queerly new ways of knowing both the human and other animals.

Perhaps Voigt's poem does not embody the most extreme ends of animal studies scholarship, in which the human is thoroughly dismantled and displaced. But it does offer a course corrective for those who attempt to categorize nonhumans in any simplistic way. The ostensibly taxonomizing impulse of the poem—*this is a groundhog*—is a ruse. Voigt's poem mocks any normative and singular way of knowing, not least because of language's instability. Moreover, when language's slipperiness is met with a nonhuman's evasive being, the writer can only offer swaps and exchanges via figurative forms like metaphor and simile. As seen throughout this bestiary, nonhumans are forever getting out of the human grasp, queering the possibility of certainty at every turn.

NOTES

1. Young and Akbar, "Kaveh Akbar."
2. Voigt, "Groundhog." Cited hereafter in text.
3. Saussure, *Course*, 856.
4. Baker, *Writing*, 1, 2.
5. Weil, *Thinking*, 4.
6. Baker, *Writing*, 8.

HO
RSE

Horse

horses bridge states of vulnerability

I

Horses have a rich and multifaceted legacy within U.S. culture, both literal and figurative, and this chapter thinks with a group of representations of them, especially as they are tied to particular landscapes and histories of nation-building. Horses (in part) enabled westward expansion and its ideological underpinning Manifest Destiny, not least through their roles in transport and labor; horses were conscripted into the American project.[1] Can we imagine the colonization of the continent without the horse as one of its principal facilitators? Yet horses have also been central to many Indigenous cultures, for longer time periods even than historians have imagined. Recent scientific studies show horses were used and integrated into Native tribes in the sixteenth century (not the eighteenth) after the Spanish reintroduced them to the Americas in 1519.[2] Horses have maintained a complex role in Indigenous cultures of the Great Plains and beyond, such as their centrality to Lakota "spirituality, science, and cosmogony."[3] Thus, to think horses in the United States is to think them in a variety of ways depending on their proximity to various ethnic and racial groups.

In the Western literary and film genre where we see representations of colonial "wilderness-taming," horses abound; yet as Jane Tompkins famously argues, horses are everywhere and nowhere, always on-screen or on the page but continuously ignored and overlooked. This chapter counters the Western's vanishing of horses—their physicality and emotionality—by reading several literary texts in which horses are central to the narratives' thinking about race, gender, and sexuality in the United States. In foregrounding the work that horses do—as Tompkins puts it, the literal and thus extensive symbolic work[4]—we can understand some of the ways that they are central to U.S. imaginaries of the non/human. Put another way, the horse is our way in to thinking about non/humans at the intersections of race, sexuality, and gender.[5]

Horses have frequently been seen and figured as nonhuman animals that embody duality—body/mind, reason/passion, wild/tamed—that speak to the heart of human exceptionalism. Philip Armstrong writes that images of humans riding horses have often been seen as "reason reining in the passions," while that image's "inverted form" shows us people driven by feeling. Horses have, for many, emblematized some post-Enlightenment concerns, capturing an "image of the bifold nature of the human as it was commonly understood: animal flesh and immortal soul; brute body and knowing, judging mind."[6] The horse enables a confrontation with (one version of) human duality. We might also note that horses actually have bilateral vision, seeing two images at once.[7] Thus, at both a literal and metaphoric level, horses manage to contain a two-ness that is itself a mirror to humanistic queries of the self: wild and tamed, thinking and feeling, body and mind, flesh and soul. Of course, these binaries were also central to the project of U.S. westward expansion. The "taming" of the landscape and its Indigenous inhabitants was legitimized through recourse to the "wildness" of the people and their environments. In the literary readings that follow, I use this doubleness to show how the horses in two of Ada Limón's poems, Kristiana Kahakauwila's short story "The Old Paniolo Way" (2021), Mary Gaitskill's *The Mare* (2015), and Percival Everett's *Wounded* (2005) are fundamental to the connecting of humans and nonhumans across gendered, racialized, and sexual lines.

Throughout this bestiary, we see the entanglement of humans and nonhumans in ways that I suggest are queer, but in this chapter I want to frame horses as nonhumans that do the work of bringing humans and nonhumans together because and in spite of their embodied differences (racialized, gendered, sexualized). This chapter reads horses as *mediating* creatures who act as bridges or contact points between kinds and forms of life, and varying species. Indeed, much of the critical material used in this chapter rests on metaphors of connectivity, not least Tompkins's sense of horses in Westerns as representing a "connection to nature, to the wild" because in part "the body of the horse stands beneath the body of the rider, between the human being and the earth."[8] For Tompkins, the horse bridges or mediates the human's relation to the landscape because it is literally and metaphorically between them. In a different way, and with reference to questions of race and racialization, Joshua Bennett appraises horses, as they appear in Frederick Douglass's writing, via images of connection. Bennett writes that horses are "a bridge par excellence between the human and non-human" because they are "saleable, living beings" akin to how enslaved Black people were. And while horses were used "for labor, entertainment, and breeding," they nonetheless "possess an interiority that is, by the rule, denied." Even with this *likeness*, for Douglass there is a different treatment of Black people and horses: "There are structures in place for the care and sustenance of animals that simply do not exist for the enslaved."[9] Thus, for Bennett through Douglass, the lives of Black humans and horses might be sutured together in this historical moment, but that does not mean some kind of equivalence, but rather an opening to think through hierarchies of livability, as explored in the introduction.

We see the connections between horses and enslaved people in Toni Morrison's *A Mercy* (2008), too, when Jacob Vaark, a white Dutch farmer and trader in 1600s colonial America, witnesses a horse being beaten. At this moment in the narrative, Jacob is beginning his journey into the trading of enslaved Black people, after having gone to Maryland to settle a debt with a plantation owner. Vaark sees "a man beating a horse to its knees. . . . Few things angered Jacob more than the brutal handling of domesticated animals. He did not know what the sailors were objecting to, but his own fury was not only because of the pain it inflicted on the horse, but because of the mute, unprotesting surrender glazing its eyes."[10] Morrison is keen in this novel—filled with other non/human relations at a moment in history when racial and identity categories were in flux—to highlight Vaark's uneven sense of anger at violence done to humans and nonhumans. He has no problem enslaving a Black woman, nor having poor and Indigenous indentured servants on his farm, but he does see the horse as having an emotional and interior world that evokes sympathy. As in Douglass's account, the horse's status above Black people both confirms a species hierarchy and the dehumanization of certain racialized populations through comparison and connection.

For Bennett, Douglass, and Morrison, horses manifest as figures relational to Blackness, or what Sharon P. Holland might call a condition of vulnerability. Holland is interested in the ways we can "map a relation among blackness/human/animal that doesn't always already see animality as descent or vulnerability as the negative consequence of biopower." Looking at a text like Solomon Northup's *Twelve Years a Slave* (1853), Holland argues that we need to reimagine relations of race and animality, so that instead of describing Northup in that book as being treated "*like* . . . an animal" which maintains the animal's subordinate position ("leaving open the possibility for disregard"), we think of him treated "*as* an animal—a semiotic ordering that holds open the possibility of ethical relation, of relationship."[11] To see Blackness and the animal in relation (as proximate) is to reconfigure species hierarchies and reimagine the traffic of meaning across species lines. Holland extends that argument further in *An Other* (2023), where she considers the relations among "hum:animal:blackness" that "d[o] not carry the stigma of dichotomous difference or solipsistic sameness," and puts emphasis, as I do here, on "relation rather than difference."[12]

Vulnerability—shared though not identical—between and among non/humans has been further theorized by Judith Butler, whose imagining of queer alliance in precarity helps us see the horse's role in mediating a range of identities in contemporary literature. In their suite of books from *Precarious Life* (2003) onwards, Butler suggests that the normative frames within which lives become recognizable and apprehendable *as lives* structure which lives are worth grieving, which lives have worth in the first place. In later books, Butler asks how we think of "life" (within and outside of normative frames) when the "human" is a contested category. Because "the human is a historically variable concept, differentially articulated in the context of inegalitarian forms of social and political power," and because the human is "constituted through its basic exclusions, haunted by those figures that do not count in its tally," then we cannot, Butler argues, use "the human" alone as the analytical ground for human rights or equity claims.[13] To see the precarity and vulnerability of all life is to "take up a position outside of [the human's] terms" in a form of "sociality and interdependence."[14]

Central for Butler is an acknowledgment that the human has never been singular—that it relies on certain exclusions to maintain its borders—and that life is permeable and interrelated with all kinds of non/human forces and beings. If "the human animal lets us rethink the very conditions of livability," it might do so through a focus on queerness as a category of coalition and nonnormativity. If "queer does not designate identity, but alliance," then we might invoke it as we "make uneasy and unpredictable alliances" in the fight for justice across species lines.[15] In this chapter and beyond, I want to think about the ways that queerness emerges in the textured territory between and beyond the so-called human/nonhuman divide (in the "bridging" work of horses); and in light of Butler's theorizing, I see that queer terrain as an acknowledgment of shared but differential vulnerability and precarity. Horses, in the texts I consider here, negotiate much of this imaginative work.

II

A few brief examples of horses in relation to gender, race, and sexuality will then open out to a longer discussion of Everett's *Wounded*. In each of these texts, the horse either literally or metaphorically acts as a bridge between marginalized people and questions of normativity. For instance, Ada Limón's poetry frequently turns to the nonhuman—dogs, trees, birds, horses—to think about a human's place in broader ecologies and other non/human entanglements. In two particular poems, Limón thinks the horse in relation to gender's multiplicity. "How to Triumph Like a Girl," from *Bright Dead Things* (2015), begins in a childlike (and gendered) equine admiration: "I like the lady horses best," the speaker says, because they are so competent. But quickly that veneration turns into identification and then a non/human merging, as the speaker imagines the female horse ("this big dangerous animal") as part of her. Its large heart, "giant with power" sits beneath her "delicate / skin." The speaker's desire for the horse's equine particularity is both a transformation of gendered stereotypes—the horse is dangerous, large, powerful—and human exceptionalism. The speaker wants the horse's innate knowledge that it will "come in first" in whatever race it is running, as if the poem is celebrating a horse rather than human exceptionalism.[16]

Limón picks up this imagery later in "Full Gallop" (in *The Carrying* [2018]) when the speaker, after a night of sex, dreams that "I chop / all the penises off." Laying next to a lover, the speaker says that, part of me is haunted—

a shadow baying inside me
who wants to snap her hind leg
back, buck the rider, follow

the fugitive call into oblivion.[17]

The speaker's ambivalence about the person she's lying next to—there are longings of both castration and desire—becomes a haunting that is materialized in both the em dash and the stanza break that follows it. The "shadow" is an unnamed horse that wants to "buck" its rider and flee into freedom. Limón's poem "gallops" into the distance by embedding the horse within the woman: a non/human figure that is (d)riven from within by something wild and other-than-herself. The speaker is confronting the unknown and unidentifiable (the equinity is not named) part of herself that is textured by a queer excess. In both poems, Limón sees the horse-within-the-human or human-as-horse at the site of gender and sexuality's vicissitudes. The horse bridges understandings of self and other across species lines.

Two other examples from fiction push this notion of the bridging horse further. In Kristiana Kahakauwila's story "The Old Paniolo Way" from *This Is Paradise* (2013) a horse farm in Hawai'i serves as the backdrop to a family narrative of death, tradition, and sexuality. When Pili returns home from California to tend to his dying father, he is confronted by the figure of the paniolo, or Hawaiian cowboy.[18] Pili's queerness is kept secret from his father, Harrison, and (he thinks) to his sister Maile. Yet this visit back confronts Pili with his sexuality in a Hawaiian context: He "was unsure of his desires and himself" back at home. Harrison's carer, Albert, also turns out to be queer, and he forms a bond with Pili on the visit. At night, once Harrison is asleep, they sit out on the porch whispering about their lives. Their desire is kept outside and hidden, but it is also transferred onto the site of the nonhuman, as they first have sexual contact in a pasture after feeding the cows. It is as though Pili's introduction of Albert to the cattle—the latter afraid at first—enables them to find their quiet moment alone. Like in the other texts looked at in this book, the nonhuman often paves the way for queer erotics. Their tussle ends quickly, though, as Pili is reminded of his father's mortality: "He'll die soon, won't he?"[19] The nonhuman animal leads to sexuality, which leads to death, as if mingling the three. Later, they finally do have sex in the barn's hayloft, which "smelled of horses" (199). Pili shows Albert horse-training items like a form of foreplay. Queerness is put outside and also into spaces of the nonhuman, coding them together.

Harrison's slow death also brings up issues of paniolo identity and the tug between tradition and modernity. The "ol' paniolo way" of the title means looking after horses in the manner of Pili's ancestors, but also to "find one good woman."[20] The straightness of the paniolo identity is also gendered, as Maile, Pili's sister, cannot occupy that role (when they were younger, she only rode the horses, rather than trained or tended them as her brother did [187]). Maile also wants to raise the horses in a new way, feeding them from racks rather than the floor, as has been the traditional method. The horses in this story mediate all kinds of gender and sexuality norms against the backdrop of a dying patriarch (and patriarchy). In a flashback, Pili remembers being schooled by his father about māhū, trans or third-gender people in Hawai'i. As a child, Pili has to reject that identity wholly, to the point that any element of queerness is kept secret from his father. Part of the issue with the term is that, as Janet Mock writes, māhū could be someone "who embodied the diversity of gender beyond the dictates of our Western binary system."[21] The term was colonized like the multitudinous genders it indexes, as well as the country it is from. Tangled in this web, Pili embraces and embodies his queerness largely on the U.S. mainland rather than in relation to Hawaiian categories.

Kahakauwila's story uses horses as bridges between different kinds of sociality: As a backdrop to familial inheritance, secrecy, and cultural norms, they remain silent witnesses. But they also enable—through inference and association—normative and nonnormative worldviews. For Harrison, the paniolo way of rearing cows and retaining a heterosexual masculinity is transformed into something more capacious by his daughter's new ideas for horse and cow-raising, and his son's queer desires. The farm is a non/human stage for mediating queer identities, both on and off the islands.

In ways akin to Kahakauwila and Limón's texts, Mary Gaitskill's novel *The Mare* (2015) depicts some of the ways that a horse becomes a non/human bridging figure. The novel has several narrators, principally Ginger (a white woman living in upstate New York) and Velvet (a young Dominican American girl living in Brooklyn), as well as Ginger's husband Paul, and Velvet's mother Silvia. The oscillation between narrative voices means that we are constantly witnessing a kind of dialogue on the page, where different emotions, interests, and perspectives play out often in disharmony. This is important as Gaitskill's novel is invested in the ways that communication is possible between and beyond humans.

Ginger and Paul, in their late forties, are thinking about having children and so, in a way to "trial" parenthood, take part in a scheme where Velvet comes to stay with them on weekends. As Gaitskill writes in her long essay *Lost Cat* (2017)[22] (which is also about non/human relations), she and her husband actually took part in the Fresh Air Fund, which "sends poor urban children (nearly all of whom are black or Hispanic) up by bus to stay with country families (nearly all of whom are white)." Gaitskill, in this memoir-essay, explains the "real" background to *The Mare*, in which a brother and sister were sent to her home upstate to experience a rural life. She notes, somewhat tellingly, that the scheme has an "aura of uplift" but actually "reeks of pain," an acknowledgment that many of the children being sent to other families experience various kinds of trauma, whether familial or societal. This white liberal fantasy of "saving" poor kids of color is but one part of the story. Gaitskill writes that she and her husband were "aware of the race-class thing" but thought that they "could override it," which I take to be a dubious assertion that sociocultural differences are merely things to be skated over rather than reckoned with.[23] *The Mare*, one could argue, is a potential literary interrogation of those very real dynamics.

There is much to say about the novel's muddying of binaries (adult/child, rural/urban, white/of color, money/poverty) but it is worth reflecting on the horse-human relation that drives much of the novel. While staying with Ginger and Paul, Velvet becomes invested in a local horse farm and a particularly boisterous horse that everyone calls Fugly Girl.[24] In time, looking after the horse becomes a way for Velvet to settle into the rural life and be calm around the white couple. Oscillating between social and cultural spaces, always classed and racialized, Velvet pushes back on those around her for obvious reasons. It is clear, too, that as an abused teenager herself, Velvet identifies with the horse, who has "scars on her face."[25] Velvet's mother, Silvia, is physically and emotionally abusive—they hit each other on numerous occasions—but Velvet is also cast aside by friends and older teen boys.

The novel shows how Velvet is neglected in ways like the horse is and asks one of the ranch workers to explain why they use crops on them. The woman, Beverly, says that "it's all psychological. It doesn't *really* hurt" (131). Velvet sees the intimate relation between training and punishment, a blurry line that speaks to her own upbringing. She says to Pat, the farm owner, "If hitting is okay sometimes, what is abuse?" (171). Ostensibly asking about Fugly Girl, Velvet is as much inquiring about her own experiences. Indeed, she quickly renames the horse Fiery Girl in acknowledgment of their similar temperaments; she turns ugliness into power. Gaitskill is quite explicit throughout the novel about the ways that this young girl of color finds kinship and identification with this horse and attempts to make sense of their place in the world.

The stories told to Velvet about the horse are always about her potential danger. The trainers say she is "not a person. She's an animal. . . . That is one thousand points of unpredictable power" (65), and "she could kill you" (66). When Velvet claims the horse loves her, Pat says "Don't be a fool. . . . She's an animal" (243). While the white adults are correct in that the horse is not without her behavioral issues—one day when Velvet is annoyed and takes Fiery Girl out, the horse throws her to the ground—Velvet does connect with her in ways that the others do not. Indeed, after sustaining head injuries from being thrown, Fiery Girl licks Velvet's hair, and even though "she was scared, . . . she still came back to see if I was okay" (242). That companion-species care is deeply connected to the enmeshed processes of racialization and animalization that the novel tracks.

Velvet is not only tied to Fiery Girl through their shared positionality. Velvet is frequently animalized herself: Her mother says that she yells "like a stupid animal . . . like an elephant or a cow" (304), and when she fights with her mother, she "cried and hit wild" (400). At the end of the novel, when Velvet finally rides Fiery Girl in a show, she too embodies the horse's feelings: "I wanted to move, to kick and bite" (419) as they both wait for their round in the show-jump to start. The novel is interested, like the other examples above, in the ways that horses bridge human-nonhuman relations, particularly at the overlaps between race and gender. Fiery Girl enables Velvet to be more herself even if those around her do not understand that self. The human-horse relation allows for identification and understanding that are not reducible to racist animalization. Rather, even while Pat suggests that the horse "doesn't care who you are, how much money you have, where you're from" (33), as if transcending the trappings of race and class, *The Mare* suggests that it is precisely *because* the young brown girl and this "ugly" or "fiery" horse share the experience of marginalization that they connect.

We see in *Lost Cat* that Gaitskill admits to awkwardness around race and class. The novel itself seems to work through (or at least stage) that ambivalence. The characters are constantly negotiating their relations to one another, as they try to create bonds of sociality across difference and similarity. Ginger admits, "She was ours!" (17) when Velvet first stays with them, a possessive declaration that creates faultlines between all the parties. Later, both Beverly and Ginger reveal racist intentions: the former noting that "even" Velvet, "the tough black girl from the city—or Puerto Rican, or whatever she is" (224) is too sentimental about horses; and the latter, thinking that maybe Latinx people are more lazy and emotive, says that "everybody was right. I'm racist. At least now I know" (351). Gaitskill depicts both as white women who say they want to reach across racial divides even as they are trapped in their vision of white supremacy. Ginger's acknowledgment, too, sounds like a faint gloss of Gaitskill's own feelings as a white woman taking children of color into her home and then writing from a Latinx girl's point of view. The novel leaves this issue suspended.

Yet the novel hurtles toward its ending, where Velvet finally rides Fiery Girl successfully in front of Ginger and Paul, the trainers, and her family. In this final scene, tensions seem to be temporarily ironed out through the human-horse bonding. Silvia, for instance, sees a "beautiful girl riding like a saint with a sword" (430), a declaration that is way beyond her previous reproach about the horse-riding. Even though it is clear Velvet will not return to Ginger and Paul's home, there is some mediation of sociocultural barriers through the non/human relation. As with Kahakauwila's story and Limón's poems, Gaitskill partly depicts what Jopi Nyman has called a "horsescape." Writing in relation to Jane Smiley's novel *Horse Heaven* (2000), Nyman defines horsescapes as "sites of human-animal encounters," which are imaginary scenes with the horse central to Americanness and its potential undoing. Horses here are "agents of transformation" in that they reconfigure human and nonhuman alike through the intimacies of "shared action" and the "recognition of relationality."[26] We see this relationality through the various above texts, as each reckons with U.S. narratives of race, gender, and sexuality across a range of landscapes and milieux. For Limón, womanhood and sexuality are recast in and through the horse; for Kahakauwila, gender and sexuality relations are rethought within Indigenous and American contexts; for Gaitskill, race and gender are woven into horse relations. In the final part of this chapter, a final example pushes these ideas further in the specific context of the American West.

III

Percival Everett's *Wounded* rethinks the Western genre in a queer non/human framework. The novel concerns itself with various kinds of wounds: bodily, psychic, social, cultural. Dead cows, a legless coyote, a traumatized horse, a stupid horse, a murdered white gay man, a dying Black man, and much else litter this novel's pages. John Hunt, the novel's protagonist, is a Black horse trainer living in Wyoming with his uncle, Gus, twenty-five horses, and eventually his new fiancée, Morgan. His equine world opens questions of non/human connections. The horse's mediating work, like that discussed above, gestures to a larger non/human world that is scarred by vulnerability.

Wounded follows Hunt as he is confronted by past and present violence in the West. When the novel opens, one of his ranch hands, Wallace (perhaps with a cognitive impairment), is falsely arrested for murdering a young gay man. It turns out Wallace is also gay, and he ends up hanging himself in the police jail. David, the son of John's old school friend comes to Wyoming with his boyfriend Robert to memorialize the murder victim. While at John's farm, David bonds with John, seeing him as both a new father figure (his own is homophobic) and an object of desire. In time, the dead gay college student is not the only victim of violence and discrimination—Native people that live near John are targeted; nonhuman animals are killed; and David is eventually kidnapped and tortured and then dies. All of this is at the hands of neo-Nazis in the area, a resurgent white supremacist movement that directs its hate and violence against all kinds of humans and nonhumans. Indeed, central to *Wounded* is the enfolding and linking of violence done to marginalized people and nonhumans.[27]

These relations in and with the rural West are evoked from the very start of the novel: "By definition a cave must have an opening large enough to allow a human to enter. The cavity can be wind- or water-eroded. It can be miles and miles deep. But it must let a person enter. And that is what is scary about caves, that one can enter."[28] Here, the nonhuman (the geological) is defined in relation to the human: A cave would just be an indentation in the rock if humans could not fit within it. This is not merely a definitional concern for the novel but an affective one too—John thinks the cave "scary" because it can be entered. In other words, the possibilities of non/human interaction are in some ways fraught, not least because of the unknowability inherent to nonhuman forms.[29]

Such unknowability is more clearly seen in relation to horses (and horse hybrids, to call back a previous chapter). John's role as a horse trainer is central to the novel and as such the imaginative work of horses is central to the figuring of woundedness.[30] Three horses and one mule recur in the narrative, all under John's care: an easily annoyed mare, a large Appaloosa that kills John's ex-wife Susie, a "stupid" mule named Pest given to him by Native neighbors, and a difficult Palomino called Felony who is foisted on John to train. Each of these horses has their own personality, their own stories in relation to humans, and a connection to vulnerability. As stubbornly themselves—often the horses refuse to do what John wants from them, sometimes they seem in concert with him—the horses mediate a non/human framework for the book, where the nonhuman (like the cave) is always outside of human grasp, not ever fully knowable.

For the purposes of this chapter, I want to think broadly about horses, and as such, I am folding Pest the mule into my remit. Acknowledging that mules aren't quite horses—they are horse-donkey hybrids—I also want to see Pest, who is lovingly embraced by John, even while he is *a pest,* in relation to the rest of the equine world. As noted in the introduction to this book, categories and taxonomies are shifting and fluid; I do not take the "horse" to be one single thing, yet to talk of the way it moves through texts means talking about it sometimes generally. It is worth saying here that the mule has a long history in relation to Black literature and thought. Joshua Bennett writes that Zora Neale Hurston, for instance, includes mules throughout her work to stage not simply an image of the mule (linked to mulatto) as a figure of raced and gendered labor oppression, but also as a creature that generates multiplicity.[31] For Bennett, mules, in Hurston and elsewhere, index questions of "value" but also gesture to "persistence" and "abundance" in spaces and "*forms of human and nonhuman life* that are traditionally marked as nonsites, as vitalized forms of death."[32] Put another way, as the protagonist of Everett's short story "Little Faith" (2015) says, "the lucky ones of us can have mules."[33]

From the start, the horses and mule seem to both metaphorize (and refuse to metaphorize) the human dilemmas. In an early scene, for instance, Wallace enters the barn where John is working. The dog's ears are "cocked," alert to Wallace's presence, while the "antsy mare" is "cranky" that her legs are being attended to (3). These nonhuman animals sense and forebode a tension that ripples through the book. Except, perhaps, the mule, who always finds a way to escape his paddock. John tries to return the mule to his neighbor Daniel, who refuses: "You ever see an Indian riding a mule? Not even in the movies" (95). Daniel underscores how nonhumans are figured in the popular and cultural imagination and declines to perpetuate those narratives. The mare and the mule already become freighted with cross-species associations.

The horse that is a fixture in John's mind, though, and that *seems* to prefigure the violence to come, is the Appaloosa. In flashback, we find out that the horse is not fully trained and throws Susie, John's ex-wife, to her death. When she's on the floor, the horse kicks out and makes contact with Susie's helmet; she dies almost instantly. This short scene not only underscores the possibly fraught relationship between humans and nonhumans (through training, or the lack thereof), but also the enormous power of horses, and their ability to inflict harm. Claude Julien reads this moment as instructive for John: "Does he now devote his life to animal training because he is haunted by Susie's death"?[34] In other words, is training horses a way to curtail future tragedy, future death, or a way to control the uncontrollable? John commits to horses as a way to avoid other kinds of commitment too. Morgan jokes with Gus about John's inability to discuss sex and emotion: "You ever notice how comfortable this man gets when the subject is horses?" (31). Horses become a way to both avenge or work through the past, while also halting the present and future.

The "monstrous" Palomino, Felony, that is given to John to train—all "dumb muscle and bad attitude" (22)—epitomizes the complex interrelations of the non/human. The horse "spooks under saddle and attacks when he's not" (23), and as such is difficult to ride, train, and interact with. Felony's problem, John says, is "not so much that he thinks he's a person as he doesn't know that people aren't horses. That's a bad thing" (68). The "bad thing" is ostensibly the species line hierarchy, in which humans can train horses to do certain things, to manage behaviors. But another way of reading this is that Felony does not discriminate across species lines, does not separate out horses from humans, or even humans from nonhumans. This blurriness makes him a threat to (some) humans, but Felony's strangeness also figures something of the *wild* that courses through *Wounded*, the ways that the unknown, the precarious, the queer—not conflatable but connected terms—cut across species lines.

In their ability to be trained (or not), John's horses metaphorize a tension between the wild and the domesticated.[35] John's training is, as it were, a reining in of the horse's wildness. Considering the novel's focus on woundedness and cross-species violence, training could be seen as an attempt to tame the wild or at least make sense of it. (Horses are not "supposed to make decisions," John says. "You've got to redirect the animal, break the routine" [19], which both works and does not for him). If, as we saw at the start, horses do dual metaphorical work in the United States, in *Wounded* they point to the human's (John's) inability to fully gain control over the uncontrollable forces of violence so deeply tied to ideas of U.S. land, the West, species exceptionalism, heteronormativity, racism, and so on. The horses in all their variety—stupid but loyal, dangerous and threatening, difficult—mediate something of the desire to control the wild, even as wildness is pervasive. At the center of Everett's novel are the killings of two gay men. Both are at the mercy of an American wildness that is usually not associated with the term: unchecked white supremacist violence. Where the wild is often yoked to Indigeneity and other ethnic/racial categories that are seemingly "opposed" to order, here the wild is the threat of violence from the heart of whiteness. Horse training might be a way not only of overcoming the loss of a loved one (John's ex) but also the losses that keep on coming.

IV

Central to the novel are the killings of the young gay man and (eventually) David, both of which—but the former in particular—evoke the murder of Matthew Shepard in 1998. In that way, *Wounded* is a work of cultural memory, recalling the homophobic attack on Shepard (in the same state, Wyoming), in which he was beaten and left to die in the desert outside Laramie.[36] Shepard's killing made (inter)national news and eventually led to the 2009 Matthew Shepard and James Byrd Jr. Hate Crimes Prevention Act, signed into law by Barack Obama. Byrd was a Black man lynched by white supremacists in Texas in 1998. They dragged his body behind their pickup truck for miles until he died. Both Byrd and Shepard were lynched in parts of the United States associated with the practice that reached its heyday in the early twentieth century (South and West). Their killings—like many of the killings of Black and queer people since—caused national outcry but similar national forgetting once the next tragedy occurred. This pair of hate crimes frame Everett's novel, which is concerned with the interconnected violences done to various Others. By metabolizing the two lynchings (Shepard's in particular) as memory, Everett stitches the non/human into a larger U.S. geography and history of violence.

The opening homophobic murder is a lynching by hanging, which Everett in turn connects to the nonhuman animal: He is "strung up like an elk with his throat slit" (12). The murder recalls other lynchings in the West and South but is here framed with species implications. Morgan says to John, "People are just animals anymore," to which he replies, "No, they're people. That's the problem" (13). Morgan indicates humans are *merely* animals, reduced to something like a violent base state (though the "anymore" might suggest things were once different). But John's point—"they're people"—highlights his distinction between the kind of killings that humans and nonhuman animals might do. He implies the former kills often out of hate, the latter out of necessity. The violence of *Wounded* is relentlessly human. The gay man's killing draws people from across the nation to the town, including David and Robert; they attend a vigil in the town (a smaller version than the one that happened for Shepard), but in Everett's novel it goes awry as the neo-Nazis turn up and intimidate David and Robert.

The murder is detailed in the press as "symptomatic of some rural or Western disease of intolerance," which John tweaks: "Yes, it's called America" (34). The novel critiques (up to a point) the idea that regions like the West are more prone to violence, to racism, to homophobia than the rest of the nation. This is true of most kinds of U.S. regionalism, of course; the U.S. South suffers the same fate as the West, as it is the "nation's region" in Leigh Anne Duck's famous phrase. Indeed, John underscores this point when later, as David and Robert arrive for Wallace's public vigil, he says that he's experienced racism in Wyoming ("of course I have. . . . This is America") but the only time he has the n-word used against him is in Cambridge, Massachusetts (52). Everett insists on us seeing the violence of this landscape as *part of* the nation, not separate from it. In mediating Shepard's murder (and recalling with it Byrd's), Everett places those deaths in a larger national narrative of violence against anyone that resists white heteronormativity. The antiqueer violence, as we will shortly explore, is on a continuum with other kinds: "Nobody's got the hate market cornered in this country," John says (67) wryly, as if to stop Robert (and us) from separating this murder from other attacks.

Indeed, a complicated move that *Wounded* makes is to link up this homophobic (and later, racist) violence against humans with violence done to nonhumans. I say "complicated" because there are ways of reading this book as conflating or equating different kinds of species violence. The book is a nuanced examination of multispecies life, but it is possible to see a flattening of human and nonhuman difference in the broad and complex cast of the novel. One day, on a trip into the plains, John finds a wounded coyote pup, burned after someone had "poured fuel down into the animal's den and tossed a match" (45). While farmers might have done this to protect livestock, the neo-Nazis are likely responsible. According to Michael K. Johnson, the land itself registers a racialized reading of the act: "On the red soil, the black was out of place" (45). "Red" and "black" in this interpretation gesture to racial and ethnic categories, and Johnson suggests that the Western landscape is here "reconfigured as a site that recalls southern lynchings," which in turn "mirrors" the "cruelty of the murder of a gay man that precedes" the coyote's burning.[37] While I would not necessarily suggest that the act evokes lynching per se, the "coloring" of the site of violence itself ties the violence done to the coyote to the other violence committed in the book. This scene, among many others, highlights the cruelty of violence done to nonhuman animals (we see it elsewhere in Gus's turn to vegetarianism).

The coyote pup is then enfolded into John's non/human domestic world: Zoe, his dog, "stays put" beside her (48), and Gus quickly "form[s] an attachment to the animal" (47). Both dog and humans take to this wild nonhuman creature, but the bonding arouses questions about her suitability of living indoors around others, and issues of training (which overlap with John's horse training). The coyote's burned leg is amputated to prevent infection, but if "left in the wild," John notes, "she would have been healthy." Instead, "because she was in our care she now had to be protected from distemper, parvo" (80), and other diseases. It is bringing wildness—as John sees it—into the human world that makes such wildness vulnerable to humanity. By attempting to domesticate the coyote, its behavior and very health is altered. John and Gus "socialize" the pup because they cannot return her to the wild. This wildness-in-domestication is another of the dichotomies that we have seen horses symbolize.

As the coyote starts to nip and bite, John tells Gus to "flip her on her back as often as you think of it. Hold her there until she doesn't struggle" (106), a training strategy that enables the pup to be around humans and other animals. Everett is suggesting that domestication is an ongoing process, a strategy of dewilding certain behaviors so that creatures can *live together*—a corollary, we might say, of his own personal dewilding in order to become closer to Morgan. Everything is fine with the coyote until David's father Howard and new girlfriend show up at the ranch during a snowstorm.[38] David runs off after they get into a fight and almost dies of hypothermia in the cold—John rescues him with the newly trained Appaloosa. (Indeed, it is the Appaloosa who killed Susie that "saves" John and David in the snow [152]). But it is later, when David goes missing a second time, that Howard returns and is bitten by the coyote. It rips "his hand open with her teeth," in a way that echoes everyone else's frustration with Howard. John says, "I felt like biting him too" as a way of "dealing with the fear" (195) about David. The coyote's wildness, ever-present even while domesticated, emblematizes the feelings of fear, anger, rage, and confusion that spill across species lines in the novel.

The burned coyote is but one creature, then, in a larger network of non/humans threatened by the neo-Nazis. Everett enmeshes different kinds of violence throughout, not to elide any differences between them, but to show the connections of discrimination across species lines. For example, when cows are shot on Native land, John's neighbor Daniel White Buffalo says that "shooting a cow is a big deal. . . . That's two thousand dollars lying in that gulley" (93). The cow is both livestock and livelihood. Later, another cow is shot—the "head was a bloody mess"—but this time, "written in the snow" alongside it, "in cow's blood, were the words *Red N*—" (111). The slur not only conjoins anti-Blackness and anti-Indigeneity—central to U.S. racism and nation-building—but also but yokes human and nonhuman. Clara Monday, another neighbor and tribal elder, says that "someone put a bullet into the slope behind her" (129) as she was out on her horse. These attacks put Black and Indigenous people in relation to the nonhuman animal, as the cow is killed just like they might be. The Nazis responsible care not for species difference.

The precarities, deaths, and wounds that we have been charting in *Wounded* are not new to the Western landscape. Through its history, the West has been seen as a site of violence, regenerative of white Americanness, in Richard Slotkin's famous words (1973). Movie Westerns place the romanticized white male cowboy as a "figure of unshakeable virtue in a lawless region of brown savagery."[39] Yet, the cowboy—killing Native people and Mexicans, along with no end of horses, bears, and bison[40]—is in Everett's fiction somewhat transformed. Though a horse trainer, John becomes the hero of the frontier, allying himself with other marginalized people from the forces of white supremacy. As Hiram Pérez has argued in *A Taste for Brown Bodies* (2015), the cowboy has always been an outsider character who "begins his career as a cattle thief and outlaw figure in many ways queer." The cowboy's queerness (he is homosocial, outside of reproductive time, itinerant, anti-industrial) is then conscripted and licensed by the nation to do the racist violence central to statecraft. His "sexuality is quietly sanctioned by the nation" (16, 138, 140, 143).

The book plays with generic conventions of the Western from the start: When John hires Wallace, he does so "in spite of his obvious surprise at discovering I was black" (5). John and his uncle stand out in this landscape as Black ranchers and horse trainers, living together across generations, eating soy bacon instead of elk chili. Everett invokes and plays with genre conventions not simply as literary play, but as a way of reimagining national mythologies. Johnson argues that Everett's Western fiction (of which *Wounded* is just one example) shows the West as a "complex and ambivalent place," sometimes exemplifying the nation's ills and sometimes offering a (romantic, nostalgic) escape from them.[41] Everett's engagement with the Western is a form of what Neil Campbell calls the post-Western. It is "post" because, for Campbell, such texts are "haunted" by the old West and the past more broadly; it is not a surpassing (post) of it. The post-West is entangled with the region's mythologized landscapes, even while we acknowledge that the West was never as fixed as dominant representations claim.[42] More specifically it is the "traces, silences, and scars" of the West that now yield "loss, yearning, and mourning."[43] *Wounded* is keenly aware of Western tropes and conventions, even while it tries to query and upend them.

At times, the book reworks the West queerly: literally in its relation to gender, sexuality and race; and metaphorically through its reimagining of both the West's social and physical landscapes. Yet, as Campbell notes, "there is often the sense that in revising by inclusion (the black Western, women's Western, or ethnic Western), one simply slots new groups into the existing framework with the same primary values and ideologies, thereby maintaining the overall hegemony."[44] The faces change but the stories remain largely the same.[45]

I want to think briefly here about the landscape itself before addressing the final violent acts of the novel, to circle back to the non/human work that the horse evokes. Throughout *Wounded*, often when John is on a horse, the Western landscape is depicted in romantic terms. Describing the nearest town to his ranch—a sprawl that he "was never quite prepared for"—John thinks that it "used to be a village, a real Western town. Now, it's working on being just like anyplace else" (11). The mournful tone is not simply about industrialization flattening the "wild" landscape, but also a fear of capitalist hegemony and rampant Americanization that disappears the "real" old West. Later, in a more reflexive tone, John thinks that "it was dramatic land, dry, remote, wild. It was why I loved the West. I had no affection necessarily for the history of the people and certainly none for the mythic West, the West that never existed. It was the land for me. And maybe what the land did to some who lived on it" (45). John is rooted in the landscape itself (its *wildness*) but not the historic violent ideologies that have attended that place. Yet, as Johnson notes, the final sentence in that quote loops us back to the mythic West's effects on those that live there, "a variation on the 'Turner Thesis,'" in which the open frontier enables a purer form of U.S. democracy.[46] Thus, as a post-Western, *Wounded* queries the West as an idea, even as it is seduced by it.

As the novel moves toward its perhaps inevitable conclusion, the West as violent frontier is again conjured up. David goes missing while out driving in the snow. Though the police and sheriff try to find him, only John and Gus can perform in the *true* cowboy role. John takes Zoe and the coyote out into the snow and finds the car David was driving near to the hole he found the coyote in, as if Everett is underscoring their related precarious fates. For the "first time" in his life, John sets out with a rifle (186), conforming finally to his role on the frontier. Gus goes with him into a "rugged canyon" on the "edge of the reservation," a place so dry "that no one cared to go there" (198). This remote liminal site, partly on Native land (a deliberate re-intrusion on Indigenous territory), is where the neo-Nazis are staying. When Gus and John get to the trailer, they see a Nazi flag on the wall and the white men throw various epithets at them, both racist and homophobic. The violence quickly escalates as Gus dominates the scene, shooting one man and tying up another. This gives John time to find David's body in the creek, which was "like a cave" (203), bringing us back to that relation between human and land at the novel's opening. He finds David and takes him to the hospital, though he is unable to be saved and soon dies.

Eventually Gus returns to the ranch with an Indigenous neighbor, Elvis, who has been drawn into the region's violence. Though we do not witness it, Gus has clearly killed all the men. Elvis intones to John, capturing the novel's concluding tone, "This is the frontier, cowboy. . . . Everyplace is the frontier" (207). That final image, of an older Black man (formerly incarcerated) and a Native American returning from the wilderness after killing neo-Nazis for the murder of a gay man is a clear example of the post-West. The characters and situations of this Wyoming frontier are very different from its past depictions. Yet, even while the novel "is predicated on making the familiar characters and scenarios of the genre unfamiliar," the ending nonetheless reinscribes the frontier as a place of individualized justice, murder, and revenge.[47] Even if white cowboys are swapped out for Black and Native ranchers, and white damsels are swapped out for queer men, can the frontier change?

What is the West or post-West with the non/human at its heart? By partially reframing the human exceptionalism of the West(ern), Everett puts emphasis on the entanglement of vulnerable life in the shadow of the white supremacy that haunts and inhabits the landscape. Though the remnants of the old West are still present in *Wounded,* it is possible to see that historic ideology as fundamentally different to what we read. Even Elvis's invocation of the frontier is layered as he says that it is here and *everyplace,* as if acknowledging both the localized meanings of that term and its more national scope. Everyplace is the frontier because racist and homophobic violence cannot be contained within one landscape or history. The West's traditional victims remain, but there is also the possibility of queer alliances (in Butler's words), as queer and Black and Indigenous peoples work together to protect one another. Moreover, in their attention to the nonhuman world, this mix of outsiders claim multispecies cooperation too.

The horses, unlike in traditional Westerns, are not cast aside and killed, mere surplus to settler colonialism. Rather, here they are fully realized and complex interlocutors: stubborn, unwanted, wild, silly. The horses (and the mule and dog and coyote) stand among the humans as they make sense of the violent and precarious world around them. The novel's immediate focus on antiqueerness is linked to the neo-Nazi violence that is also aimed at people of color as well as nonhuman animals. Everett's point is that the West has always been a site of multitudinous violence, but by centering non/human relations—principally via the horse—a new ethics of resistance to white domestic terrorism might be possible. When John is out looking in the snow with the coyote, he notices that her pawmarks are odd given that she only has three legs. John identifies with her as he talks to Morgan: "I'm that three-legged coyote. . . . I can't recognize my own tracks until I stop moving" (188). That "gap, that space, that break in her track" is only present "while she was still there" (185), John says. The physical and metaphoric break in this novel is the acknowledgment of absence right under one's feet. John does not always notice that absence while he continues to move. For him, that absence is the loss of Susie, the loss of David and Wallace, the loss of safety, even the losses of horses in his care. There is a gap, a space, a break in Everett's post-West out of which all manner of vulnerabilities and precarities seep.[48] In *Wounded*, those corporeal and psychic wounds are managed and mediated by non/human relations. But it is the horse that begins and grounds such bridging work.

NOTES

1. One reason for the horse's centrality to human narrative and mythmaking, especially in "The West," is that they were central to everyday life. Horses enabled and actualized transport, leisure, sport, farming, and broader industrial change.

2. Curry, "Horse Nations." This summary article offers an overview of the findings cited below.

3. Taylor, Librado, Icu, et al., "Early Dispersal," 1.

4. Tompkins, *West of Everything*, 90.

5. As explored in "Dog," horses saturate the English language too; from "dark horse" to "horse sense" and "high horse" or "hold your horses," there are so many ways in which the horse becomes a metaphorical frame for understanding human action. See Elaine Walker's *Horse* (2008) for more.

6. Armstrong, *What Animals*, 7.

7. Slicer, "Joy."

8. Tompkins, *West of Everything*, 93.

9. Bennett, *Being Property*, 2.

10. Morrison, *A Mercy*, 26

11. Holland, "Vocabularies," 206, 208.

12. Holland, *An Other*, 5.

13. Butler, *The Force*, 59.

14. Butler, *Notes Toward*, 42.

15. Butler, 134, 70.

16. Limón, "How to Triumph," 3.

17. Limón, "Full," 70.

18. The history of the paniolo is a transnational one, as the figure only arises when cattle are first brought to the islands, and then Mexican vaqueros teach Hawaiians about tending, raising, and killing cows. The paniolo gains its own identity that intersects with but diverges from the Mexican and U.S. incarnations. The word paniolo is itself a distortion of español.

19. Kahakauwila, *This is Paradise*, 190, 213.

20. Kahakauwila, 217.

21. Mock, *Redefining Realness*, 102.

22. Published as a single short book in the UK in 2020.

23. Gaitskill, *Lost Cat*, 17, 18.

24. Velvet's name calls up both the protagonist of Enid Bagnold's *National Velvet* (1935) in which a young girl rides her horse in the Grand National disguised as a boy, as well as Margery Williams' *The Velveteen Rabbit* (1922) in which a stuffed rabbit wants to become real through its owner's love. The former calls up questions of queering gender and the latter highlights love and care as markers of ontology, both of which play into Gaitskill's Velvet.

25. Gaitskill, *The Mare*, 23. Cited hereafter in text.

26. Nyman, "Horsescapes," 219, 224, 231.

27. This is a set of themes explored elsewhere in Everett's work. For instance, in the story "Little Faith" (in his 2015 *Half an Inch of Water*), a veterinarian with a loyal dog and a penchant for horses becomes embroiled in the story of a deaf Indigenous girl who goes missing. He sets out into the Western desert to find the girl (on his horse) and is trapped amidst an array of rattlesnakes. (Rattlesnakes crop up in other Everett fiction too, notably *Telephone* [2020]).

28. Everett, *Wounded*, 3. Cited hereafter in text.

29. There are many scenes in the book set in the cave; it's a site of exploration (John keeps trying to get further into the cave), of sexuality (John has sex with his girlfriend there), and of tension (is it where John takes David when he finds him in the snow; where they both huddle naked to maintain body heat; and where David then kisses John). Read alongside Plato—a philosophical touchpoint that Everett is certainly aware of, given his other work—the cave in *Wounded* might also be

seen as a figure for thinking about what the human characters can actually *see* in this violent West: the real or merely its shadows.

30. Everett used to train horses for over a decade. In an interview with the *LA Review of Books*, Everett said training is "like a novel. One thousand two hundred pounds, and it doesn't have to do what I want it to do" (Jama-Everett, 2023). Everett is gesturing to the relationship between writing and training, whereby both involve attempting to control the (potentially) uncontrollable. Seeing the horses in *Wounded* in relation to the imaginative act is a line of thinking outside the scope of this chapter.

31. Mulatto, coming from the term mule (as hybrid) is a derogatory term applied most often to women of mixed heritage, often the child of a white man and a Black woman. For a recent embrace of the term, see interviews with Danzy Senna; e.g., Lucas, "Danzy Senna" (2024).

32. Bennett, *Being Property*, 116, 117.

33. Everett, "Little," 8.

34. Julien, "The Real," 247.

35. Training is an idea that crops up in other Everett work, especially with horses. But it also occurs in his experimental poetry collection, *The Book of Training by Colonel Hap Thompson of Roanoke, VA, 1843* (2018). In these poems that voice a Virginia enslaver in 1843, Everett scathingly approaches questions of the "training" of enslaved people. In the opening poem—each of them "annotated" by an unseen hand, another enslaver we imagine—Thompson discusses writing his manual about the "training of our black animals, / my text on shepherding them / from animal existence / to human coexistence with us" ("My Name is Colonel Hap Thompson). There are thus many ways to read the training of these horses in relation to a larger story about non/human entanglements as they are shaped through slavery's animalization of Black people.

36. Shepard's killing has had other literary incarnations—the Tectonic Theatre Project's verbatim plays *The Laramie Project* (2000) and its follow up *Ten Years Later* (2009).

37. Johnson, "Looking," 50.

38. Johnson usefully suggests that the sudden snowstorms in the novel are symbolic of the endemic and threatening whiteness in the region (50).

39. Pérez, *A Taste*, 16.

40. The bison, of course, was nearly hunted to extinction in the nineteenth century by white people colonizing the West. Manifest Destiny was a project not just of displacing and killing Native people but also decimating the landscape and those other nonhuman animals in it.

41. Johnson, "Looking," 29.

42. Campbell notes in *The Rhizomatic West* (2008) that it was always "defined by complex connectivity, multidimensionality, and imagination" (3) so the post-West is, in a way, extending that tradition.

43. Campbell, *Post-Westerns*, 14, 14–15.

44. Campbell, *Post-Westerns*, 15.

45. Other texts, from Quentin Tarantino's *Django Unchained* (2012) to Jane Campion's film *The Power of the Dog* (2021), Lauren Groff's *The Vaster Wilds* (2023) to Téa Obreht's *Inland* (2019), or more queerly inflected texts like C. Pam Zhang's novel *How Much of These Hills Is Gold* (2020) or even Annie Proulx's "Brokeback Mountain" (1997), have been debated in this context too. *Wounded* is but one example of a larger trend in U.S. fiction and film where the West is fixed in the cultural imagination as a space hard to traverse.

46. Johnson, "Looking," 49. Other critics like Michel Feith, however, read that scene differently. He writes that the "individual relationship to the land" here has a "quasi-mystical intimacy" that is clearly a Frontier ethos, but one that does not dovetail with the "mystifications of nationalism and jingoism." Feith, "Philosophy Embedded in Space," 96.

47. Mullins, "Counter-Counterstorytelling," 458.

48. With more time and space, we might also think that "break" along with Fred Moten's oeuvre.

TAX
IDE
RMY

Taxidermy

taxidermy queerly arranges (taxis) the skin (derma) between and across non/human forms

I

In Jeff VanderMeer's *Hummingbird Salamander* (2021), a taxidermized hummingbird and salamander—the former "tiny" and "frozen" in flight, "dead but somehow alive, able to be wounded"; and the latter "startling" and "posed in a sinuous way, like a living river," and "almost seemed to smile"—draw Jane Smith, a security analyst-turned investigator, into a world of eco-revolutionaries.[1] Each taxidermized creature is a clue and a gateway to more information about the shadowy world of one woman's attempt to reimagine a planet wrecked by climate change. For Jane, the hummingbird and salamander gesture to something beyond their specific forms: The hummingbird is placed gently in its box because it is "somehow alive," and the salamander is "reassuring" in its smile (199). Like medieval bestiaries, these creatures symbolize beyond their individuality. Jane is desperate for meaning in this cryptic world after she's handed an envelope with a key to a storage unit, and she finds that meaning in the bird and lizard.

Noticeable in the two descriptions is their vitality: "iridescent feathers" (13) and "almost bright gold" (199). Both are full of beauty and vibrancy, even though dead—a tension at the heart of taxidermic practice. We might call this the vibrancy of matter, as Jane Bennett does: the way she notes a pile of "stuff" (a dead rat, a stick, a bottle cap) "shimmied back and forth between debris and thing." The stuff commanded "its thing-power" through an "energetic vitality."[2] It is the glittering brightness of these dead creatures, seemingly innocuous but materially charged, that gives them a talismanic quality to Jane Smith. But the hummingbird and the salamander in this novel point, in the end, to an era of mass extinction (see the final chapter of this bestiary).

The narrative we have been reading, we find out at the novel's end, is timed to be released by Jane a hundred years after its completion; as such, the story is coming from the far-off past and is already gone. Not only does the novel use taxidermy as a plot device, then, but the novel itself becomes a kind of taxidermy, encoding life in death. The question of extinction in the novel thus scrambles (queers?) temporality: We only know about the strange utopic world of ecowarriors long after that world has (likely) disappeared. The end of the world might thus be ahead of and behind us, a matter not just for our conception of futurity but of presentness and history too. Thus, the question of what we know now (or what we *will* know, in the future anterior) is deeply connected to the stuffed nonhuman forms that drive the narrative's thriller plot. The inert but *lively* taxidermy creatures ask, as Rachel Poliquin does, "What does it mean to be dead but not gone?" and are they "animal or object? Animal and object?"[3]

A similar set of questions are asked in the opening of Ocean Vuong's *On Earth We're Briefly Gorgeous* (2019). The narrator Little Dog, writing to his mother in a language she does not understand, recollects the time that, outside some bathrooms at a highway rest stop, they saw a taxidermy buck, "its antlers shadowing your face."[4] That shadow of death casts a foreboding light over the novel which is so suffused with violence in the past and present. Little Dog's mother, Rose, says, "Can't they see it's a corpse? A corpse should go away, not get stuck forever like that" (3). Death, for Rose, should be mourned, the body interred; remnants of death should not linger in the present, even if that is exactly what she experiences in terms of memories of the Vietnam War. Seeing his mother's reflection in the buck's eyes—as if joining the two in some kind of bond—Little Dog notes that it was not the "grotesque mounting of a decapitated animal that shook you—but that the taxidermy embodied a death that won't finish, a death that keeps dying as we walk past it to relive ourselves" (3). The ongoing death—akin, perhaps, to a kind of melancholia, an unfinished and unending mourning—is also connected to the bathroom where they want to literally expel that which the body does not need. The body of the buck is intimately linked to the human bodies, especially this queer Asian American boy and his mother, both of whom are figured as animalized outsiders in this new country. Death's ongoingness, embodied in the taxidermy animal is much like VanderMeer's salamander and hummingbird; these are creatures who are dead but not gone, both subject and object, liveliness within death. The central texts of this chapter—Matthew Griffin's *Hide* (2016) and Kristen Arnett's *Mostly Dead Things* (2019)—ask similar kinds of questions about the non/human, encoded as they are in taxidermy forms.

II

I am reading these two novels in light of Sarah Bezan and Susan McHugh's concept of "taxidermic fictions"; they argue that "Stretched, stitched, and stuffed, taxidermy hides [skins] themselves *hide, conceal, and secret away their stories*," and also that literature has the ability to narrativize that which taxidermy often cannot.[5] Literary texts are but one taxidermic form that enables us to ask questions about the practice's cultural meanings and histories. Taxidermy's ambiguous meanings and status—preservation or destruction—are, in this chapter, queerly inflected. In both Griffin's and Arnett's novels we see how the disrobing, stuffing, and reanimating of dead nonhumans is a queer practice. It is queer in the sense of destabilizing and reimagining identities, entwining gay lovers physically and emotionally, eroticizing the dead, and lingering beneath the flesh.[6] Like the book of which this chapter is a part, taxidermy indexes the processes of both conservation and annihilation, valuing the nonhuman by holding it still, but only because its stillness is deathly. Like the archive (of which this book is a kind), taxidermy is committed to a form of still life as we witness the simultaneity of ossification and enlivenment. For both Griffin and Arnett, taxidermy is a way of holding both concepts open, in a form of disavowal. Taxidermy keeps family members and pets alive but also dead. Taxidermy also enables non/human entanglement, across species lines, where that entanglement is fleshed by sexuality, race, gender, and other identity markers.

The history of taxidermy is a long and layered one, and I won't rehearse it here (others have done that work[7]). But within this bestiary's larger purview, taxidermy has a complicated relationship to race and gender (in particular), as it took off in relation to colonial expansion. While we can see taxidermy—and related practices—in various parts of the world across history (it was coined in the 1803–4 *Nouveau dictionnaire d'histoire naturelle*), its rise as a form of collecting and displaying humans and nonhumans accelerated with empire-building. As Antoinette Burton and Renisa Mawani, citing Alice Would, write: "Animal taxidermy that was proudly displayed in public and private spaces became 'physical symbols of the power of the British over colonised lands—and colonised wildlife.' Thus, animals and animal parts were status symbols of masculinity, femininity, race, and class mobility through consumption, display, desire, and the relentless quest for military conquest and white settlement."[8] Taxidermy's very substance and technology are enlaced with histories of subjugation and destruction through hunting and other means. (We return to this topic in the chapter "Hunter").

As a form of displaying the "still and silent token[s] of the exotic" from colonized lands, taxidermy propped up the colonial logic of mastery over the nonhuman (which extended, of course, to those humans outside the concept of "Man").[9] Both humans and nonhumans were put on display at the height of empire. Ethnological exhibitions (or "human zoos" as they were called) displayed people of color from around the world to white Western audiences; the exhibited people's supposed "wildness" and "savagery" were part of the spectacle. In this way, the taxidermized nonhuman animals were put in relation to these live human subjects, both as exotic objects to be observed. Taxidermy manifests across non/human lines.

The stuffing and exhibiting of nonhumans has similarly been historicized through white colonial thinking; as Giovanni Aloi notes, when critics distance taxidermy from other forms like mummification in ancient Egypt, the former is "validate[d]" as a "rational" and "secular" form—and thus an authorized (white) scientific "epistemic tool"—and the latter is seen as somehow backward.[10] In all, then, taxidermy is *stuffed* with histories of exploitation and exoticization, with capture and deathliness. To reimagine taxidermy, as Griffin and Arnett do, is thus in part to reckon with or to distance that history. Taxidermy in these novels is about sexuality and gender in particular, but the novels secret(e) them into taxidermy's forms and processes.

Poliquin summarizes taxidermy's main goals thus: "to flaunt a hunter's skill or virility, to contain nature, to immortalize a cherished pet, to collect an archive of the world, to commemorate an experience, to document an endangered species, to furnish evidence, to preserve knowledge, to decorate a wall, to amuse, to educate, to fascinate, to unsettle, to horrify, and even to deceive." Both Griffin and Arnett represent taxidermy from within these categories: In

Hide, taxidermy draws two gay men together at a time when their love was impermissible, and it attempts to keep part of their relationship alive as they age and become sicker; and in *Mostly Dead Things*, taxidermy functions as a way to keep a dead father (and his ideologies) alive, as well a way to recast him and his legacy anew. These two texts have been chosen not because they are exemplary of taxidermic fiction but because they speak to the queer memory-work of taxidermy as a "narrativ[e] of longing" and a "gesture of remembrance."[11] Both books encode desire for the past within their queer storylines.

III

The title of Matthew Griffin's novel signifies in multiple ways: It is the hide (from the German *haut*), the skin of nonhuman animals used in taxidermy, and the cultural stories the hide itself secrets away; it is the skin of humans, particularly marked and tattooed; and it is the process of hiding that the two gay men in the novel undergo all their lives. Theirs is a literal hiding away (in a house up a track far removed from other people), as well as an emotional one (they obscure their sexuality for years). As such, Griffin sutures together the secrets of sexuality and queerness with the secrets of the skin, both human and nonhuman. If *taxis* means ordering, then Griffin's novel illuminates that ordering via a multitude of skins.

The novel focuses on the relationship between Frank Clifton and Wendell Wilson, who meet just after World War II. Frank is a laborer in the town, and Wendell is a taxidermist. Their long relationship (almost sixty years) is told by Wendell as the men are aging in the North Carolina countryside. In between this present-day storyline—where Frank has a stroke and slowly deteriorates, becoming ever more dependent on Wendell—there are flashbacks to when they met in their early twenties and their relationship bloomed (and where taxidermy is central to their coming together). *Hide* thus oscillates between present and past, keeping the men both alive and close to impairment and death. As they age, the next chapter reinstates them and returns them to the scenes of their initial romance and love.

Symbolically, then, the novel is a kind of taxidermic form, by preserving lifelikeness in death and keeping the past suspended in seeming perpetuity. It's a kind of narrative weaving, which mimics the stitching up of a nonhuman body. As Pauline Wakeham puts it, "While taxidermy recreates death in the image of life, its hyperrealist tactics of reincarnation effectively inscribe the fatal sign of mortality upon the bodies it claims to revivify."[12] In its form and method, taxidermy reveals the deathliness at the heart of its life-making, and the novel, I argue, mirrors this. Put in Caroline Levine's terms, the affordances of *Hide*'s form are such that the book replicates or plays out some of the inherent tensions about temporality and life in the taxidermy it is depicting.

If taxidermy is about the literalization and symbolization of non/human entanglements, in *Hide*, Griffin shows how that entanglement can be queer or is tied to queer attachments. The protagonists and their dog Daisy form a queer family in the North Carolina wilderness. Their world is one textured by the non/human, not least because their house is filled with taxidermized creatures that customers fail to collect from Wendell. The walls are claustrophobic with them, highlighting the potency of the form and practice. Frank's aversion to dead things (he "could never bear to see an animal hurt") is an inversion of Wendell's continued sense of the world as something to be transformed in death.[13] But he also sees humans and nonhumans as much closer together than others might. Wendell's customers, he thinks, spot his queerness (indeed, *they* look at him queerly, "a little askance") and see him as if he "might secretly be dead as the animals on the wall, and just made to appear otherwise" (121). His projection onto the customers testifies to a sense of himself as dead in life *because of* his queerness.

The language and logic of taxidermy also runs throughout the novel (not just in queer ways); it is as if Wendell's point of view is one of disassembly and stasis. When Frank must see numerous doctors, for instance, for different ailments, Wendell thinks: "They keep dividing us up, down and down into parts too small for a knife blade" (14). On the day that Wendell and Frank first meet, the town is covered in ice, as if to be "preserved" (19), and when icicles fall to the floor, it "sounded like the world coming undone" (21); and on that day, Frank's coat itself is "unraveling" and "cobbled together" (20). Later, a storm makes it sound like "the house is about to come apart" (80), and when his mother dies, Frank cries "great, heavy sobs" that make Wendell think "they would shake him apart" (114). This lexical focus on taxidermy's mechanics is one way for Griffin to show how central the practice is to the world of these two men. The novel's focus on the two men's gay relationship is underscored, or perhaps fleshed out, by the art of dissecting (as well as the more sexualized notions of stuffing and mounting; more on these in relation to *Mostly Dead Things*).

Central to this novel then is the (queer) intimacy of taxidermy: the interweaving of the human and nonhuman (non/human) that connects sexuality and gender, as well as questions of species. I will shortly read a scene in which this comes to the fore. But for now, considering everything we've seen about taxidermy so far, the form is no liberatory practice: it is steeped in power, (white) supremacy, and attempts to contain and aestheticize the nonhuman wild. Yet it finds a kind of corollary for the two men hiding away from the world in the rural U.S. South.[14] The two men hide their sexuality (and their relationship) from the outside world, including family members, neighbors, and the public. Their house is set back miles from any main road or other people, and when they go anywhere, they take separate cars so as not to rouse suspicion. Even in the first present-day scene, when Frank is in the hospital, Wendell pretends to be his brother, both to conceal their relationship status and to be an "official" family member able to get into the hospital room.

The novel can be seen then as one ultimately about masking one's identity. Simon Dickel reads Griffin's novel in light of Didier Eribon's *Insult and the Making of the Gay Self* (1999), which focuses on the "habits gay men . . . form from an early age to cope with homonegativity"; that is, in a punishingly heteronormative world, gay men are "socialized into forming self-oppressive habits."[15] Dickel sees this self-abnegation throughout *Hide*, where Frank and Wendell hide their sexuality for fear of insult, where insult indexes all kinds of violence and persecution. Frank is proud of the fact that no one knew his sexuality, even in the army (120), and the specter of homophobic violence, largely from the state—"men being arrested," "fired from their jobs, evicted from their homes," and "sentenced to prison, or sent to the sanitarium" to undergo conversion therapy (121)—is never far from these men's minds, even in old age as society seemingly "progresses." Indeed, at one point Wendell rants about openly queer (proud?) men who are "cavorting half-naked in leather harnesses" (122) and later being diagnosed with HIV and AIDS. This shocking moment (out of the blue) testifies not only to Wendell's internalized homophobia but also the ways in which he distances himself and Frank from other queer men: the "*Homosexual*," he says, "sounds like another species" (122). Far from the Foucauldian sense, Wendell sees queers (mainly gay men) as another type, an "ancestor of decent men, dragging its knuckles through the dust of evolution" (121). Queers are, to Wendell, some aberration in human development *as well as* some other kind of species altogether. And, of course, this thinking has a corollary with the ways in which people of color have been animalized and tied to figures of savagery, wildness, and devolution throughout history.

The stigma of gayness/queerness runs through the novel in stark ways. For Dickel, the novel's focus on the "habits of hiding" offers no way out for these men; the characters, in his words, have "little agency" and "no space" for "recognition or gay emancipation."[16] While I query Dickel's idea that a novel should do anything in particular, let alone forge a liberatory politics, I do want to argue that *Hide*'s enlacing of non/human bodies is (to some degree) queerly generative. For, even when the characters are trapped by their fear of heteronormative society's judgments and punishments, within their non/human world of taxidermy and pets, life-worlds that cut across species lines can (haltingly) flourish. Like taxidermy itself, things are held still in their liveliness. This is not emancipatory per se, but it is a queer take on the way that non/human bodies are deeply interconnected and dependent on one another: a queer ecology, even amid death.

Yet the novel oscillates between taxidermy's liveliness and deathliness, and its associations therein with queerness. In a key chapter where Wendell and Frank—during the dismantling of a whitetail buck corpse—open up to one another and eventually have sex, the exposure of history and non/human bodies are deeply connected. In this scene, taxidermy enables, licenses, and perhaps even arouses the possibility of sex between the men.[17] I want to spend some time on this section, unpacking the way its language and imagery moves and builds because it exemplifies the larger novel's thematic concerns (Dickel, too, explores this scene in depth but with a different focus[18]).

Late in the evening, at a time when Frank does not usually show up, he comes to Wendell's shop. Attempting to salvage a buck's skin after a man runs over the animal, Wendell has to get the "hide off . . . before he spoils" (57). Frank and Wendell see the scene differently: "Living things are disgusting," Wendell says. "You mean dead things?" Frank replies. "The difference . . . isn't very great" is Wendell's retort (60). Not only are non/human boundaries fluid here; so too are the governing lines between life and death, especially through the form of taxidermy.

In broaching the subject of Wendell's family—"I wasn't any of the things my parents wanted me to be" (61)—the two men approach a new emotional intimacy. This slight acknowledgment of Wendell's otherness (which we can read as, in part, his queerness) is his explanation for why he left home at such a young age. Frank's desire to know more is animalistically translated in his "wild" eyes, like the gaze of a "starving dog" (62). Here, the intense focus on the dead buck allows Wendell to open up, because he can focus his immediate attention elsewhere; opening the carcass allows him, in turn, to open up too.

Because Wendell cannot or will not say more about his past *out loud* to Frank, he instead takes Frank's hand in his own and puts it into the buck's carcass, beneath the skin. Wendell hopes that "it would tell him . . . all the things I couldn't say"; this physical gesture unleashes a thirty-four-line sentence in which the overwhelm of his familial history is densely articulated, from his "mother's magnolia perfume" to nostalgia for "evenings full of warm, wild wind" (62). The sentence itself, unfurling silently beneath the animal's skin is its own kind of "wild wind" that moves across the page. The dead buck between them is a conduit for their physical proximity and intimacy. It is here—at the intersection of the unspeakable, the queer, the non/human—that sexuality flourishes further. Dickel describes this "shedding of skin" as an opening of the "alterity of the other's body."[19] I would go further and say it is *because of* the taxidermy that this alterity is confronted.

Frank's arm is "rigid and shaking" as Wendell "work[s]" their hands together; the sexualized language heightens as Frank's fingers "[stay] stiff" (63). They reach the shoulder of the buck, where the skin is so thin that they could "tear through" it if they "pushed any further" (63). The threat of breaking through is not only erotic (encoding the "skin" of a condom, for instance), but potentially destructive of the buck's skin, itself a kind of displaced (human) dermic fissure. We might read in this moment, too, the kind of "shattering" nature of (queer) sex that we saw in "Animal," as the narrator of *We the Animals* both came apart and was newly "made" through sexual acts. That shattering, in light of Freud and later queer studies from Leo Bersani and Tim Dean, is sex's scrambling of bodily and psychic coherence, where the "separateness and hence the distinguishability of bodies" is undone.[20] In this way, the men's hands beneath the buck's skin—the carcass itself joined into the sexualized act—threaten to "tear" or "shatter" their own internal coherence because of their blurred entanglement. As Frank and Wendell pull out of the carcass, the "world felt raw and exposed" (64), signifying threefold: They are coming out (of the closet), coming out of Wendell's past, and "pulling out" of the buck's (a man's) body.

Wendell then takes Frank's body into his hands, substituting one buck for another. (As a sidenote, this is the only sex scene in the whole novel, something Dickel notices and regards as striking). Wendell traces Frank's tattooed muscles, themselves covered in wild tableaux: "On his biceps, clouds unwound from a dark skein about the buck's antlers," and across his collarbone, a sky is filled with a "flock of birds of all kinds, . . . their bodies and beaks overlapping" (64). It is as if Frank's body is an extension of the nonhuman world, as well as a representation or index of it; a copy, as it were, of taxidermy's craft. The nonhumans are both enlivened (in flight, overlapping) and static (the tattoo is fixed on the skin). The focus on the skin too is a way for the novel to link non/human hides and the permeability of the flesh, both by taxidermy's knives and through queer desire. Naomi Segal (glossing Didier Anzieu) notes that the skin "has a double surface," and is thus a complicated "structure of surfaces" that are interpenetrating, looped, and enfolded; the skin, in this view, helps us understand the body differently, not as something with a deep core to be penetrated, but as a shifting set of planes.[21] The men's bodies are not simply coming together through sex and taxidermy, but are revealed to be radically and queerly interpenetrating (again the specter of bestiality emerges). They open one another up, anew, *via* the buck's skin: Taxidermy is the medium of the skin's layering.

Yet the skin is also charged with other connotations. The focus on Frank's tattoos is registered throughout the novel, not only here in the sex scene. Earlier on, we learn that Frank always wears long-sleeved shirts, even in hot weather, to hide the tattoos. He does this, Dickel notes, because the tattoos mark him as different, even when he is passing (successfully) as straight.[22] When he first shows the tattoos to Wendell in a park, Frank notes that "they make me look like a criminal" (38). For Dickel, Wendell inks his homosexuality into the tattoos as if being gay is a crime (and it is for much of their lives), and if tattoos index criminality, then both are bound together in the skin. As such, the hide must be hidden beneath clothing, in a mirror image of Wendell and Frank's hiding of their identities from the rest of the world. That otherness (or queerness) of being different, criminal, gay, and so on is underscored by, or rather interlaced with, the nonhuman. For the tattoos are like "woodcut prints" all "tangled together": "It was hard to separate," Frank says, "the markings on his skin from the shadows of the branches that overlaid them" (36). Frank cannot tell "one from another" because of the "knotted chaos of his skin," full of flora and fauna (37). The nonhuman forms are out of scale and are not fully contained by their thickly lined borders. (So many skins are entwined here, including the tree's bark, the human skin, and the representations of other nonhumans.) In other words, the knotting of gayness, criminality, and the skin is a queer one, in all of the senses of nonnormativity and its social excesses. But more importantly it is queer *at the site of* the non/human.

After the men have emerged from the buck's carcass, Wendell pulls Frank's penis free from his pants, which is "barely curved like the branch of an antler, long and hard, the velvet just rubbed away from the bone" (65). Even the penis here is non/human. Based on a simile, the description further enlivens the organ: The "musk" is "unruly, wild," a scent that lingers like an animal's marking (65). Not only is their sexuality wild in the sense of its nonnormativity, but the very flesh of their bodies is rendered queerly in wild terms: made up and out of the non/human world. As Frank enters Wendell, he waits "rigid" (echoing that word used earlier in relation to Frank's arm) "until [Wendell's] body believed he was just another part of itself" (66). The corporeal entanglement reaches its apex here as, one inside another, the bodies fuse together, as if "naturally" part of the same organism.

By descending together into the buck's carcass, literally getting beneath its skin—because they cannot overtly or always get beneath their own—the men become entwined with it and each other. The buck enables and allows, through a form of mediation like we have seen in "Horse," the men to explore their own inarticulable queerness. The non/human entangling is queerly erotic and, concomitantly, destabilizing; as Halberstam argues, the wild "questions the hierarchies of being that have been designed to mark and patrol the boundaries between the human and everything else."[23] This wild scene scrambles the hierarchies of flesh and desire, interior and exterior, past and present, living and dead. *Hide* shows us how taxidermy might enable or lay the groundwork for queer non/human connections: how the overlaps between species—literally via the body—engender all kinds of nonnormativity. Next, I turn to *Mostly Dead Things*, in which Arnett similarly reveals how the practice of taxidermy can be a mode of queer expression and a connection to the messiness of desire and memory.

IV

Kristen Arnett's *Mostly Dead Things*, as its title suggests, is about those inert things that thrive, and those alive things that perish. If taxidermy is about preserving a kind of aliveness in death—most of the customers in this novel wanted a creature "larger than life, as if the animal might reanimate and attack"—then taxidermy also allows the characters of *Mostly Dead Things* to elongate, transform, or reimagine death across species lines.[24] The novel centers on Jessa-Lynn Morton, the queer daughter of a taxidermist who kills himself before the novel opens. Jessa-Lynn takes over her father's shop, principally because she feels devoted to his work and legacy, but also because her brother Milo has no talent for it. At the same time, Milo's wife Brynn (and Jessa-Lynn's secret girlfriend for most of their lives) has run off, leaving Milo with her son from another relationship, Bastien. As such, the novel is saturated with loss and death: the suicide of the father, the loss of a wife and girlfriend, as well as innumerable dead creatures that litter the shop and the humid Florida landscape they inhabit. Both Jessa-Lynn and her mother, Libby, use taxidermy to different ends: Jessa-Lynn to continue her father's legacy, and to keep him (in a way) alive; her mother by sexualizing and transforming standard taxidermy creatures into erotic tableaux, remaking her husband's life and work.

Like *Hide*, *Mostly Dead Things* progresses through a present-day narrative and flashbacks, and like Griffin's text, those flashbacks detail blossoming romance and the learning of taxidermy. Indeed, the flashback chapters all are named after nonhuman animals and their Latin names, such as "Ursus arctos—Brown Bear" (273). In this way, the past is mediated and organized *by* nonhumans, and the practice of taxidermy becomes central to Jessa-Lynn's own biography. Where other children had "stuffed animals," she and Milo had "mounted bass and antlers covered with Varathane" (3). Not only does the novel use this dual structure to interlink the past and present, but it moves through two parts, "skinning" and "mounting," as though replicating the steps needed in taxidermy. The novel skins its characters, laying bare their internality, before mounting them by its end. Thus, like *Hide*, Arnett's novel is not just about taxidermy but rather uses it *formally* to investigate the queer boundaries of non/human connection.

From the start, the two modes of taxidermy (the father's and the mother's) are contrasted. While we learn about Jessa-Lynn's father teaching her the art of taxidermy in the past, the present is full of Libby's transformative artworks. In this way, Jessa-Lynn is twinned with her father: The book's opening is a pedagogic encounter not just with taxidermy but its attendant gendered norms. He shows Jessa-Lynn how to "slice the skin" with "tenderness" and "love" (3)—which already frames the act as an emotionally relational one—and when she does it well, he whispers "*You're a natural. Just like your dad*" (9). Milo does not take to taxidermy in the same way, though we might expect him to. Instead, Jessa-Lynn's "female masculinity" (to put it in Halberstam's words) suits her, or acculturates her, to the form: she and her father have the "same type of body: naturally muscly and built like bulldogs" (113). You needed the "*right body for it*" (113), her father says; "*You're like a mole,*" Brynn notes (136). Not only is the dense physicality needed for taxidermy ("standing upright for hours" [136–7]) linked to muscularity, and thus coded as stereotypically masculine, but that gendering is also then linked to nonhuman animality (bulldogs, moles). It is as if the "masculine" work needed to take apart certain creatures is creaturely from the start.

Where Jessa-Lynn and her father are thus twinned, they also use the logic of taxidermy as organizing principles for life. Again, if taxidermy is about arranging and ordering, it is also about control over the other, especially the nonhuman other. Jessa-Lynn and her father turn to taxidermy ultimately to hold things still, both literally and figuratively, as a way of regulating the world. As we know, the father kills himself after bottling up all his fears and unvoiced concerns. Jessa-Lynn is not only his protégé but his extension: not just "expected to take over everything" and carry the burden, but she "just needed to be Dad" (23). Inhabiting his body and his outlook, Jessa-Lynn's world is shaped by taxidermy. She notes that she is the "kind of person who'd wish death on a creature just so I could make it my own" (97), an acknowledgment of her desire for life through death, or control through obliteration. Twinned with this deathly impulse is her and her father's secretive nature; she hides for years a relationship with Milo's wife, Brynn, a queer coupling that is pushed underground, which itself is stitched to the nonhuman. In the early days of their romance, Jessa-Lynn shows off to Brynn with her taxidermy: "My hands commanded the flesh," bringing the "animal back to life" (42), a coded sexualization of the craft. Their sex in turn is both taxidermized—"Every nerve ending was exposed and frayed" (39)—and then animalized—the sounds they made were "wounded, animal noises, whimpers" (40). As such, queer sex is tangled not only with secrecy and infidelity, but also the violence of taxidermy and its rearranging of non/human forms.

The other women in the book are similarly complicated. When Jessa-Lynn meets Lucinda Rex,[25] the gallery owner who takes interest in Libby's artwork, she struggles with Lucinda's ostensible polish amid the messiness of her usual queer desire. She is used to "thinking about [a woman] in terms of how I might disassemble her" (50), or she likes to "picture her mounted like a dead animal" (51), a pathology that stitches together desire that must be hidden with queerness and the control inflicted through taxidermy. Lucinda turns out to be not so polished; we find out that she is already married (and separated), but also eventually burns down the art gallery—full of Libby's installations—to get insurance money. As should be clear, all the characters keep secrets, act out, and live in the shadow of taxidermy's ultimate violence and aesthetics. So connected is Jessa-Lynn to taxidermy and its worldview, that she is figured often as the one who is "mostly dead," wandering in a hungover haze through stuffy rooms and the store, as well continually feeling out of place: "Nothing fit right. Everything I owned felt uncomfortable" (24). As a recourse to this deadliness-in-life, Jessa-Lynn puts all her faith and control in taxidermy itself: a non/human feedback loop.

As I have been arguing, Jessa-Lynn and her father are interested in the "proper" or normative mode of taxidermy, but Libby reimagines the form altogether. Here I want to focus on Libby's creations as central to the criticality of *Mostly Dead Things*. Though taxidermy, Aloi notes, has "never been accepted by the artistic canon" as "high art"—principally seen as a craft, as a form of work outside of lofty artistic practice—Libby is the person in the family to remake taxidermy in her own way.[26] She takes the taxidermized creatures—largely completed by her husband—and rearranges them into sexualized scenes, such as "alligator skulls with panties stuffed in their open mouths" (19). Jessa-Lynn is personally shocked but also offended on behalf of her dead father; she sees Libby's efforts as a "wreck" of his work (18). "I knew," she notes, "my father would mind someone dripping lube on his prized mountain lion" (19), a line that is both comic and tragic.

Libby's reworking and restaging are clear responses to the father's death: Where Jessa-Lynn tries to model his work with accuracy, Libby sees it as her duty to experiment with and repurpose the creatures to her own ends. If, as

Poliquin argues, taxidermy "always exposes the desires and daydreams surrounding human relationships with and within the natural world," then Libby's artistic practice reveals desires about her relationship to her now-dead husband as well as the nonhuman worlds that he invested in.[27] To some degree, Libby uses the nonhuman material to make non/human representations that are saturated with questions about sexuality and gender. The work is queer in both antinormative sexual content and in its splaying of subjects, objects, and materials together (the works are often hybrid forms, as explored elsewhere in this book). In one setup, a panther is placed behind a goat, as though penetrating it; in another, a futon is draped with her mother's linen, and on it placed a raccoon "gowned in a satin negligee, bridal veil" over its face. Next to the raccoon is a bear "in a roomy pair of custom boxer shorts made from two pillowcases" (19). The work is wild, as described by Jack Halberstam: Wildness is the "*disorder* of things, the ways of being that resist expert knowledge, that fail to resolve into identity forms" and are expressed by "eccentrics, and recluses."[28] Libby's art is a disordering of Jessa-Lynn's and her father's practice (and literal products); it is also a form of art-making that resists expertise (it is not the traditional work of taxidermy); and the sex scenes play with the boundaries between human and nonhuman as a way of holding open identity's fixity (a queer move). Jessa-Lynn, too, in this terminology, might call her mother an "eccentric." As such, the wildness is Libby's way of overcoming both personal and cultural histories.

But beyond wildness, I want to frame Libby's artwork as overlapping with (if not exemplifying) "rogue taxidermy," as analyzed by Miranda Niittynen, or "speculative taxidermy," as theorized by Aloi. Both concepts help us see how queerness shows up at the intersection between the non/human, especially as it occurs through reimagining taxidermy. *Speculative taxidermy* is art where "visible animal skin (or its representation) is critically adopted as a defining indexical relationship between animal presence and the medium of representation itself." Such art explores "shared physical and ontological vulnerabilities concealed by the naturalization of past human/animal institutionalized relationships." In other words, speculative works query the stories that taxidermy hides within its hides by reflexively foregrounding its means of production and meaning-making. Artworks that are or use taxidermized nonhumans (or even representations of them) ask "questions about what taxidermy may be or do in order to unravel complex interlinks between humans, animals, environments, discourses, and practices."[29] Like Libby's arrangements, this artwork is explicit about its *use* of stuffing and mounting nonhumans; explicit about the ways that taxidermy works, and the cultural stories that is embedded within it.

Relatedly, *rogue taxidermy*, for Niittynen, is a cross-temporal mixup of artistic styles and genres (among them surrealism and "pop" aesthetics), which is "environmentally conscious" and "ethically sustainable," always interrogating the dominant Western narratives that have "produced and perpetuated a distorted image of animal/human difference." Niittynen looks to (queer) women artists such as Sarina Brewer—who, I would posit, could be a close model for Libby—that reorient taxidermy away from its masculine roots and style. In opposition to Jessa-Lynn, who wants to continue her father's male-centric legacy, Libby (re)genders that legacy from her own worldview. Rogue taxidermy not only demasculinizes the form but also reworks its colonial legacies by using decolonial imaginaries and methods; it goes rogue by responding to and tearing apart (often literally) its material histories. By "breaking the established and strictly policed borders of 'proper' interspecies intimacy"—think about the panther and goat having sex—rogue work embodies new ways of seeing and thinking the non/human.[30] Jessa-Lynn stands against this speculative-rogue style because it "pervert[s]" taxidermy's normative form: where "the animals [are] whole and lifelike," as if they "could step off the mount" at any moment. Libby's alternative work shows the nonhuman animals as "mangled and misshapen, slopped together like trash," which "took away their dignity" (107).[31] Jessa-Lynn's language reveals the very disavowal at the heart of taxidermy: She literally makes forms with dead—killed, murdered—carcasses that are stripped of dignity and life. Libby's art simply foregrounds and magnifies that reality rather than stuffing it with falsity.

Both rogue and speculative forms are also concerned with the enmeshed nature of human and nonhuman animals, as well as the queerness that often lingers at that porous borderland. For Niittynen, artists like Brewer create queer aesthetics in their taxidermy creations—in representation and formal play—because they "mock both the *over*representation of racialized and gendered sexuality as testimony to deviant 'bestial desires,' but also the *under*representation of animal sexual behaviours, especially those not conforming to the normative framework of reproductive heterosexuality."[32] In other words, artists like Brewer (and Libby) use cross-species erotics and messy formal modes to queer the history of non/human relations and the calcifying role of taxidermy in this history. Moreover, as Aloi continues, "The semantic ruptures proposed by the manipulation of form, engage in speculation on the interconnectedness" of non/human networks of power, ecology, and culture.[33] While on a narrative level it would seem that Libby's artworks are just creative expressions in the face of loss—about, "merely," familial dynamics—Arnett's novel does seem be asking larger questions about the relation between humans and nonhumans and the landscapes they find themselves in.

The "semantic ruptures" that happen through formal rupture in the artwork allow Libby (and the novel as a whole) to question the interpenetrations of patriarchal power, cultural narratives of hunting and capture, the values of the artworld, and the complexities of gender and sexuality. Libby's big show, hosted and encouraged by Lucinda, plays with—in Libby's words—"similarities between sex acts in the animal kingdom and those in modern suburbia," as well as "grief and anger" (166), drawing together non/human worlds. In this show, a water buffalo is "festooned with whips and paddles," and is ridden by a mannequin in a "tight suit made out of patent leather, showing off lean muscle" (167); the mannequin is a mockup of Libby's dead husband. This cross-species, bestiality-inflected BDSM scene illustrates, for Libby, "the repressive nature of relationships and sexuality," as well as the connections between BDSM "and how modern domestic marriages set us up for cyclical punishment" (166). Of course, even Libby's reading here is not quite accurate, because her comic and evocative taxidermic pieces are not simply critiques of masculine dominance and feminine submissiveness, in the same way that scholars of BDSM reveal some of the more liberatory pleasures that its various practices enable.[34]

In that light, there are various ways to read Libby's work. Seen one way, Libby is the water buffalo, ridden by masculine dominance; in another, she is showing the white patriarchal trappings of taxidermy, whipping nonhuman animals into submission; in another, her dead husband is a queer leather daddy, enjoying illicit cross-species pleasure (not unlike that which he got from the processes of taxidermy); in another, the plastic (human-made) mannequin's relationship to the (natural) hides, and the leather outfit—once animal, now a garment—is a critical one. Though Libby sees her creations as principally being about exposing her husband (and straight husbands in general) as "controlling and repressive" (292) and also as a "prude" in public (306), her work actually contains numerous rogue and speculative threads that make them radical and queer. Taxidermy in her hands is transformative, unshackling the form from its violent roots, all the while using and deploying nonhuman bodies. Interrogating the fungible lines between humans and nonhumans, some queer taxidermy can rethink and reimagine the borders between both, which have been deliberately hidden away by taxidermy's very mechanics.

V

To close the archive on taxidermy seems to be an ironic task because the form is always trying to enliven that which is already shut down.

At the end of *Hide*, Wendell taxidermies (some of) the carcass of their dog Daisy, who dies when Frank accidentally runs over her with a lawnmower. (We will come back to this scene in the "Dog" chapter of this book to dwell on it in relation to other canine stories.) In that moment, the stuffing and mounting of Daisy is a way of preserving her, giving her death meaning, and stopping—however briefly—the workings of time. After the fire in *Mostly Dead Things* where Libby's installations are destroyed, Jessa-Lynn sifts through the show's "detritus" like an "administrator of a burn unit," trying to find what is salvageable from the "aftershocks of trauma" (283). Jessa-Lynn finds "bat wings" and "bird torsos" amid the wreckage, as well as a pair of her parents' handcuffs (306). Libby goes into extreme mourning (not washing or eating), as though grieving both the loss of the artwork and her husband all over again: "I put everything I had into that work," she says (292). Her art is a way to bridge life and death, herself and her husband, the human and the nonhuman. When the gallery goes up in flames, so does one version of her imagination. However, once Jessa-Lynn, Milo, and Libby all confront each other more openly ("Neither of us can deal with anything because we refuse to let anything go. We learned it from Dad,"[35] Jessa says to Milo [311–2]), they are able to collaborate through taxidermy for the first time.

They produce a new show in which Jessa-Lynn stuffs and arranges the nonhuman animals and then gives them to her mother to stage. This partnership is still fraught but at least joins mother and daughter in a form that was so rigorously tied to the man in their life. Jessa-Lynn notes how Libby "anthropomorphized" the animals, which she usually balks at, and thinks is "bizarre" (351), but for both of them there is a "wild kind of freedom" (352) in the process. This wildness, I argue, touches on and dialogues with the queer: both in speculative and rogue forms, the entangling of non/humans through taxidermy's technology enables a queer cross-species relationality. While not free from the dominant hierarchies of human control and animal death—taxidermy fails to break free from that while still using "real" carcasses—their practice is a step toward something like reimagining species boundaries and human exceptionalism, however haltingly. In Aloi's words, and to return to the hide, speculative artistic forms render "the preserved animal skin into a charged interface tracing actual human/animal agential relationships." This interface, a metaphoric skin, questions non/human boundaries in a way that foregrounds "interconnectedness, intra-action, materiality, and indexicality."[36] In other words, the queerness of the interplay between non/humans (the messy glue of that slash, if you like) is made manifest through taxidermy's form and function, its representational strategies and its processes of materiality.

The "different kinds" of intimacy (295) that Jessa-Lynn confronts when thinking about her relationships with Milo, Brynn, her mother, father, and Lucinda are ones stitched with, by, and through taxidermy's queer species intimacies. Though taxidermy is no eco-utopic or world-shattering process, it is a form of seeing the (forward) slash between the human and the non-human anew.

NOTES

1. VanderMeer, *Hummingbird Salamander*, 13–14, 199. Cited hereafter in text.

2. Bennett, *Vibrant Matter*, 4, 5.

3. Poliquin, *The Breathless Zoo*, 9, 5.

4. Vuong, *On Earth*, 3. Cited hereafter in text.

5. Bezan and McHugh, "Introduction," 132.

6. As well as VanderMeer's novel, there is a flurry of texts out there that focus on taxidermy (and its symbolic potential), including, for instance, Lydia Millet's *Magnificence* (2012).

7. See Turner, *Taxidermy*.

8. Burton and Mawani, "Introduction," 8.

9. Wakeham, *Taxidermic Signs*, 19.

10. Aloi, *Speculative Taxidermy*, 46.

11. Poliquin, *The Breathless Zoo*, 16, 17.

12. Wakeham, *Taxidermic Signs*, 18.

13. Griffin, *Hide*, 57. Cited hereafter in text.

14. Another argument could be made here about both novels being set in the U.S. South. It may be that these novels were chosen because of my previous southern studies bent—rather than anything inherently southern about taxidermy or representations of it—but there are things to be said, outside the scope of this chapter, about the North Carolina and Florida locations of the novels. In both, temperature and heat play a factor in the preservation process; and in both, there is a sense of non/human relations that correlates with long-standing cultural narratives of the U.S. South as being particularly rural and agricultural.

15. Dickel, *Embodying Difference*, 144.

16. Dickel, *Embodying Difference*, 144, 145.

17. Though I do not have much room to discuss it further here, the specter of bestiality appears in this scene, or at least my parsing of it. The intimacy of the men with the buck's carcass is connected to the sex they have afterwards. There is a long-standing connection between bestiality and other forms of queer/nonnormative identity. As Colleen Glenney Boggs notes of colonial America, "At stake in the criminalization of bestiality was the production of gendered subjectivity and ethnic citizenship" (*Animalia Americana*, 51); and as Halberstam notes of the early modern period, the "clustering of crimes against nature to include both anal sex between men and sex between men and animals" shows a) both the links between queerness and species lines, as well as the fluid definitions of "crime, nature, and sexuality" in this era (*Wild Things*, 15).

18. He interestingly misidentifies the buck as a rabbit, though.

19. Dickel, *Embodying Difference*, 157.

20. Dean, *Unlimited Intimacy*, 22.

21. Segal, *Consensuality*, 44.

22. Dickel, *Embodying Difference*, 154.

23. Halberstam, *Wild Things*, 4.

24. Arnett, *Mostly Dead*, 6. Cited hereafter in text.

25. We might, as an aside, think about this name in relation to the nonhuman Latin names throughout the book. As "King Light," Lucinda is for both Jessa-Lynn and Libby a kind of queer masculine torch in the darkness.

26. Aloi, *Speculative Taxidermy*, 20.

27. Poliquin, *The Breathless Zoo*, 16.

28. Halberstam, *Wild Things*, 15.

29. Aloi, *Speculative Taxidermy*, 23, 24.

30. Niittynen, "Animal Magic," 14, 16.

31. This neat dichotomy, too, evokes or stages the dialogue between literary realism and the "non-realist" licenses of other genres. Both realism and its alternatives have their own inherent scaffolding and realism in particular is as constructed (i.e., not "transparent") as any other genre. But here Jessa-Lynn grasps for the truthfulness of realism as a way to avoid the "reality" of her taxidermic practice.

32. Niittynen, "Animal Magic," 34

33. Aloi, *Speculative Taxidermy*, 24

34. While practices of BDSM (bondage and discipline, dominance and submission, sadism and masochism) have been pathologized and marked as disordered sexualities, thinkers such as Freud, de Sade, Masoch and beyond—up to contemporary scholars of Black women's sexuality like Ariane Cruz—have shown how the sadist is at least in control of a power-play as the masochist is, the roles as intimately entwined as they seem divergent.

35. A tagline for taxidermy itself, perhaps.

36. Aloi, *Speculative Taxidermy*, 24, 25.

MOUN
TAIN
LION

Mountain Lion

mountain lions are shapeshifters

I

The mountain lion, also known as a puma or a catamount or even (in states like Florida) a panther, is—in its name alone—a kind of shapeshifter. Such nomenclature connects to the creature's nocturnal and crepuscular nature, a liminal and shadowy creature of night and the night's edges. Mountain lions roam across the Americas, from Canada to the tip of South America, proving to be simultaneously everywhere yet hidden in twilight landscapes. Mountain lions see humans more than we see them. In this short bestiary entry, the mountain lion's connection to (queering and/or trans-ing) gender is explored through Henry Hoke's novella *Open Throat* (2023), a very short book written in fragments without punctuation from the "first-person" (first-creature?) perspective of a queer mountain lion living in the Los Angeles hills. Before that, I want to make brief reference to Lucy Ellmann's *Ducks, Newburyport* (2019) which is quite different in scope—it is 998 pages long—but shares similar formal and thematic concerns, if from a more normative angle. Ellmann's novel is comprised (almost) of one sentence, broken up only with commas and the refrain "the fact that," which tells the first-person story of an Ohio woman going about her day, ruminating on domesticity as well as U.S. life and culture. Interspersed in this narrative is a short tale about a female mountain lion, which is written in full sentences.

In both texts, the mountain lion's connections to gender and sexuality are seemingly linked to the author's formal experimentation. The affordances, to use Caroline Levine's words, of these literary forms (both condensed and expansive) might just be the reimagining of non/human relations: ways of substantiating cross-species imaginative leaps. Or, put the other way around, the presence of queerness (in thematic and formal terms) itself informs the forms of these novels. What forms are "capable of," in Levine's words, the affordances inherent to those structures, seems both to come from the non/human entanglements and the ways of approaching queerness at such an intersection.[1] In both novels, the inner lives of mountain lions are depicted—in ways that many of the texts in this bestiary do not attempt—as a way of thinking about non/human concerns, like identity and place. Even though Ellmann's novel has an Ohio woman in first person and the mountain lion in third, that latter voice is still highly focalized, foregrounding a nonhuman interiority that runs alongside the human's. I turn to that book first as a way in to thinking about Hoke's more radical presentation of gender.

The switches between narrative voices in Ellmann's novel are consistently upending—from human to nonhuman animal, from third to first person, from one long sentence to sharp, clear lines. The mountain lion's psyche is made viscerally clear from the start when she is nursing cubs: "When you are all sinew, struggle and solitude, your young—being soft, plump, vulnerable—may remind you of prey."[2] The sibilant entwining of care and violence runs throughout the book, and the mountain lion's ambivalent feelings for her cubs is made explicit: their "furry closeness" (11) is as much warming as it is stifling. The cubs constrain her in the den when she would like to be off hunting alone. A flashback to the cubs' conception is rendered just as precisely: A sensitive male cat edges toward her until she is ready, and then "at her urging, he clung to her until she was all fuck, and every point of connection between them made her come" (241). Ellmann's attempt to make sense of the mountain lion's experience of pleasure could easily be described as anthropomorphized, but nonetheless that "all fuck" (verb-made-noun) gestures toward an embodied and affective state beyond language, a state barely capturable for humans either.

The lion's desire for aloneness ultimately comes true, however, as the cubs are stolen and taken to a zoo; she spends time hunting for them, until she too is taken into the facility. (It is worth thinking about this section in relation to the "zookeeping" in this book's "Animal" chapter.) The frantic search leaves her hungry and exerted and puts the mountain lion in close contact with more humans than she is used to: she is overwhelmed by roads and cars, confused by the human "vertiginous form[]" (938), and notes that men are "noisy, clumsy animals" (406). The strangeness of humans and their encroachment into the wilderness (even the wild areas "between the cracks" [786] of urban geographies) are ironically skewered at the end, when the mountain lions are reunited. The zoo, in which the nonhuman animals "no longer . . . exist for themselves," and are turned into "spectacles" (949), sees the "introduction" of the adult and baby cats as a triumph. Not knowing they are bringing the cubs to their mother, the zoo officials "congratulated themselves" on this "fostering coup" (959). Throughout this section, the free-indirect discourse of the narrator seems to be from within the mountain lion's perspective, knowingly reflecting on both the practice of zoos and the paucity of human knowledge about other animals. Even with all the lions back together, "in private or in wilderness, she was alone" (949), a sentiment easily shared by the mountain lion's human counterpart.

Most notable is that the narrative voices of human and nonhuman overlap, or more precisely, the lion's voice interrupts and pierces the dense flow of sentence-less text from the Ohio woman's kitchen. Ellmann suggests, by entwining these non/human stories, that the roles of motherhood or "femaleness" seem to run across species lines in essentialist terms, where both human and mountain lion do everything for their children (where, indeed, femaleness equals motherhood). Both mothers are loyal and protective of their families, while also craving and feeling disconnected from social structures. Both see the constraints of institutions, but mothering overtakes all; the last lines of the lion section are "she would love them and save them . . . and never let them go" (959). Ellmann's novel, while formally and linguistically daring, nonetheless are a normative figuring of women primarily as mothers and caregivers, even in a strong feline form. The detailing of the woman and lion's conceptions of gender dovetail to near essentialist or at least diminishing modes. While the affordances of the epic novel are expansiveness and detail, the book relinquishes the complex questions of gender and sex that it sets up. Yet the entwining of the non/human nonetheless pressures us to think sex outside of an anthropocentric frame; the enlacing of stories requires new frames for thinking gender's trans-species forms.

II

In Hoke's *Open Throat*, a mountain lion roams the Hollywood Hills, looking down over Los Angeles, contemplating the wild; human-nonhuman relations; family and upbringing; as well as a changing planet. The backdrop to the novella is anthropogenic climate change and the ravages of the planet: "Things are changing," the mountain lion says, as they wish for "water to come from the sky or anywhere else."[3] We will return to the mountain lion's vision of a humanless planet in the "Extinction" chapter, but Hoke's novel places non/human queerness within a much broader context of ecological destruction. *Open Throat* ultimately puts emphasis on the connections between nonhumans, the potency of language, and the possibilities of queer sexuality and gender. The novel is narrated by the mountain lion who, while sexed as male, seems to understand their identity in less fixed ways, and is attributed femaleness by the one human that the lion comes to bond with. For this chapter's purposes, I use *they* as the lion's pronoun, a) because the book's jacket and marketing copy does so, and b) because I think that Hoke's presentation of the lion is meant to make us question binary designations of sex. *They* thus holds open meaning and signification for this slippery mountain lion.

Told in short fragment chapters that are written in what look like poetic lines, the novel's form offers a glimpse into the mountain lion's psyche in all of its (un)becoming. Put another way, the affordances of the novel's poesis are a way of grasping language from within a nonhuman body that cannot be articulated simply in human language. When Thomas Nagel asked in 1974, "What is it like to be a bat?" and had to grapple with the fact that he could only imagine what it would be like for *him* to be a bat, not what it is like "for a *bat* to be a bat" (the "resources of [his] own mind" are "inadequate to the task"), Hoke attempts the psychic and corporeal leap into a mountain lion nonetheless.[4] When, late in the book, the mountain lion is discovered hiding out in a house (aided by the daughter of the household, Jane), the lion acknowledges that "I have no idea what it's like to be a person and be confronted with a me" (132). As they reflect on their state of being, they attempt to scratch words in the floorboards to articulate that they are not a threat to Jane's stepmother. The lion admits that they are just scratches, but maybe "someday I'll be able to write what you're reading" (132). Even though we are indeed *reading* the voice of this mountain lion, this moment reveals to us that the grammarless lines of the novel are formal ways of approaching the lion's interiority, their fragmented thoughts and impressions of the world.

Language seems to be one way that the mountain lion begins to make sense of their own queer or trans selfhood. (Let me come back to transness later in the chapter.) Throughout the book, human language is grasped for and is yet elusive: The mountain lion hears residents talk about "ellay" (LA) and the fear of "scare city," a mistranslation that is also a kind of double meaning about the worries of food and energy scarcity in the contemporary United States. After descending from the Hollywood Hills because of fire (which I will come back to), the mountain lion first stops at the LA Zoo and then ends up in the basement of a wealthy home belonging to the Slaughters (an on-the-nose name). The daughter, Jane ("little slaughter") helps protect the lion in the family basement and importantly offers them language and a name. The lion gets "most of [their] words" (110) from Jane, a revelation that suggests something of the novel's interest in non/human worlds. *Open Throat* suggests that the mountain lion can *acquire* language from humans, can indeed make more sense of their world through English words, even if those words cannot be written, spoken, or articulated. The book is asking us to imagine—as in Nagel's framing—what it might be like to be a mountain lion who is now aware of themself through language, something that we can only begin to think about through the novel form.

Moreover, the power of language also helps us see some of the mountain lion's queerness. As if understanding the lion's fluid identity, Jane refers to them in feminine terms and names them "heckit" after Hecate, the goddess connected to magic, the night, femininity, transformation, and transition, and who has a triple-bodied form.[5] Hecate's mythic connections to Greece, Egypt, and other cultures seems only to underscore her capaciousness as a goddess of the magical and the liminal. Like mountain lions, Hecate moves between the night and day. Thus, Jane encourages the mountain lion to reimagine gender and sex through human language and naming. When Jane's father eventually sees the lion he says, "*You keep saying she she what the hell jane . . . I can see its goddamn dick*" [138]. This scene is a kind of mirror to the ways that human transphobia is running rampant in the political and media landscape of the United States and elsewhere. The emphasis on physical appendages as indexes or signifiers of some immutable sex is the elder Slaughter's attempt to pierce the self- and other-fashioning of "heckit" and their human interlocutor.

Indeed, the mountain lion does not tell us any other name—"my mother gave me a name I can't share" (32), "my father gave me a name I won't repeat" (33), and "I can't tell . . . my real one" (102)—both because the name is "not made of noises a person can make" (102) and, I suggest, because it amounts to a *deadnaming* that the mountain lion experiences as a kind of violence. By "deadnaming" I refer to the discriminatory practice of calling trans people not by the name they use, but by the one first given to them, perhaps when they were alternatively sexed or gendered. Though I am yet to make a full case for the mountain lion's transness, I want to suggest transness here as an open category, not one of movement between one binary sex position to another but as a destabilization of category altogether (as discussed in this book's introduction). The novel begins thinking about the vicissitudes of gender and sex in relation to the vicissitudes of language.

Hoke puts pressure on, but does not try to answer, the difficult question of nonhuman queerness. *Open Throat* uses the mountain lion perspective to probe human and nonhuman worlds, not least in relation to sex and gender. What sense does it make, for instance, to talk about mountain lions *as* queer and/or trans, or as gender nonconforming, as though those human terms—already fluid, contested, and not always able to capture the nuances of human identity—could simply be applied to nonhuman animals? I say this not to throw into question our discussion so far but to reframe some of the novelistic concerns in broader discourse. As Hannah Boast argues, talking about "gay frogs," for instance, "risks anthropomorphism" because this term is "derived from human social categories, experience, and identity."[6] Similarly, in a review of some animal studies texts, Susan McHugh writes that "human ways of being may provide useful analogies for beginning to make sense of the strangeness of other animals' lives, but when used as a measure of social agency, they also set precise limits to what can be known about 'the' animal." For McHugh, talking of queer animals is both generative and problematic, due to "the inadequacy, at one extreme, of using animal research to naturalize queerness and, at the other, of imagining that anthropocentric queer theoretical perspectives can adequately come to terms with species . . . life." Pushing beyond language of the non/human and the non/heteronormative is a way, for McHugh, of thinking across and beyond animality and queerness.[7] And as Stacy Alaimo argues—after scholars like Joan Roughgarden and Myra J. Hird, who see gender and sex diversity everywhere in the non/human world—dominant and normative modes of social theory "tend to minimize the significance of queer animals" (where queer signifies in multiple ways).[8] As such, thinking the queer nonhuman is vital to our destabilization of species supremacy and normalcy altogether.

More particularly, trans studies engages animal studies to think not only about the multitudes of life on the planet that do not conform to binary heteronorms but also about the ways that transness can further open up questions of bodies, lives, identities, and forms. As Hird argues in "Animal Transex" (2006), because of the planet's endless gender and sex variation, binary sex—and the separation of nature and culture that attends antitransness, where the trans and queer are unnatural deviations—would make "little sense" to most organisms. In this way, Hoke's mountain lion merely fits into nature's nonnormative plurality anyway. Additionally, Hird writes that transness is both a classification and a resistance to classification: a "movement across, through, and beyond," as well as "between and within matter," so that a "well-defined, inviolable self" is shattered.[9] This concept is picked up in later scholarly work such as that on "tranimacies" (where transness is enmeshed with gender, the animal, and animacy), or "tranimalities" (where trans*ness envisions new non/human futures). That latter term, from Eva Hayward and Jami Weinstein, uses the asterisked trans*—as outlined in this book's introduction—to point to the multitudinous ways that trans signifies and extends its reach. Tranimalities look to "trans-infused apprehensions and engagements with the expansive world of possibility opened up by non-anthropocentric perspectives."[10] If, too, as Hayward and Che Gossett put it, "trans does not have to reify that category of 'the Human,'" but opens outwardly, then Hoke's novel offers some imaginative routes to do that.[11] Through the nonhuman "I" voice, Hoke offers us a mountain lion that confronts transness as it is experienced variously, both on the lion's own terms and in relation to unstable categories of human queerness too. Giving voice, speculatively, to a trans mountain lion pushes us to think beyond our normative models of subjectivity and identity.

III

Open Throat, through its staging of non/human relations, queries and embraces the power of language to think queerness across species lines. Queerness here relates both to designations of sex and gender (as well as its blurring and destabilizing of them) and a broader sense of a marginal position relative to the white cis-heteronormative—and, we might add, *human*—sphere. In this section, I want to think about the connections between humans and nonhumans in the novel for their gay and queer inferences in light of this earlier theorizing.

From the novel's opening, the mountain lion is linked to the disenfranchised and the outsider. They live in the hills near what they call a "town," a camp of unhoused people. Because the lion sees themselves as similarly Other, they relate to the people there as worth protecting; for instance, they kill a coyote that attempts to eat one of the camp's dogs ("you are welcome I think to my sleeping people" [43]). That "my" puts the mountain lion in the role of protector, near those on the fringes, outside of the city below, from which hikers come. Those hikers describe their trips to therapy, saying things like "*that's the trauma talking*" (40) and "*everything is gay now*" (51). Here, the novella mocks a particular human proclivity to both generalization and a kind of traumatology, where any anxiety is folded into the overarching category of trauma. The mountain lion does not pass comment, but the novel suggests that the wealthy Californians who hike the trails and discuss their emotional lives are miles away from the struggles of the unhoused and the marginalized. In other words, while the mountain lion is drawn toward those cast outside of normative society, they nonetheless have a view on a stereotypical LA population who are caught up in their human-focused and narcissistic gaze. Even if "everything is gay," it is certainly not all queer.

Another non/human connection is with a sexuality that is almost consigned to the hills, pushed out of the way. The book's opening scene sees three people near the mountain lion's cave engaging in BDSM acts: A woman films a large muscular man whipping another man's testicles. The man with the whip has bulging neck veins, which the mountain lion senses. The lion also twins the *sexual* whipping with the torture of nonhuman animals ("sounds like the torment of all big cats" [4]), which sets into motion the lion's desire to eat the man. Later on, the same man sets fire to one of the tents in the camp of unhoused people and burns the "town" to the ground, inciting murderous rage in the mountain lion. The opening lines of the novel—"I've never eaten a person but today I might" (3)—forebodes the book's end when the lion tears into "the whipping man" on the city streets. Queer sexuality is embroiled in violence, as the whipping yokes both consensual and nonconsensual sadism. The human sexuality is also linked to nonhuman torture as the lion cannot discern between different kinds of corporeal violence. This is but one element of the non/human mesh that is queerly rendered.

A second, more erotic, scene occurs further into the novel when two men go into the rocky hills to have sex. The mountain lion watches the men and figures them—as throughout this bestiary—in queer non/human terms: One man "leans in to the other's neck to bite" (60), as if in an act of consumption; "on their knees," one man "has his hands planted flat like my paws against the dirt" (61), drawing their bodies into alignment; and the "shape they form," in doggy- (or catty-?) style, "is like my shape" (62), the mountain lion says. Not only are the humans rendered creaturely in their sexual activity, but the three of them are drawn into sexual harmony as the mountain lion purrs loudly in the cave while watching (62). This vicarious sexuality is erotic to the lion. The men also remind the mountain lion of another big cat who once shared a dear carcass with them years before. The "kill sharer," as he is called, eventually dies on the freeway, but the memory of this other lion ensures that the narrator "can't let go of him easily" (61). Our mountain lion imagines the "warmth we would make together with our eight paws and two dangling parts" (64), acknowledging a shared anatomy if not shared sense of self. The gay human sex enfolds the mountain lion into a constellation of desires: for the sex act, for queerness, for sharing flesh, for the memory of a lost "love," for connection. My contention is that the novel sees queerness—of sexuality, of identity, of social positioning, of nonnormativity—in those moments where the human and the nonhuman are connected. It is the slash of non/human that *Open Throat* seems to be most interested in. This is not simply a novel of imagining the animal Other, but rather one of viewing non/human worlds from a nonhuman perspective, seeing categories like sex or processes like climate change from a queerer point of view.

As the novel reaches its visceral conclusion, the mountain lion is tangled more than ever in human worlds and imaginaries: "I feel more like a person than ever," they say, "because I'm starting to hate myself" (115). In this way, human self-consciousness breeds a human condition of self-critique, not lost on queer and trans outsiders. Forced out of the Slaughter home, Jane takes the lion in her car to escape. As they see "the whipping man" eating his lunch outside a café, the mountain lion is torn between a romanticized life with Jane—there is a dream sequence before this in which they explore Disneyland together, paraded atop a celebratory float, living a joyously queer (yet impossible) life—and one in which they tear open the man's neck. The latter is what their teeth are "meant to do" (152), even if that makes them vulnerable to other humans. The mountain lion ultimately chooses to leap at the man. They acknowledge it is a "terrible choice but I'm making it," "just like a person" (152) would. Again, their *animal* instinct is equated with *human* action, as if the two are not so separable.[12] As they attack, the mountain lion says, "This is what a goddess looks like" (153), a final image of feminine power mixed with non/human violence. Such more-than-human femininity is both bestowed and evoked by Jane; in naming the lion heckit, she has enabled them to (re)imagine their sense of self. Helicopters soon descend on the bloody scene and the mountain lion is likely to be killed, seen as a purely or only a "threat" (156).

The final image is of the mountain lion retracting their claws as they "try to become the kitten at the center of myself" (156), a strange ending whereby the mountain lion attempts to revert to a childlike state. This internal incohesion—between wanting a queer life of escape, with humans that understand their alterity, and with "giving in" to their instincts to attack (albeit to attack those who have harmed others)—ends with the lion regressing. That childhood state of confused identity is one that offers a balm amid chaos. We can only speculate whether they live or whether they are captured and or killed. Throughout *Open Throat*, the mountain lion has chosen to live and act in the margins and has consistently been misunderstood by most of the humans around them. At the book's end, they are maligned once more. They do not get to live the "queer" life that they imagine because the normative world cannot see them for who they really are. Yet, when given language and the tools of self-experimentation by a young girl, this queer/trans mountain lion is able to figure an alternative world, a nonnormative non/human existence.

NOTES

1. Levine, *Forms*, 6, 10.

2. Ellmann, *Ducks, Newburyport*, 11. Cited hereafter in text.

3. Hoke, *Open Throat*, 9, 8. Cited hereafter in text.

4. Nagel, "What Is It Like," 439.

5. We might connect this back to the mountain lion's multiple names/terms.

6. Boast, Theorizing the Gay Frog," 663. Boast tracks the figure of the gay frog as it has been picked up by far-right figures in the United States, like Alex Jones (of Infowars fame). In Jones,' and others imagining, the *gay* frog is "created" by environmental contamination, as if same-sex behavior in nonhumans can only be a byproduct of toxicity, and in turn, that human queerness is somehow unnatural. (Boast's argument reflexively skewers each of these points).

7. McHugh, "Queer (and) Animal Theories," 155, 156, 167.

8. Alaimo, "Eluding Capture," 56. Roughgarden, *Evolution's Rainbow*; Hird, "Animal Transex."

9. Hird, "Animal Transex," 41, 37, 38.

10. Hayward and Weinstein, "Introduction," 201.

11. Hayward and Gossett, "Impossibility," 17–18.

12. We see this elsewhere in *Wounded* ("Horse"), for instance.

DOG

Dog

dogs are leashed to (non)normative worlds

I

Dogs are *a man's best friend*; one can be *put in the doghouse* if one does something wrong; one can *go to the dogs*, if things get worse; one can be *dog tired* and a *dogs-body* if one must do all the tiring work; one can be *sick as a dog*, if ill; *dog-eat-dog* worlds are savage; *dog days* are the hottest, the most languid, maybe in decline; one can be an *underdog* or even *top dog*; one *can't*, though, *teach an old dog new tricks*, because we are so resistant to change. These idioms proliferate because language—at least the English language—is so saturated by canines, both literal and figural. Not only are there extensive canine figures of speech, but they also signify so differently (often in contrary ways). Such multiplicity will be central to this chapter's literary texts. This polyvalence is also relevant to the dog's own species status. As Susan McHugh writes, there is an "ongoing struggle of defining what a dog is" because this species "has the largest range of body types and sizes of any mammal," the "broadest geographic range," "the longest history of human domestication," and the ability to "produce fertile offspring with other species." The dog's definitional instability skewers "species-centered notions of history" and scrambles modes of taxonomizing.[1] With this in mind, to talk of *the dog* in this chapter is to acknowledge the term's capaciousness while also trying to home in on the specificities of particular canine representations in the United States.

Such a toggle between the general and the particular is saturated by human variability too. In Mark Doty's memoir of non/human illness and death, *Dog Years* (2007), dogs are said to exist "in relation" to humans as their identity is "built around" people and our worlds.[2] In this view, the dog is what Donna Haraway calls a companion species: Humans and nonhuman companions "make each other up, in the flesh," through love, even though each party is "significantly other to each other, in specific difference."[3] To "make each other up" means to co-constitute, but it also means—for this bestiary chapter—means to imagine and construct the dog (and human) in language. As companions, dogs are not only relational but also, as the narrator of Sigrid Nunez's *The Friend* (2018) says, "the epitome of devotion." The "devotion to humans, so instinctual that it's given freely even to persons who are unworthy of it," is part of the dog's wide appeal[4]—though another character in her later novel *The Vulnerables* (2023) thinks that dogs "love people so much" because of the way they are bred, gesturing to how humans have *made* dogs into devotees of humans regardless of their "worth."[5] In Doty's memoir, though, he asks why people "love a species so dependent on us" (30), when we often (in his eyes) balk from such neediness. Already, in thinking the dog's relationality, we run into what Alice Kuzniar calls the trap of sentimentality. Kuzniar notes that because (some) humans are so attached to dogs, particularly because of their status as "loyal pets"—and vice versa—we risk, in writing about them, falling into easy tropes rather than figuring a knotty language of attachment.[6] Through the below literary readings, we will grasp for a flexible lexis.

While the dog has so far been imagined as a well-loved nonhuman animal, we should note here that a) not all dogs are treated and seen as the same; and b) not all humans have the same kind of relation to dogs. To speak of man's best friend might better be written as Man's best friend, where Man calls up what Sylvia Wynter and other Black studies scholars see as one white ossified version of humanity. Because of the dog's history in enforcing racial and ethnic regimes of terror—think, for instance, of the police dogs and fire hoses used against Black Americans in Birmingham, Alabama; or before that, the dogs used by enslavers across the U.S. South—populations not racialized as white have a more complex relationship with the species. Because, as McHugh puts it, "dogs seem unthinkable outside the context of human culture," they bear much imaginative and associative weight, as their identities both produce and are produced by human interaction.[7] As Bénédicte Boisseron puts it, "Contact with a specific human race and gender will determine whether the dog is perceived as a threat or as a loving companion to humans."[8] For example, pit bulls, while not an actual breed but more of a "type," associated with particular physical features and behavioral characteristics (all of which are not singular to that type), are frequently connected to Black men in the United States, joined together imaginatively and emotionally as innately dangerous, a threat. Greyhounds or golden retrievers, on the other hand, are whitened in various ways—the former as a "regal" and "moneyed" breed (both coded as white), and the latter as warm and playful, part of a heteronormative (white) imaginary. Both humans and dogs are mutually constructed in this way; Erin Tarver calls this a "metonymic feedback loop."[9] This chapter will thus think about that feedback loop in relation to the social, cultural, and imaginative worlds of humans and dogs, especially as those worlds are striated by race, gender, and sexuality. "Dog" posits that *because* canines are intimately braided into human life—in homes, workplaces, even our language—they also have the capacity to queer human identities as well as notions of connectivity and intimacy.

More than other chapters in this bestiary, I survey a wide variety of literary texts (as if to echo the complex and multifarious relations and connections between humans and dogs). Through brief readings of Matthew Griffin's *Hide* (2016), Danzy Senna's story "The Land of Beulah" (2011), Phil Klay's story "Redeployment" (2014), Ocean Vuong's *On Earth We're Briefly Gorgeous* (2019), Garth Greenwell's *Cleanness* (2020), Mark Doty's *Dog Years* (2007) and then Danez Smith's poem "dogs!" (2020), the chapter figures the dog's richness and variety. In cycling through questions of intimacy (by revisiting *Hide* and its relation to taxidermy); and racialization (Senna, Klay); we then move to gender and sexuality (Vuong, Greenwell, Doty), before seeing in Smith's poem a threading together of all the above.

II

To think about the human-dog relation as one of intimacy and interconnectedness, it is worth beginning at the end, with a dog's death. In the "Taxidermy" chapter, we looked at Matthew Griffin's *Hide* for the way it uses taxidermy as a way of literally and figuratively getting under non/human skins, especially as they are substantiated by gender and sexuality. The protagonists, Wendell and Frank, aging gay men living in the U.S. South, are both tied to nonhuman animals throughout the novel. Wendell, in particular, was a taxidermist and the final section of the novel concerns his working on their dog, Daisy, who is accidentally killed by Frank. By this point in the novel, Frank's physical and cognitive health is deteriorating; from the start, he often calls Daisy "Fancy," the name of their old dog, blurring them together. In addition, the novel forebodes Daisy's death at the end of the novel, as earlier on she jumps out of their car and "smashes her belly on the asphalt."[10] The book circles around scenes of non/human injury.

Against advice from his doctor and Wendell because of declining health, Frank mows the lawn and accidentally runs over the dog Daisy, who had been circling him. She lunges once too often at the mower and Frank dismembers her. Wendell describes the moment viscerally: It is "the worst sound I have ever heard," a yelp and "underneath it all the wet, dull thud of blade lodging in flesh, of flesh tearing" (202). The sharp t-d-f alliteration running through the sentence heightens the violent affect. The dog is "severed" and her organs "are spilling out, one leg's cut clean through" (203). This moment of intense bodily undoing is not (as usual) from Wendell's hand, but from the mower.

Wendell inevitably taxidermies Daisy as a kind of memory object, and thus there is a long process of corporeal disassembly: "With a grapefruit spoon I scrape the brain from the inside of her skull" (207). Griffin's level of detail here focuses not just on craft but also the *ordinariness* of the process, as Wendell uses household items. Daisy's death is made intimate, domestic. The taxidermy, too, is another example of non/human interconnectedness—dog brains and grapefruit, as well as the use of coyote eyes, because "it's hard to get good dog eyes" (229). The novel's focus on taxidermy is as much about keeping things alive as it is confirming their death. But Wendell confronts his own investment in the form quite directly: "This is what is takes to hold on to something. To keep the things you've loved" (207). Memorialization happens in this novel through a visceral investment in transforming a torn-up carcass into an aesthetic object for the wall. Dogs, unlike the other nonhuman animals in *Hide*, are given a special kind of status, turned into mnemonic objects even in their cross-species and incomplete forms (the full body cannot be salvaged). The stuffing and mounting of Daisy's body gives the death meaning denied to the book's other nonhumans.

If dogs, in this light, "stand in for a bridge—the bridge that joins persons to things, life to death," as Colin Dayan argues, then they might also do the connective work looked at in the "Horse" chapter.[11] Like the horses that bridge and suture human/nonhuman worlds, so do dogs—in some texts—help humans understand questions of ontology. Though again, this happens not in a unified or singular way, given the various ways in which non/human bonds are racialized, gendered, and so on. Comparisons between the treatment of Black people and nonhuman animals have often been instrumentalized in some animal studies scholarship. Rather than contribute to this comparative model, scholars like Boisseron think about connection and alliance across species lines. Her work wants to reanimate links between Black people and dogs (hence her book's title, *Afro-Dog*) that refuse simply a "comparable state of subjection and humiliation," and think instead of "defiance" against negative treatment.[12] I have written elsewhere, in this light, about how a writer like Jesmyn Ward represents the complex and multifaceted links between dogs and Black people in the U.S. South.[13] In *Salvage the Bones* (2011), for instance, Ward ties her main characters Esch and Skeeter—siblings living in rural poverty in Mississippi as Hurricane Katrina approaches—to the pit bulls in their life. For Esch, the dog China is pregnant like she is; for Skeeter, China is his fighting dog, but also his daughter, and his love.

Danzy Senna's short story "The Land of Beulah" looks at how one Black woman and a stray dog come to have a fraught and vexed relationship in the shadow of racialization. The dog "bridges" much about race and gender in the United States. Jackie, the story's protagonist, finds a dog abandoned on the street and forms a bond with it that is partly identificatory and partly abusive. She thinks that the dog "didn't look mixed" but "like some breed that hadn't yet been discovered."[14] The dog is one of the "stray mongrels all over Brooklyn" (37) that she treats with disdain. But that disdain seems to come from, Senna intimates, the ways that Jackie sees connections between herself and the dog. People on the street guess the dog's "background" by scrutinizing "her appearance and behavior." Yet, everyone sees "what they wanted to see," depending on their own identity. "White people swore she was a Gordon setter," for instance; Puerto Ricans and Koreans think something else (35). This projective taxonomizing is built in to the human imagination, Senna implies. As Boisseron puts it about pit bulls in particular, "like the issue of race in humans, the pit bull exemplifies how much more 'dog' and 'breed' have to do with human perception and social construction than with science."[15]

The story pushes this idea further by mirroring Jackie and the dog. She is a mixed-race woman, who was born "looking like the missing link between Sicily and Libya." As such, "cabdrivers liked to claim her as part of their race just before they asked her if she was married" (39). As Zadie Smith notes on the story, Senna is interested in the "subtle shape-shifting always at work, as characters respond to one another on the basis of superficial signifiers which, in a culture gone visual, seem to mean everything."[16] Jackie's racial indeterminacy (at the visual level) becomes something that others latch onto, in ways akin to that of the dog. Moreover, this "claim" on her race is also sexualized so that her race becomes entangled with her sexuality and gender. Put another way, the "superficial signifiers" used to read Jackie are intersectionally loaded so that her ambiguous racial identity is automatically tied to her desirability.

At the heart of the story is the strained relationship between Jackie and the dog, especially as we find her in the aftermath of a relationship. Kip, her ex, is a Black man who wants Jackie to celebrate her Blackness (like wearing her "wiry curls" out so that "people would know" [39]). He only dates Black women—did not "believe in race mixing" (39)—but at the story's end Jackie sees him out with a white woman. The story gestures toward ideas of racial "purity" and racial signifiers, only to entangle them with canine/species ones. Jackie's racial and gendered self-consciousness is transferred onto the racialized dog (a "fucking dirty mongrel" [53]). Almost immediately Jackie abuses the dog, at first after it pees on her "snowy white duvet" (42)—a racialized "stain." The story details animal abuse,[17] from kicking to beating, and even small slaps and leash-tugs, which Jackie thinks of as "small acts of violence" that help "quell her rage" (43). The story articulates links between abuse and care—Jackie "loved" the dog, both "extreme hatred, extreme love" (55)—in ways that reveal the projections and identifications between human and dog. Jackie takes out on the dog all of the complex emotions of dispossession that she herself feels and tries to mend them at the same time.

The "ritual" of daily violence—which Beulah "barely seemed to feel" (53)—is a manifestation of so much misogynoir that Jackie has experienced, even if the story does not always say that outright. One moment of clarity, however, comes when Jackie notices a hole on Beulah's nose—possibly from being pierced—that instantly "reminded her of shackles and chains, of mutilations too deep ever to heal" (48). She cries into her bed at this realization but does not process the historical link she is making between the previous abuse of Beulah (that she is recapitulating) and the abuse of enslaved Black people from whom she is descended. The story surfaces this historical connection (not comparison, as Boisseron would say) between states of subjection only to have Beulah completely disregard its significance. Senna intimates that the internalization of anti-Blackness is so absolute that when its correlatives in a cross-species dynamic appear (or any other dynamic) it is hard to see: Jackie cannot link her own oppression with what she enacts on the dog.

The story ends with Jackie physically and emotionally changed by her time with Beulah. The dog transforms her, not necessarily for the better. She does not attend to her appearance, nor change her clothes, nor wash. Her feet become animalistically "tough as hooves" (59), and she ends up "raceless and ageless" (60), as if stripped of her identity. Jackie's time with the dog awakens not only historical and contemporary forms of oppression that affect her but also a desire to disappear into obscurity and a lack of identity. Senna's story poses complicated questions about the bridges between humans and dogs, especially when racialized and gendered dynamics inflect that relationship. Because the dog's mixedness provokes feelings of shame and confusion in Jackie, the racism and sexism she feels are transferred onto the dog, making the cross-species connection one of violence and subjugation rather than understanding and care.

Turning from this story of a Black woman and her dog against the backdrop of history to a white solider and his dog against the backdrop of war, we see another dimension of this canine racialization. "Redeployment," the title story of Phil Klay's collection about U.S. soldiers in the Iraq War, uses the figure of the dog dually: as mediating those lives that are valuable and those that are disposable. Sergeant Price, the white soldier narrating the story, thinks back on his time in combat as he attempts to reassimilate into U.S. life, before being "redeployed." Like much U.S. war fiction, the story prioritizes the soldier's estrangement both from the war and from his trip back home; the emphasis is less on the sociopolitical context of war, nor the tragedies of his (and America's) killings.

The story opens with the blunt and wry sentences, "We shot dogs. Not by accident. We did it on purpose, and we called it Operation Scooby. I'm a dog person, so I thought about that a lot."[18] The callous way that the soldiers kill the dogs is echoed in the staccato sentences and the jokey "Operation Scooby." That he is a "dog person" means only that he "thought about" the killing, rather than processing what it might mean. They kill the dogs on "instinct," because they see a "skinny brown dog lapping up blood" (1). The *brownness* of the dog is, I would argue, key to understanding this story as the narrator notes, "It wasn't American blood" the dogs were drinking, "but still"; this then becomes the "the last straw." From then on, "it's open season on dogs" (1). Were the dogs to lick American blood, who knows what violence might erupt. By drinking human blood like water, the dogs confront the soldiers with something aberrant and cross-species, but it also is part of a string of associations between dogs and Iraqis. The narrator says, suddenly shifting to second person, "you don't think about it" (killing), but rather about "who's in that house, what he's armed with, how he gonna kill you, your buddies" (1). Allyson Booth sees this scene as about the "self-reproach of a dog person for having hunted dogs like game . . . and an understanding of what it means to be hunted."[19] Yet what Booth does not say is that Klay's story shifts effortlessly between the killing of dogs to the killing of Iraqis in ways that clearly conflate the two. The brown dogs—abjectly drinking blood—index the (male) Iraqis who are all a threat to the soldier's "buddies" (not comrades or fellow soldiers, but friends, a telling detail).

Not all dogs in the story are so disposable. The story later introduces another dog, a Labrador called Vicar, who "belongs" to the narrator and his wife back in the United States. Vicar, as the name connotes, is a Christianized figure, and not othered in the way the dogs in Iraq are. When the narrator gets home, Vicar is sick: He is "grayer than before," with tumors on his legs, and cannot move without being in pain (9). He is slowly dying, throwing up often. These scenes are interspersed with the narrator's attempts to shift back into U.S. life, having sex with his wife, watching television, and going to the mall. He wants to go back to Iraq, "because fuck all this" (11). The "all this" refers to what he sees as the bland overwhelming Americanness, or the absence of warfare: its comradery, intensity, and purpose. Vicar's sickness is enmeshed in the soldier's inability to be "at home" and, in so many words, killing dogs elsewhere. When they realize they have to put Vicar down, the narrator decides he will do it rather than pay a vet.

The killing of Vicar, a pet, is made peaceful and deliberate, in contrast to that of those previous dogs. Taking him to a stream because "it's pretty" (14), the narrator has a flashback to the war and he freezes. He notes, less comically this time, that "something in me is going to break if I do this" (15), an acknowledgment that killing might change him profoundly. He makes three deliberate shots—"how it should be done, each shot coming quick after the last so you can't even try to recover, which is when it hurts" (16)—that are the "ethical" choice, in that Vicar will not feel the pain, cannot "recover" at any point. Booth reads this story slightly differently than me, seeing the story as a confrontation with the soldier's "difficult" role of both killing and potentially being killed.[20] The possibility of being shot is entangled with the way that the soldier can easily shoot someone else. Booth's reading implies that Klay's fiction is a complex look at war, yet I would argue that the story only reinforces—through its use of the dog—normative modes of killing and living. The first dogs were killable because they stood in for Iraqis, who for Price are imminently killable because seen always as a threat. Yet Vicar is only killable as an act of mercy. He is enfolded in the same Christianized U.S. framework that legitimized the nationalist wars in the Middle East in the first place. Rather than helping us see the ambivalence of war, I would suggest Klay's story underlines the ways that certain lives, via nonhuman figures, are hierarchized in this American imaginary.

The use of the dog figure during the "war on terror" era is not confined to short stories like this. We also see them used, as Colleen Glenney Boggs writes, at the Abu Ghraib prison in Iraq. While the dog is not sexualized in Klay's story—it is used principally in a racialized way—at Abu Ghraib, U.S. soldiers used literal and figurative dogs in ways that braided race, religion, sexuality, and gender. Boggs examines, in *Animalia Americana* (2013), the relation between soldier, detainee, and guard dog—a triangulation that "places the categories of humanity and animality, of 'the' human and 'the' animal, in shifting relation." Animality, for Boggs, is a "structural position" opposite to (but also less than) humanity, and thus humans can be rendered in terms of animality just like nonhumans; in other words, animality is not synonymous with the nonhuman. Entangled in these positions are the specters of bestiality and sodomy. Boggs's book tracks the historical conflation of these terms, where bestiality connotes either a human having sex with a nonhuman animal *or* with a human positioned, or seen, as an animal. Sodomy's historical overlap with bestiality ties queerness to animality and animality to queer people (men in particular). At Abu Ghraib the U.S. soldiers used this cultural imaginary to degrade and dehumanize the prisoners. By using the real guard dogs, as well as dog leashes on the prisoners, in addition to real (and implied) sex acts, the soldiers depicted the prisoners *as animals* but also called up both bestiality and sodomy in their actions. The link "between being 'animalized,' 'sexually deviant,' and 'homosexualized'" was part of the soldiers' template of torture.[21]

Here we see how literal and imagined dogs—prisoners *as* dogs, prisoners *with* dogs—are used within the U.S. military, not least against largely Muslim inmates.

In short, Boggs writes, because nonhumans (dogs) "can be instrumentalized to enact state violence and to produce animality," the prisoners are "hyper-animalized in contrast to the guard dog." Thus, to animalize the detainee—to put them in the structural position of animality, through their degradation and treatment—*via the dog* in its literal and figurative form both blurs the human/animal distinction but also shows the dog as an "intermediary." For Boggs, the dog "abjects" the prisoner but also "calls attention to the process by which such abjection occurs."[22] In highlighting the mechanics of dehumanization, the dog bridges subject positions *and* the very construction of those positions. Boggs points out that the use of dogs to degrade a human subject to a dog-like position (on a leash, caged up, engaged in acts of bestiality/sodomy) actually loops back to reveal how such human violence happens. Rather than a nonhuman specter in this prison, the dog calls attention to itself and those lives around it. Through Klay's story and Boggs's summary of Abu Ghraib, we see how the Iraq War proves a testing ground for America's animalization of racial others and the cultural stories needed to prop up that nationalistic war project. Klay's story tried to humanize the U.S. soldier through putting into hierarchy certain kinds of racialized dogs, and by using the dog in its literal warfare, the Abu Ghraib soldiers use markers of animality to dehumanize and violate Iraqis. In both examples, race, sexuality, and gender are implicated in one another through literal and figurative dogs because of the animal's capaciousness for bridging non/human worlds. The dog carries so much symbolic weight as it traffics across human environments and identity categories.

III

Having thought about the racialized dynamics of human-dog connections, I now turn to a few examples of dog narratives that foreground gender and sexuality (as well as race). Where dogs, in Klay's short story, index the kinds of lives worth protecting or killing—thus showing *some* dog positions as inherently subordinate—Ocean Vuong considers a canine position in relation to a queered human one. In *On Earth We're Briefly Gorgeous*, the protagonist Little Dog is named as such because, in the Vietnamese village where his mother Rose grew up, "the smallest or weakest of the flock, as I was, is named after the most despicable things."[23] As in the rest of the novel—explored elsewhere in this bestiary—Little Dog's position as young, slender, feminized, and queer informs and is informed by his name. The "despicable" things one could be named after—like "demon, ghost child, pig snout, monkey-born," and so on (with "little dog being the more tender one")—are so chosen to spare the weak child from the evil spirits that roam over the villages. The "hideous and ghastly" name *protects* Little Dog. Early on, he realizes, "to love something . . . is to name it after something so worthless it might be left untouched—and alive."[24] The "worthless dog" or, as some might say, a "mutt" (a term that has its own racialized connections, as we saw in Senna's story), is that negatively, if complexly, valenced kind of dog.[25]

Thus, Little Dog's queerness—in the sense of his gender and sexuality, as well as his seeming "tenderness," all interpenetrating—produces an animality that further lowers him in a species hierarchy. Where the name Little Dog is meant to protect him, it also negates or at least queries his personhood. That the dog is central to this figuration is interesting, not least because of how obedience, loyalty, and other "canine traits" come up in relation to his queer sexuality, as explored in the "Hunting" chapter. There, we see how Little Dog's sexual position (largely as a bottom) is connected to feminization—he is called a "girl" and "bitch," that latter term clearly canine-coded as well as misogynistic. For Vuong's complex novel of interspecies life, to be a dog is to ultimately be *lesser* because one is already, as the queer human, lesser—the two become braided, mutually informing. Yet that marginalized position, as we will see in "Hunting," might also produce other kinds of power and agency.

In Garth Greenwell's *Cleanness*, dogs emblematize various forms of queer intimacy, both desired and not. In the book's final section, the protagonist, an American teacher working in Sofia, Bulgaria, goes out clubbing with two of his ex-students. The intimacies between these men are fraught and shifting. When the teacher finally heads home, aware that he has transgressed some kind of power boundary—a theme central to the book—he finds Mama Dog on his doorstep. She wanders the campus, no longer able to be a proper guard dog. The dog wants treats and rubs, and finally the narrator gives in. They share intimate moments (placing foreheads together, the dog head-butting the narrator's jeans, licking his face). Even though she is not allowed inside the house, the narrator lets her in—another of the book's threshold crossings—and they fall asleep on the hallway floor. In the morning they will feel better, he thinks, "though I feared I wouldn't feel better, in body and spirit" (222). It is not simply the hangover that has the narrator feeling this way but the multiple forms of exposure he has experienced in the book, from the pedagogical to the political and the sexual. Mama Dog puts her paw on his chest, and he knows that it would "leave a mark": the mark, if you like, of cross-species intimacy. This final image (and line) of the book suggests that human-canine positionality—the narrator letting the dog into the house, letting her nuzzle him, leaving her mark on his body, laying as equals on the floor—is key to understanding *Cleanness*.

The narrator's remark to the dog, "You're filthy, . . . but I love you" (221), is a kind of recall to earlier sections of the novel in which the narrator engages in BDSM-related sex. Two sections, "Gospodar" and "The Little Saint," mirror one another as sex scenes that go to places the narrator does not want and does not expect, respectively. In both, the sadistic/masochistic dynamics at play are deeply tied to animality. Mel Chen notes that some BDSM cultures "engage in enriched animal figuration," which often "deploy accoutrements of animalness—dog chains, dog bowls—to engage in elaborated relations of power."[26] Chen notes that, rather than simple animal representations, BDSM often invokes and plays out canine/animal positionality. The men in *Cleanness* are not becoming dogs; instead they produce a kind of animality that is neither "human" nor "animal" but the queer excess often attached to both categories.

In "Gospodar," which means master (or teacher) in Bulgarian, the narrator goes to a man's home for sex. In the dom/sub scene between them, the narrator becomes the "bitch" and a "good girl," which is a "humiliation" because to "seem like a woman" is the "worst thing" (26): an internalization of both misogyny and homophobia that began in the narrator's childhood. The power play between the men quickly takes a turn away from what is *wholly* consented or fantasized, as the narrator inhabits a subordinated role: He moves around "on all fours" and a chain is forced around his neck, "the kind of leash you use with difficult dogs" (30).[27] The narrator does not enjoy this "pageantry" (30) per se but does find pleasure in "being made an object" (31). Such objecthood—which, for the narrator, slips into a kind of animality—is echoed in "The Little Saint," in which the narrator is now the man in a position of power, the dom to a Bulgarian sub. This younger man nuzzles into the narrator's crotch, as if emulating a dog, in a "kind of animal instinct" that is the pleasure of "being marked" (passively, rather than actively *marking*; 180). The man is frequently tied to a nonhuman position: His movements shift from "animal" to more "precise," as if animality is everything excessive and unregulatable. When he fellates the narrator, he "shak[es] his head a little as if to work me in deeper, like a dog worrying a toy" (190). Where the scene builds to a climax of near-sadism on the narrator's part—an analysis for a venue other than this chapter—"The Little Saint" frequently invokes the nonhuman and canine to dramatize the ways in which queer sex destabilizes human boundaries altogether. By *queer*, here, I mean the fullness of nonnormativity, or the ways that *queer* works to upend all kinds of identities.

To circle back to Mama Dog, the final moment with a *real* dog—not the specter of a dog or the subordinated animality it indexes—is a form of cross-species dialogue that unsettles and destabilizes all of the species hierarchy that came before it. Rather than being cast as animal in the submissive sexual role, the narrator confronts animality in the flesh, as it were. Mama Dog connotes all of the dichotomies of the book thus far: wild/domestic, free/unfree, clean/unclean, human/other, care/abandonment, touch/distance. In breaching the boundaries of these binaries, Mama Dog forces the narrator to see his world messily, more queerly. The hard oppositions set up in the stories are prized loose by the dog's familiarity and insistence on corporeal presence.

In the examples, then, from Vuong and Greenwell—like those racialized ones above—dogs are often used in literary texts to open up questions about ontological boundaries, barriers, and possibilities. The dog's position maps onto the queer human's position (often literally, via sex) and animal studies theory has seen a similar move to the erotics of canine-human relationality. In Haraway's famous vision of companion species, that intimacy is corporeal as well as emotive. The dog's "saliva," for instance, mingles with the human face as their "darter-tongue kisses" become "irresistible." The *love* at the heart of these companions is also coded with "sexual and generative connotations always ready to erupt," such as "to consort, to keep company"; indeed, that "eruption" is clearly climactic.[28] Carla Freccero makes similar points about her Basenji dogs, which she loves "in part for their beauty": She has a "shameless investment in their sleek and muscular slender bodies." Freccero's relation to her dogs is one in which her gendering/sexing "commingled with theirs, my identifications, desires, and kin networks entangled with them," which in turn is tied to racialization and nationhood, as the Basenji index a spectral Africanness for her.[29]

For both writers, the dog-human connection is one structured by the complexities of desire, sensuality, and the body. It is what Kathy Rudy, in her article "LGBTQ. . . Z?" (2012), describes as the disavowed phantom of bestiality. Rudy's argument is—like the playfulness of her title—an attempt to help us think beyond the narrow confines of the terms "animal," "sex," and "love." If, she suggests, we can eat, kill, train, pet (etc.) nonhuman animals, why is sex with nonhumans "unspeakable"? Her point is not that sex with nonhumans should be celebrated, but that "sex" is so unstable a term—particularly in light of queer studies, which has done much to scramble our notion of sex, sexuality, and desire in toto—that to push aside the *idea* of bestiality is in itself revealing of the way we conceive species and sex. Like Haraway and Freccero, Rudy describes the intimacy of her relationship with her pets (six dogs specifically) and speculates on what it means to "love" them. "I can't figure out," she writes, "if that love is sexually motivated" in that it is, in some ways, difficult to "cordon off sexual desire from all the other desires that move our lives." If, as Rudy notes comically, "I get more affection from my dogs than I ever did from any girlfriend," what does affection mean across species lines? What does "desire" mean in this context? Rudy's essay pressures so many of our definitions—importantly, of course, through the figure of the dog—to "constitute a new way of being with another species" and unearth our "cultural anxiet[ies] about our own animality."[30] Rudy's dogs reveal so much about the boundaries humans set up to delimit how we understand ourselves and each other.

While this bestiary is full of intimate human-animal relations (where "relation" is read broadly), it is notable that for critics like Rudy, it is the dog through which questions of desire and love are often worked out. (It is not via snakes or gerbils, for instance.) It is arguably because the dog is so enmeshed in human worlds—in people's homes and lives and families—that they can translate some of the cross-species language we use to make sense of the world. The endless projection onto dogs from humans is indicative of the way that dogs are also comforting and familiar ciphers for non/human affects. This chapter is attempting to show how dogs are so often embroiled in human frameworks, from race to sexuality, from language to desire, because of their everyday intimacies with many of us. It is their presence in so many homes, especially in the United States, that make them available for all kinds of human narrative. Rudy's essay ends by pointing to a number of literary texts, like Mark Doty's explored next, that show us not "an identity called bestiality" but rather a "world transformed by human/animal love," where that "love" is multifaceted and even ineffable.[31]

Bringing some of this chapter's threads together, before moving to our last example, Mark Doty's *Dog Years: A Memoir* explores human-dog relations in connection to queer intimacies, death, and sexuality. In the memoir, Doty tracks the entangled lives of dogs and humans, as he adopts a golden retriever, Beau, as company for his partner, Wally, who is dying of AIDS-related illness. The men have another older dog, Arden, a black retriever, and while the book is about the life and death of his two dogs, it is also haunted "at the edges of the narrative" by "Wally's slow death," as Daisy Henwood writes. After foregrounding the inevitable losses that we will read (and that readers will likely have encountered in Doty's other memoirs and poetry), the memoir "backtracks, and begins to tell the stories of adopting, caring for, moving around, and losing both dogs, against the backdrop of Wally's illness and death," offering us a "sense of control" over the narrative of loss.[32] In other words, Doty's recursive narrative structure prepares us for the inevitability of multispecies death, and in particular the dogs are both proxies for Wally's death as well as being fully fleshed creatures with their own mortalities.

Dog Years narrativizes some of the queer worlds that take form when Doty and his partner live with two dogs and cats. One of these worlds is the family's move from Vermont to Provincetown, where their "presence as a couple was both welcome and ordinary, a community where Wally's HIV diagnosis was nothing unusual" (63). As such, the book's coastal geography is not simply pastoral idyll but temporary queer haven. The particularity of Provincetown—its openness to LGBTQ+ people throughout history—corresponds to the possibilities of a queer multispecies family, as per Haraway, Freccero, and others mentioned earlier. This gayness is even rendered comic: When Beau bulks out and becomes more muscly, Doty jokes that he is "becoming a Chelsea boy, ready for a circuit party" (118–19). Even the dog has a gay human corollary.

The intimacies between humans and dogs in this memoir are multifaceted. The dogs, unlike in some of this bestiary's other texts, neither symbolize nor overbear the death of Wally. Instead, the various lives are in dialogue with one another. As in Rudy's essay, Doty's memoir thinks intimacy and desire in complex ways. Arden is Wally's "guardian" and "animal counsel" (73), as well as his caregiver. The book is clear about the messy ways that dogs and humans *show up* for each other. On a trip to Mexico, Doty and his partner form a bond with a stray dog who steals their heart. He writes, "you can know an animal—or a person, for that matter—in an instant, really, though your understanding can go on unfolding for years" (195). Not only does the parenthetical "or a person" destabilize our usual humanist sense of who is capable of knowing and being known in the first instance, but Doty's narration of their dog-human connection spills into a discourse of love that we might expect for humans.

With the fragility of these bonds ever-present in the book, *Dog Years* is an attempt to make sense of death within non/human worlds. For instance, Arden sleeps all day with Wally as he is dying, though minutes before Wally goes, Arden "jumped, fell of the bed with a loud *whunk* on the old wooden floorboards, and slunk off" (83).[33] It is as if, Doty intimates, Arden knew that death was imminent. The dogs do not just sense death but also echo the human suffering: Beau's sickness is "weirdly familiar, uncannily like Wally's illness, the way he's going" (146). Both dog and human struggle with infirmity to the point that they are near identical. It is as if love and death are the emotional worlds that bridge dog-human relations, making them not so different at all. In Nunez's *The Friend*, the narrator thinks—akin to Doty—about how dogs understand suffering. "It is widely believed," the narrator says, "that although animals don't know that one day they'll die, many of them know when they're actually dying. So at what point does a dying animal become aware of what's happening?"[34] Doty suggests that his dogs do indeed know what death is, at least instinctively, bestowing on them an emotionality perhaps otherwise overlooked.

Indeed, nonhuman emotions form a key part of *Dog Years*. Doty reflects on a dog's understanding of "limit": "How much can we know what they feel, to what degree is any description a matter of twisting their animality into a mirror of ourselves?" (140). Living with nonhuman animals, and attempting to *write* them, always risks projection or anthropomorphism, Doty argues. Yet he is "convinced that what they experience *is* emotion—and that some of the terms we'd use to describe a human character (observant, thoughtful, desiring) are the best we can do to name their not quite knowable inner lives" (53). In this way, the memoir is an attempt to "name" the "inner lives" of dogs as well, perhaps, as humans too. Human interiority is also notoriously hard to translate into language. Mary Gaitskill, in her memoir *Lost Cat* (2017), describes how for a family member, the mourning of a dog—rather than a human death—opened up routes to grief: "The dog he could feel, and through the door of that feeling came everything else."[35] In other words, the dog's availability for mourning enables or provides a bridge to other kinds. It is notable that all of Doty's cross-species identification and entanglement is through the dog, one of the most apprehendable nonhumans in the United States. The dog's long-standing relationship to humans means that it is primed to be easily assimilable—domesticated, if you like—into human-centric worlds and frameworks. In this light, it is significant that the book casts aside the two cats that live in Doty's homes—they appear twice, briefly—as if the story of love and loss has no room for creatures that are (perhaps) not as easily folded into the narrative of loving companionship?[36] Dogs are, for Doty, the nonhuman animals most suited to his tale of queer loss and love.

Doty's memoir reveals, as Joseph Anderton writes, that "writing the self can involve writing the other in the same way that writing the other can involve writing the self."[37] In other words, by confronting his dogs' animality, Doty is able to confront his own; or, in seeing the overlaps between human and nonhuman worlds, the boundaries between both are broken down. It is no coincidence that this self/other writing happens queerly, or within a queer world. Doty's memoir suggests that queer family—forged through care and interspecies dependence—undoes non/human hierarchies and their attendant normativity.

IV

To conclude, and to tie together some of this chapter's concerns about how dogs bridge and suture non/human worlds, especially at the site of racialization, gendering, and queerness, we turn to Danez Smith's poem "dogs!" from their collection *Homie* (2020). The poem is concerned above all with the ways that dogs figure various human-nonhuman connections, especially as they are raced, gendered, and queered. The long thin poem, split into short stanzas, cycles through cultural references, sociocultural contexts, and the speaker's own present as a dog barks in an apartment above them. In all, the poem helps thread together some of this chapter's main concerns: how dog and human worlds are braided at the site of Blackness and queerness.

In an early stanza, Smith's speaker articulates two definitions: "dog" and "dawg," tying together Black men and canines, in ways akin to what Boisseron (discussing Josephine Baker) sees as turning "a racial slur into gold, or social currency, by making it a sign of racial empowerment."[38] The definitions mirror one another but spell out key differences between dogs (coded in relation to whiteness, and thus grievable) and dawgs (coded as Black, and thus not):

> dog (n.): a man's best friend. (see:
> fetch, roll over, K-9, good boy, put
> down.) ex. *my dog died, I had to do*
> *it with my own hands.*[39]

We might link these lines back to the discussion of "Redeployment," and the ways that dogs' deaths are given care and attention (in contrast to racial others). "Put down," of course, has double meaning, referencing both a ball or toy and being killed, but at the mercy of the dog's owner. "Good boy," we should note, recurs later in the poem, with a more sexual connotation. The second dog definition skewers the first:

> dawg (n.): a man's best friend.
> (see: blunt rolled already,
> handshake, my n——, put me on.)
> ex. *my dawg died, he did it with his*
> *own hands.* (36)

Smith explicitly ties together the two definitions. Where dogs are a man's best friend, a "dawg" is a friend because they have drugs ready prepared. In both stanzas, dogs/dawgs are objects to the man's subject. Where the canines do *man*'s bidding—fetch, roll over—so too do the Black men service *man*'s needs. The example at the end of the stanza, though, underscores a key difference: when a Black man dies, it happens "with his / own hands." Smith gestures to the way that death is either something proffered with care, or it is self-inflicted, depending on your (racialized) species position.

Other parts of the poem echo the above discussion of species grievability. The speaker says that "a dead dog is a hero, . . . a dead child is a tragedy," though this is dependent on "the color, the / nation," of such a child (21). Dead dogs are heroic and dead children are tragedies, only when those lives are normative. Only when whiteness is the governing frame do certain lives become coded as tragic. In a related way, the speaker asks: "everybody love Lassie, but what / about Sounder?" (19). The latter figure is the eponymous dog from an African American novel for children from 1969, a dog that has less cultural traction than the white-adjacent Lassie. Smith's poem is asking *how* certain animals, human and otherwise, get to count in the cultural imaginary, how certain lives get recognized and remembered. Indeed, even the speaker has to question themself when the upstairs dog keeps barking and they think of "ending his little / noisy life" but then remember that "he matters he / matters" and the dog's "brown" owner would "cry forever" (18). The mattering of life requires an active engagement with grief, from the acknowledgment of a life's dependence on others.

Of course, how lives get to "matter" is the work of racist structures and histories. As the speaker notes, "dogs aren't racist but they can be / trained to be so as can the water as / can the trees." Everything can be shaped by racism and the marking by "a pale hand" (20). In this way, dogs—like people—are not innately racist but are taught it through whiteness's all-pervasive grip on the social, what Christina Sharpe might call *the weather*. And racist history, too, ties dogs to Black people, as the poem explores links between the use of dogs during slavery and its aftermath. One stanza charts the "graduat[ion]" from "outrunning the / block's dogs to outrunning the / block's police" (19), a clear historical trajectory that ties the dog to police violence, as noted in reference to Birmingham. And later, the speaker links "dogs bred to smell the coke" and "the bomb" and "the n—— hid beneath / the floorboards" (22). Again, the dog is not merely linked to Black people to dehumanize; the dog is also a technology of surveillance and white supremacist violence. The dog is put to cultural use continually along racial lines.

Smith's poem also explores these non/human connections, though, in relation to gender and sexuality. For example, the speaker acknowledges that "i too have been called boy & / expected to come, kneel" (19), and later in a club's bathroom, in their "tightest shortest shorts" says "*i'm a real bitch* / 3 times" and puts their hand "on a man's chest & it's a paw" (21). Here, the speaker's proximity to a dog figure reads in multiple ways. Though they are "called boy" and "expected" to kneel, we do not know if this is out of desired submission or racialized/gendered coding of sexual positions and roles. But when the speaker puts their "paw" on a chest after acknowledging their "bitch" power, they seem to have more agency. In both, the *dog* position is one of sexual submission to masculinity, whether wanted or not. Smith's "dawg" is a Black masculinity not tied to heteronormativity or strict gender roles; rather, the cross-species link opens questions about an animality that is toyed with.[40] Smith's speaker continually leans in to and pulls away from the equivalencing of dogs and Black people, so as to underscore the ways in which this historical figuration is not singular but open to being reimagined.

At the end of the poem, when a police officer pulls the speaker over and asks if they know why, the speaker says, "*I'm just trying to be / me*" (22). That enjambement suggests that both *being* and *being me* are two different but related endeavors. Living, and living as oneself, are both pushbacks against white figurations of Blackness here. The following (final) stanza returns to the dog barking upstairs, and the speaker now acknowledges that they can't "hate him" as he's "alone" all day. Making noise, they think, "must be / the only way he knows he's not a / ghost" (22). Put another way, the dog brings itself into being by making noise, articulating itself—not unlike the desire "to be / me," and not unlike the speaker's poetic utterance. Both speaker and dog are in a continuous state of coming-into-being, not quite in Haraway's sense of *becoming kin* but rather in the way that the Black-queer-dog "metonymic feedback loop" (to return to Tarver) is shown by Smith to be ever evolving. While saturated with history—with the ways that dogs have been deployed to both police Black populations and to *stand in for* Black populations, and indeed to racialize and gender Black men in ways that are both desired and not—the non/human world evoked by Smith's poem, and many of the earlier examples, is such that species boundaries and lines are ever available for redescription.

If the human-dog relationship is so deeply entwined, so deeply historical and cultural, so deeply fraught by the machinations of mattering and its inherent normativity, we might think it unbreakable. But the dogs in this chapter have continually upended expectations, have faced-off human designs on their complexity. The dog's proliferation means that canine stories will continue to be told and retold. And they will always be tied, as we have seen here, to the workings of gender, sexuality, race, class, and nationhood, because they are so enmeshed in our human worlds.

NOTES

1. McHugh, *Dog*, 7, 8, 12, 14.

2. Doty, *Dog Years*, 30. Quoted hereafter in text.

3. Haraway, *When*, 15.

4. Nunez, *The Friend*, 41.

5. Nunez, *The Vulnerables*, 203.

6. Kuzniar, *Melancholia's Dog*.

7. McHugh, *Dog*, 19.

8. Boisseron, *Afro-Dog*, 42.

9. Tarver, "The Dangerous," 282.

10. Griffin, *Hide*, 105. Cited hereafter in text.

11. Dayan, *With Dogs*, xiii.

12. Boisseron, *Afro-Dog*, 36.

13. Lloyd, *Corporeal*, 139–65.

14. Senna, "The Land," 35. Cited hereafter in text.

15. Boisseron, *Afro-Dog*, 43.

16. Smith, "The *Harper's* Columns," 318

17. Though Zadie Smith seems to think the story funny, for reasons that escape me.

18. Klay, "Redeployment," 1. Cited hereafter in text.

19. Booth, "Thank You," 181.

20. Booth, 185.

21. Boggs, *Animalia*, 43, 49, 66.

22. Boggs, 73, 74.

23. It is worth noting that the girl in Maxine Hong Kingston's *The Woman Warrior* (1976) is also named Little Dog by her mother for similar reasons.

24. Vuong, *On Earth*, 18.

25. McHugh, *Dog*, 129.

26. Chen, *Animacy*, 105. Chen later in this section goes on to discuss "furries," which do not appear in Greenwell's novel, and not in this bestiary at large, but could easily form the next steps in a queer non/human imaginary.

27. For more on consent, and "limit consent" in particular, see the chapter "Hunting."

28. Haraway, *When*, 15, 17.

29. Freccero, "Death Do Us," 119, 129.

30. Rudy, "LGBTQ. . . Z?," 605, 611.

31. Rudy, 611.

32. Henwood, "Does Something," n.p.

33. This quotation is in italics in the original (it is one of many italicized interludes, or "entr'actes").

34. Nunez, *The Friend*, 168.

35. Gaistkill, *Lost Cat*, 53.

36. As someone who lives with a cat, I am wary of projecting a kind of defensiveness here about their being side-lined in the text. However, the two quick references to Doty's felines are instructive. The first acknowledges that they have been hidden from the reader: "Cats, you ask? What cats? Well, no story can contain everything" (36). Notable here is that the cat becomes part of *everything* beyond the story, rather than—in fact—the cross-species story of love and loss. The second reference is about Doty and his partner traveling across the country with all the pets, including "the two cats who do not figure in this story." They are in their plastic crates "piping up from time to time" (99). Ostensibly talking about the cats' meows in the car, their "piping up" could just be Doty's vague consciousness about hearing and seeing these nonhuman animals who must be central to the narrative he is telling but cannot find room for. Does the dog edge out the cat? Do canine narratives foreclose thinking about other (less comforting) creatures?

37. Anderton, "Dogdom," 272.

38. Boisseron, *Afro-Dog*, 36

39. Smith, "dogs!" 18. Cited hereafter in text.

40. Another stanza comically notes that "the gay agenda made *CatDog* to / offer your child's gender to their / seven-headed god," (21) a line that further teases out the queering of non/human boundaries in pop culture and their relation to gendered embodiment.

BUT
TER
FLY

Butterfly

butterflies ignite non/human relations

Like the life of most butterflies, this chapter is brief. The average lifespan of a butterfly is two to four weeks; though monarch butterflies—which flutter into the work of Ocean Vuong, the subject of this section—can live either two to six weeks (if born in summer) or six to nine months, if born later in the year. The latter are migratory monarchs, traveling vast distances before dying. The four-stage life cycle (egg, larva, pupa, imago) of the butterfly is often used in popular culture as a metaphor for change and development. In this chapter we see how Vuong continues this tradition within a queer transnational framework.

As Jessica Rapson and I noted in an article about Barbara Kingsolver's cli-fi novel *Flight Behavior* (2012), butterflies "are an obviously 'poetical' species that have long been aestheticized and used for symbolic purposes,"[1] uses that critics like Timothy Morton critique for a focus on "nature" over "ecology" (a "sadistic admiration").[2] Rapson and I push back a little to describe the monarchs in Kingsolver's novel as figures for the interrelations of the local and planetary, the porosity of place, and—ultimately—because of their displacement from Mexico to Tennessee because of climate change, as signs of ecological disruption.[3] Butterflies in contemporary U.S. writing often gesture toward the fleetingness of lifeforms in a radically changing world.

As we see elsewhere in this book, Ocean Vuong's *On Earth We're Briefly Gorgeous* (2019) is dense with nonhuman figures. The narrative, though, is bookended by monarch butterflies beginning their migration south from the northern United States to Mexico. Their migration is initiated both by small changes ("the angle of sunlight" [8]), and, as in *Flight Behavior*, by destroyed habitats. Vuong frames this novel about transnational migration and queer relationships with the monarch's literal and symbolic relation to temporality and travel: "The monarchs that fly south will not make it back north. Each departure, then, is final. Only their children return; only the future revisits the past" (8). If each adult journey is one-way and never includes a return—like Little Dog's mother and grandmother moving to the United States—then only he, the child, can go backward or reconstruct the past. The monarchs who survive migration pass a "message down to their children," so that the "memory of family members lost from the initial winter was woven into their genes" (12). What is passed down to Little Dog, one could argue, is a sense of dehumanization—"There are no animals here but us" (46)—but also the notion that inheritance is a matter of survivability, livability. This is not in the sense of a heteronormative reproductive futurity, but rather in a more local familial genre of belonging where queerness names all of those kept outside of the dominant white patriarchal norm. The monarchs, for Little Dog, both materialize and symbolize (they are not *just* "poetical") the arduousness of migration and the losses that often follow.

By the end of the novel—two hundred pages pass without monarchs appearing again—Little Dog notices a butterfly land near him.[4] It turns out to be not a monarch but a "weak white blur ready to die in the first frost" (223), a symbol of Little Dog's lover Trevor, who overdoses on heroin and fentanyl. And though this image of death is followed by another—"I can't tell you why some monarchs, on their way south, simply stop flying, their wings all of a sudden too heavy, not entirely their own—and fall away, deleting themselves from the story" (229), another metaphor for Trevor's disappearance or "deletion"—the monarchs in the final pages index metamorphosis. It is as though death and change are, for Little Dog, inseparable.

Vuong's prose poem "My Father Writes from Prison," from *Night Sky with Exit Wounds* (2016), similarly uses the image of the monarch butterfly to signal transformation through death. The speaker (the father of the title) writes home to a partner that "there are things / I can say only in the dark / how one spring / I crushed a monarch mid-flight / just to know how it felt / to have something change / in my hands."[5] The slashes appear in the poem to both indicate tentative line endings within the prose—breaks amid continuity—and to figure the prison bars behind which the speaker writes. Crushing the butterfly is, for him, about change and/through death. The end of the poem then lifts off, as it were, like the butterfly as he imagines his partner's dress and then "ignite[s]." The poem ends midline, without subsequent punctuation, as if transformed like the dead butterfly—in another kind of flight.

On Earth relatedly ends with a rush of nonhuman images, all tied together through their vulnerability.[6] Little Dog runs into an open tobacco field thinking he hears an animal (an echo of an earlier scene). Finding nothing there, he instead imagines herds of buffalo that run off the edge of a cliff, following one another to their death (an image that he and Trevor discuss at length, foreshadowing Trevor's own demise). In his mind, the buffalo run and change into other creatures: they "become moose," "then dogs," then "macaques . . . [with] brains hollowed out" and then, finally, "they ignite into the ochre-red sparks of monarchs" (241). There is much to say about the blurring together of these nonhuman animals in Little Dog's mind—the way they are all rendered disposable in the novel, are invaded by human violence—but the use of the word "ignite," as in "My Father Writes from Prison," seems to gesture to the vitality and spark of the monarchs, even as they will soon be dead. Like the speaker in "My Father," and even the monarchs in *Flight Behavior*, which in the first instance the protagonist mistakes for flames among the trees, the ignition of the butterflies thinks survivability amid curtailment, the flickers of life within precarity.

Little Dog summarizes his multispecies imagination: "Monkeys, moose, cows, dogs, butterflies, buffaloes. What we could give to have the ruined lives of animals tell a human story—when our lives are in themselves the story of animals" (242). Here the non/human, in all its messiness, comes into focus as the novel webs a network of species. Vuong calls attention to how *On Earth* itself has used the nonhuman as a proxy for vulnerable life, but with the monarch's transcendent flight toward death he nevertheless signs the way forward to an entangled non/human world of migration, queerness, and possibility.

NOTES

1. Lloyd and Rapson, "Family Territory," 918.

2. Morton, *Ecology*, 1, 5.

3. Heather Houser makes related arguments in "Knowledge Work."

4. Its wings, in an act of literary inheritance, resemble "that corner of Toni Morrison's *Sula* I dog-eared. . . . It was the part where Eva pours gasoline on her drug-doomed son and lights the match in an act of love and mercy" (223). This comparison not only stitches together the butterfly and the literary text but also links to Morrison's story of Black women's relationships, and then in turn to poverty, drugs, and children. The butterfly's tiny wings are saturated with literary meaning.

5. Vuong, "My Father Writes," 18.

6. I'll come back to the macaques in "Hunter."

OC
EAN

Ocean

the sea contains queer depths

In the "Hybrid" chapter, we saw non/human fusions as queerly hybrid, where that term partly shrugs off its colonial histories and taxonomizing fixity. In *My Life in Sea Creatures* (2022),[1] Sabrina Imbler looks at hybridity initially through the butterflyfish and then in relation to themself as mixed race. While they "don't want to . . . reclaim" a term so laden with racism, Imbler sees "parallels" between themself and the *hybrid* creatures of the sea.[2] Imbler writes about a hybrid of a threadfin butterflyfish and a lined butterflyfish, which "becomes C. *auriga x* C. *lineolatus*," where the *x* is the hybrid space between types. The *x* is "intangible and, on its own, meaningless" but not to Imbler; hybrids "will never be caught between worlds, as long as we have x; it is our world" (157). Imbler's book about sea creatures is itself a submersion into the *x*: the queer space of the between and beyond. They explore their non-binary mixed-racedness through feral goldfish, starving octopuses, Chinese sturgeon, and other creatures. While the book is as much about the things living in the ocean and other waterways, it is also about the ocean's capacity to hold so much potential beyond the normative imagination.

This chapter is counterintuitively brief given the ocean's vastness. Rather than attending to its expansiveness, I want to zoom in on two texts that think about the ocean and creatures within it from very specific vantages. Attending to their imaginative worlds with brevity will hopefully gesture to the large aquatic worlds beneath their surfaces.

The ocean covers 71 percent of the planet, and even though it is "organized as discrete units" (such as the Atlantic or Indian Ocean) "in relation to their adjacent continents," the ocean is one enormous thing that resists thing-ness in its magnitude, depths, and fluidity.[3] Eric Paul Roorda argues that the ocean is often seen as "changeless" and "without a history," because of a "terracentrism" that prioritizes land over water (even while it is outstripped by the ocean's planetary coverage), but conversely the ocean has many histories within it and is ever changing. To think in line with ocean studies, then, is to figure an aquacentric perspective.[4] In Imbler's memoir and Alexis Pauline Gumbs's *Undrowned: Black Feminist Lessons from Marine Mammals* (2020), we see two ways of thinking the ocean from trans and queer of color perspectives. In both, the authors turn to sea creatures and the waters they move in—the "more-than-human temporalities of the ocean" that Elizabeth DeLaughrey calls "sea ontologies"[5]—to paint possibilities of queer living for humans and nonhumans alike.

Imbler's memoir moves from the personal to natural history within each chapter, so that their sense (and narration) of self is entwined with sea creatures and their ways of being. For instance, they describe how the "abundance of life" (100) at the bottom of the ocean confused scientists in the late 1970s, who had imagined a paucity of lifeforms in deep sea trenches. Yet the creatures there were found to be consuming "flecks of fish that died nearer the surface," and "eked out an alternative away of life" that is not a "last resort" but a "radical act of choosing what nourishes you" (101). Akin to the motto that queer people "get to choose our families," the vent bacteria, tube worms, and yeti crabs at the ocean's bottom, Imbler writes, "take it one step further" and "choose what nourishes them" (101). In this way, *My Life* is as much about specific sea creatures as it is the ways that they (and Imbler too) find ways of living and organizing queerly, embracing the alternative possibilities that the sea's vastness (and strangeness) can offer. In that way, Imbler joins much queer and feminist theorizing of water, such as Astrida Neimanis's conception of "watery embodiment," which is a shift away from the normative figuration of the body as discrete and sovereign, and instead is more fluid and capacious.[6] As Imbler puts it, "with a body 95 percent water, you are more like a lake than an animal" (227). Given, too, that we live in a time when water crises are endemic (more droughts, *wilder* weather, floods, sea-level rise, water contamination), critics like Neimanis urge us to think aquatically, not least because water is likely to determine our futures as a human species.

Thus, if the planet and our bodies are more watery than dominant narratives would claim, what might it mean to imagine ourselves otherwise?

Thinking historically, culturally, and personally, Alexis Pauline Gumbs extends her work from *Spill: Scenes of Black Feminist Fugitivity* (2016) to other aquatic arena. *Undrowned* begins with the "unfinished" drowning of slavery's Middle Passage, and the breathing of those Black lives on board ships or underwater, as well as the liveliness all of those creatures in the sea then and now. "Breathing in unbreathable circumstances," Gumbs writes, "is what we do every day in the chokehold of racial gendered ableist capitalism," and this breathing is not confined to Black people whose ancestors were enslaved but is planetary in scale.[7] Gumbs maps a form of what Christina Sharpe calls—in similarly oceanic terms—"the wake." To be "*in* the wake is to occupy and be occupied by the continuous and changing present of slavery's as yet unresolved unfolding," Sharpe writes.[8] *Undrowned*, then, takes its Black feminist lessons from marine mammals because they are "amazing at not drowning" (2); they can survive the wake. Moving through Black feminist principles such as listening, remembering, honoring boundaries, and ending capitalism, Gumbs takes lessons from marine mammals to chart new paths forward. Each chapter is a pedagogic meditation, a way of "identify[ing] *with*" marine creatures to rethink "relations, possibilities, and practices" (9). Because marine mammals are, to Gumbs, "queer, fierce, protective of each other, complex, shaped by conflict, and struggling to survive the extractive and militarized context our species has imposed on the ocean and ourselves" (9), they are the perfect guides for her queer Black feminist theorizing.

As we saw with ocean studies' reorienting of terracentrism, and feminist water studies' resistance of embodiment as solidity, Gumbs's book thinks corporeality otherwise—as historical, dialogic, shaped by time and memory. For instance, dolphins' dorsal fins are thought to have evolved "from practice across generations" to live in the ocean's "wild movement" (44). Gumbs ties this to her own scoliosis, a spinal shift that bears the imprint of the world in which she moves. Read this way, *Undrowned* echoes Marquis Bey's framing of Black trans feminism. Bey argues that the fixity of "the body" (as a singular construction) is produced by and through normative frameworks and structures (not just heteropatriarchy, but also epistemological and ontological frames). These are, in Bey's words, "territorializing projects" that "must be subverted." Gendering and racialization as territorializing modes are antithetical to the oceanic thinking noted above that resists landed boundaries. Bey reads Gumbs's body of work as expanding "racialized and gendered lexicons of possibility," largely through "performing transness inasmuch as 'trans' denotes the vitiation of the disposition toward categorization, especially binaristic categories." In other words, Gumbs's Black trans feminism is identifiable through her commitment to reimaging not only what race and gender might be but also what might live beyond those frames of existence. In *Undrowned*, she does this by attending to oceanic creatures and the oceanic imaginary, where, Bey writes, to "unbecome humans is to be in kinship with beings across taxonomy." Such kinship is an "interspecies coalition" that might, Bey writes, "save the earth and ourselves as, not inhabitants of, but kin with it."[9] Gumbs's creative and theoretical work both queers *the human* and its (our) place within wider ecologies and planetary frames through an oceanic imaginary.

Like the South Asian river dolphins who swim sideways, Gumbs's orientation in *Undrowned* is queerly aslant. Writing, "Are you swimming sideways? . . . Are you re-evaluating what you thought progress meant?" (48), she is asking, like many queer theorists before her, what normative modes of embodiment, movement, and futurity are. Imbler, too, takes their inspiration from sea creatures who live otherwise. They ask, in light of feral goldfish set loose from their tanks, "What does it mean to survive in the wild? You can't do it without going wild yourself. We are all capable of reverting to a wilder state. . . . For a goldfish, the wild promises abundance. Release a goldfish and it will never look back. Nothing fully lives in a bowl; it only learns to survive it" (19). While Imbler is talking here of "feral goldfish" that expand immeasurably when released into waterways—and often mess up those waters for other species—their point is that the captivity of creatures, the limiting of their purview (the bowl), has deleterious effects on its existence. Set "free," the goldfish becomes other than it has been imagined by humans.

One of Imbler's lessons is this: What might it look like for humans as well as nonhumans to be set free, let loose, given the space to be something other than what has been prescribed. If one learns only to survive one's containment, rather than flourish in it, what might the ocean's freedom help bring into view? What might its breadth and depth, its shifting fluctuations, its ubiquity across the planet and the bodies on it, and its movability mean for non/humans? The ocean is everywhere, within and without us, yet cannot be pinned down.

NOTES

1. Or, in the United States, *How Far the Light Reaches: A Life in Ten Sea Creatures.*

2. Imbler, *My Life,* 154. Cited hereafter in text.

3. Roorda, "Introduction," 1; Roberts and Stephens, "Introduction," 7.

4. Roorda, "Introduction," 1.

5. DeLaughrey, "Submarine Futures," 33.

6. Neimanis, *Bodies,* 1.

7. Gumbs, *Undrowned,* 2.

8. Sharpe, *In the Wake,* 13–14.

9. Bey, *Black,* 9, 118, 138, 137.

HUNTING

Hunting

the hunter is also the hunted

I

The hunt, in the United States and elsewhere, has often gone hand in hand with national statecraft, normative human schemas, and patriarchal visions of control. For Indigenous people in the Americas, though, hunting has had manifold meanings and significances over time: Nonhuman animals were/are killed for food and for their skins (to make clothes, homes, and objects) but also as a way of continuing tradition and culture. Hunting is not the same in every Indigenous culture, but there are shared practices of killing that are attentive to species control, environmental change, and future sustenance. Many Indigenous groups have hunted with the future in mind, not simply as a "sport," as it has become for other inhabitants of the country. Yet as colonists settled the nation, hunting transformed into a different form of human-nonhuman relationship. As Antoinette Burton and Renisa Mawani argue, colonial-era hunting (around the world) was as much about the nonhuman animal killed as the logics that underpinned the act. Because "racial supremacy" hinged upon "species supremacy and vice versa," the human/animal distinction and the hierarchies it produced enabled colonial forces to decide which lives were worth living, or which lives (in Judith Butler's terms) counted as lives to begin with.[1]

One of the ways in which empire—particularly the British—exercised control over the nations it colonized was through "the hunt," which tied together and buttressed ideas of gender, race, sexuality, and class, among much else. The hunt, Burton and Mawani write, "symbolized the projected racial strength and displayed the material triumphs of empire, and at the same time signaled the vulnerabilities of British imperial manhood." Hunting purportedly demonstrated white masculinity (and the associated notions of courage and strength), but it did so as "a performative conquest over nature." Hunting not only shored up particular versions of colonial identity but also had violent material effects in the "displacement of Indigenous and tribal peoples," as well as the killing of species and the decimation of carefully tended environments.[2] The hunts brought back (to the metropole) items and materials—bones, fur, skins—that would be put to other uses, like fashion and even taxidermy.[3]

These colonial uses of hunting alert us to how the human killing of nonhuman animals has not only been about survival (meat, resources). Hunts produced, mediated, and sustained colonial worlds and imaginaries. The capturing of nonhuman animals, the performative killing of them in front of others, the display and collection of the creature's body, the consumption of those parts—all served to underscore not simply species domination but also a modulated and normative version of the human. Much of this racialization and gendering runs through this chapter's examples, too, demonstrating how the hunt has always been about producing taxonomies of life as well as the masculinization that subtends them.

In a U.S. context, the hunt has been most clearly depicted in literary texts that ossify species lines. Hunt narratives, Antoine Traisnel writes—from Herman Melville's *Moby-Dick* (1851) to the work of James Fenimore Cooper and Ernest Hemingway—have often been used in the "self-fashioning" of the nation, which "monumentalized the mythos of the intrepid and enterprising frontiersman who dominates his natural surroundings, with all its attendant sexual and gendered connotations."[4] American hunt narratives are as much about the specific human-nonhuman dynamics as they are about upholding national myths and their normative human frames. In this chapter, we look at writers interested in gender, sexuality, and race/ethnicity for the ways that they interrogate hunting and some of its American underpinnings.

Reading Blackfeet author Stephen Graham Jones's *The Only Good Indians* (2020), David Vann's *Goat Mountain* (2013), Tom Franklin's *Poachers* (1999), and Ocean Vuong's *On Earth We're Briefly Gorgeous* (2019) for the ways that they imagine the hunter/hunted dynamic—via elk, bucks, possums, macaques, veal, and more—this chapter suggests that hunting traverses and queers species lines rather than simply upholds them. Indeed, hunter and hunted are bound so tightly together in these texts that they are near impossible to separate. A queer lens is used most explicitly in relation to Vuong's novel but also in the larger schema of reading gender and sexuality's relation to race and the species line in all the texts. What happens when hunters are hunted (and haunted) by their prey a decade later, in a tale of trans-species feminist revenge? What happens when the hunt goes awry, and the human body is queered beyond recognition? What happens when hunter and hunted are seen as inextricable, as queerly dependent? These are questions that this chapter's texts explore. The chapter links to others in the bestiary, too, in its attention to species hierarchies (and their queering/inverting), to the entangling of non/human lives, and the demarcations of which lives are worthy of being seen as lives, or kinds of lives that are apprehendable and worthy of grief.

The present texts depict stories as much about killing nonhuman animals for food as they are about the sport and pastime of hunting, about the fetishization of guns, and the culturally accrued meanings of the hunt within particular families and communities. There is not much in this bestiary about factory farming and its relation to death, but there are other books out there to do this work.[5] The texts under scrutiny here are far more interested in the psychic and somatic resonances of the hunt, the way that certain kinds of hunting are made permissible or understandable via culture and history. For instance, there are differences here between hunting nonhumans (as sport, as heritage) and poaching, the latter of which by necessity requires a kind of transgression: killing something that "should not" be killed, or in a place you "should not" kill it. The texts also ask why killing some animals is legitimate but killing others is not. What are the boundaries, these texts ask, of hunting and killing? If the normative equation is hunted = nonhuman (and vice versa), what happens when humans are rendered nonhuman and are suddenly available to be killed?

II

Before analyzing Jones's novel, it is worth sketching out a little further some of the hunt's significance in a U.S. context and its relation to taxidermy, which we have explored elsewhere in this bestiary. Traisnel does much to unpack the significance of the hunt in the nineteenth-century United States, especially as it morphed into a new regime, that of *capture*. Capture, as a mode of control and power—where nonhumans are caught in representations (by photography for instance) rather than killed—moves from the specific hunt to a more generalized containment. Traisnel notes that as the nineteenth century saw huge changes in industrialization and the "closure" of the frontier,[6] as well as a growing conservationist discourse and an altering relation to the land, the hunt was "recast as a primitive anachronism" or "pastime" and instead a mode of capture took its place. Like the small cameras that were mounted to shotguns, a newer way for (white) Americans to "seize" nonhumans took hold. Without delving too deeply into Traisnel's historiography, he notes that "the singularity of the hunt is subsumed into the routinized, systematic regime of capture, under which animals become indifferentiable from one another—exchangeable, like all commodities."[7] I want to think about both this flattening and singularity of nonhuman life within the hunt, too.

Parsing the difference between hunting and capture, Traisnel writes that the hunt "supposes the copresence, however brief, uneven, and fortuitous, of the hunter and the hunted," and it acknowledges that "animals exist in their own right before the encounter with the hunter." We see how this plays out in the chapter's texts. As an atelic verb—in contrast to capture, which is telic, referring to a clear endpoint and object—the hunt means that one does not know in advance "what will be hunted or whether the hunt will be successful."[8] Rather than the unending time of capture—the nonhuman is caught and held still—the hunt works provisionally, improvisationally, and with an element of the unknown. The *hunted* can shift at a moment's notice, not just in its ungraspability but in the way that the hunter can easily become the hunted too. Capture, though, also calls our attention to another intersection of hunting and the non/human: taxidermy. Where capture is about holding the nonhuman still in its aliveness (death in life, life in death), so too do we see in the "Taxidermy" chapter how the preserving of nonhuman bodies keeps something of them vivid.

Taxidermy's links to hunting are a useful way in to thinking about non/human entanglement. In colonial times, as Burton and Mawani note, taxidermized animals were displayed publicly and privately as "physical symbols" of empire and colonial rule over "lands" and wildlife."[9] Taxidermized creatures were status symbols of power and control, as well as an index of the consumption and display of "exotic" otherness. Within a U.S. context too, hunting—as sport and pastime—often produces a kill not simply for consumption but also for the spectacle of the display which indexes and materializes the (often) masculine-coded power over the nonhuman. (We see this today with trophy hunting on African game reserves, for instance.)

In the "Taxidermy" chapter we see how that practice of stuffing nonhuman animals and posing them in "realistic" scenes is partly a desire to keep the nonhuman other simultaneously alive and dead; it gives lifelikeness to that which is gone, even species that are/were extinct. In Matthew Griffin's *Hide* (2016), for instance, the narrator Wendell ends up keeping many taxidermized creatures because the people who requested them fail to collect the works, as if the idea of the trophy became less important as time passed. In Kristen Arnett's *Mostly Dead Things* (2019), Jessa-Lynn incisively notes that the hunters who came to them with carcasses want the nonhumans awakened in poses that were "commanding" and "larger than life, as if the animal might reanimate and attack." Notably, they want this emphasis on the theatricality of danger and threat to "prove" their hunting prowess, "even if the person had shot the animal from behind as it nosed through a garbage can."[10] Jessa-Lynn here underscores one of the fantasies central to the hunt: that the "dominance" at the heart of the kill is actually luck or cunning. The final shot might be achieved "from behind" with a highly sophisticated rifle, rather than through anything like "skill." Baking that disavowal into the taxidermy form—purported power over the nonhuman, in an unequal and uneven relation—is doubly telling, as only in the taxidermized form can the creature be seen as dangerously wild, "larger than life." In other words, the dual desires in taxidermy of keeping something both alive and dead also speak to the fantasy at the heart of hunting—human power over the nonhuman that is hardly power at all but merely the specious display of it. Hunting reveals the precarity at the heart of a human's need to control nonhuman life.

III

In his novel *The Only Good Indians*, Stephen Graham Jones offers us a narrative of hunting in which non/human revenge is tied up with gender and Indigeneity. We follow four Native men—Ricky, Lewis, Gabe, and Cass—who are, one by one, killed by the spirit of a pregnant elk (Po'noka, or Ponokaotokaan*aakii*, meaning elk head woman) that they shot a decade earlier on tribal land that is reserved for elders. The novel, in Christopher Pexa's

(Bdewákaŋtuŋwaŋ Dakota) words, "interrupts settler-colonial binaries of the human and the nonhuman, the more-alive and the less-alive." As a story of nonhuman revenge of a pregnant elk against the men that would kill her (against local tribal and moral principles), the novel can be read as an indirect commentary on the sexual violence rampant against Indigenous women, as well as a twist on the history of the settler-colonial wiping-out of Indigenous people. Yet the novel resists such easy parallels and allegories, instead mining the complex overlaps of Indigeneity, gender, and species: It is, for Pexa, "an imagining of justice through a fictional tribal law that operates beyond settler frameworks of restoring rights."[11] In this way, it is a useful starting point for this chapter's examination of hunting and the non/human because: a) the hunters become the hunted, in part because they transgress certain tribal laws; and b) the hunted nonhuman evokes and indexes other gendered violences, thus voicing enlaced non/human concerns.

The novel follows Po'noka, a spirit in various forms (some physical), as she exacts revenge for her and her unborn calf's killing; the four men are picked off in turn. The first man, Ricky, is killed outside a bar. Lewis, who shot the elk originally, dies when he convinces himself that his Native coworker is inhabited by the elk head woman and ends up killing her and his own wife. He is then chased down by law enforcement. Cass and Gabe die at Gabe's hands after an evening in a sweat lodge. Po'noka is only able to transform back into her full elk self at the end when she tries to kill Gabe's daughter Denorah. But Denorah ends up leading the elk to the site of the killing, and they find the spot where Lewis buried the calf. Its body emerges from the ground (a classic horror trope), and Po'noka is able to return to their herd after transforming: "Her right leg kicks through its human skin, is coarse brown hair underneath."[12] Throughout these revenge killings, the elk head woman interrupts and destabilizes the human world. Her hybrid presence—non/human because she queerly blurs the lines between human and nonhuman, ghostly and material—is such that the four men end up being led to their deaths rather than simply being murdered by her. In other words, the novel is not interested in a simple payback, an eye for an eye, but another vision entirely, whereby the hunted creature is able to meddle in the human world so that the hunters ensnare themselves and each other.

That the non/human entanglements of this novel are precipitated by a hunt that transgresses laws is vital to our understanding of how hunting can *queer*. The four men are on tribal land that they know they should not hunt on, but do so anyway when they stumble upon a huge herd. Because it is snowing heavily, the elk cannot hear the men, and thus they hunt with an advantage (much like the examples above, where hunting is not about skill but luck). Lewis remembers, for instance, the intensity with which he unloads: "His rifle stabbed through the rolled-down window, shooting, and shooting, and shooting, only stopping to thumb another round in" (72). The sentence unfurls in a way that is uncommon in the novel,[13] the repetitions and commas elongating the frenzy of Lewis's actions, not simply a skilled hunt but an assault of gunfire and display of human power. The desires inherent in a "normal" hunt overspill here, revealing a deeper (masculinized) violence and anger aimed at the nonhuman world.

As in this chapter's other examples, contemporary hunting narratives also focus on the hunted body coming apart (and its gendered implications). Lewis's frantic shooting kills the elk but not completely; the bullet hits her spine and collapses her body and internal organs. The narrator notes, via Lewis's consciousness, "She was trying to stand again . . . , never mind that the top of her head was missing, that her back was broken, that she should be dead, that she had to be dead" (77). Again, the accumulating clauses echo the intensity and panic of the hunter who cannot fathom the elk's survival against the shot nor fully the impact of his violence. Lewis wishes for the elk's quick and simple death, not an elongated dying, which would confront him with his actions. The unraveled body is a manifestation of hunting's ontological undoing. To prop up his ego Lewis tells himself that shooting the elk again was nothing, even though "he was Indian, even though he was this great born hunter" (78), acknowledgments that reveal his own feelings of impotence. The grisly death—which is only compounded when Lewis realizes the elk is pregnant—transgresses multiple rules: killing on protected land, killing a pregnant elk, killing absentmindedly.

That the elk is female, too, leads scholars like Pexa to see the act as linking to (but not allegorizing) "settler-colonial violence against Indigenous women," which is rampant in the United States across tribal and state land.[14] Contemporary Indigenous fiction such as Louise Erdrich's *The Round House* (2012) often interrogates the ubiquity of sexual violence against Native women, who are two and a half times more likely to be victims of it than the rest of the U.S. population. Jones's novel then shows how hunting expands beyond simple human-nonhuman boundaries and is deeply enmeshed with other forms of violence between and beyond species. Mapping the novel's non/human connections requires seeing the killing of nonhumans as imbricated in other forms of patriarchal violence and control.

As this short analysis shows, the novel introduces the central themes of this chapter: that the (human) hunter can always be turned into the hunted, and that the hunter-hunted dyad is not simply a one-directional power relation between species but a more radical (and queer) entangling of bodies and agencies. Hunting is innately non/human, bringing the human and nonhuman into intimate proximity, blurring both.

IV

David Vann's *Goat Mountain* invokes ideas of Indigeneity in relation to the non/human only to keep them at bay. Vann dedicates the book to his Cherokee grandfather, "who hunted each year on Goat Mountain," in order to tie his characters—who I take to be white—to conversations about humans and land. The narrator says, "This was where we returned," and "where our history was kept."[15] The generational return connects the main characters in this novel to their generic forebears ("we" and "our"), and to the entangling of U.S. codes of masculinity with hunting's permeable boundaries between human and nonhuman.

In the novel, three men and an eleven-year-old boy go off to hunt on Goat Mountain, Northern California, in the late 1970s. Told in an off-kilter retrospective narration,[16] where the narrator describes his boyhood from a state of not-knowing, a lack of adult awareness or information ("I remember nothing" [55], he says early on, unable to translate this early experience). Such strangeness only serves to underscore the nightmarish and otherworldly days that the boy spends with his father, grandfather, and family friend Tom. On the first day in the wilderness, the group spot a poacher up on the mountain. The boy spies him through his rifle's scope and ultimately shoots the man, not entirely consciously. The novel spins out from this moment of violence that is about trespass: across un/sanctioned killings, across the non/human, across generations. Tom is intent on turning the boy in to police; the grandfather tries to kill the boy; and the father acts as an intermediary. The novel ends with another killing (of the grandfather) and this group of men fractured by ongoing violence. As Sebastian Groes writes, "A triangular relationship between natural landscape, human beings and memory forms the creative dynamo" of Vann's earlier novels, and *Goat Mountain* is no different.[17] This is a book steeped in masculinized violence rooted in the land.

Layered onto this story are brief biblical asides that invoke Cain's murder of Abel, which becomes a kind of Ur-story about the inevitability of human violence ("Cain is how we began" [17]). Such references also gesture toward the ways that Christianity was central to the wiping-out of Indigenous people through colonialization onwards. Vann's novel is interested in some of the ways that religion shapes epistemologies and ontologies of non/human life especially as they intersect with normative visions of American masculinity. Cain is the narrator's marker of an *innate* humanness, yet he does not acknowledge that this position is racially coded and gendered (we return to Sylvia Wynter's "Man"). While I do not want to dwell too much on this religious dimension, the novel poses a set of questions about morality and predestination that it refuses to fully answer.

As my summary suggests, the narrative is shaped by gendering. The hunt has always been a colonial and heteropatriarchal endeavor, a delineation of species next to gendering and racialization, and for the men in this novel, it is no different. The American mythos of masculinity is tied to the capture of other animals. For instance, the men barely drink water on the hunts, as it is a "kind of test in [the] family" (90), to prove one's strength. When the narrator finally shoots and kills his first buck, his grandfather notes, "Now you're a man" (156), which the narrator soon after clarifies: "eleven years old and now a man" (157). Here, he is both unbelieving yet committed to the gendered adulthood this hunting clan has produced. Similarly, the book's absence of women is underscored by the way that the men do not talk to the young boy about his mother. The boy asks Tom and his father what the mother was like but neither answer (133). The idea of family in this novel, Sophie Chapuis argues, is a "precarious unit, an endangered species," in part because of the absence of women (and thus ideas of reproduction).[18] The marginalization of women in the family is mirrored in the novel itself, as though hunting is solely the preserve of men and male-coded power; and perhaps it is the *effect* of women on the boy (the mother's unknowable history) that causes him to transgress so many rules.

The men struggle to comprehend the murder of the poacher, in part because the boy seems so different to them, is othered from the start. They figure him as evil and monstrous. As we see in the chapter "Hybrid," the monstrous can signal not simply the terrifying and aberrant but also the fluidly complex, the queer hybrid that is never one thing. Monsters, for Jeffrey Jerome Cohen, often police and limn the "borders of the possible," as well as "demarcate" the "bonds that hold together that system of relations we call culture." For Tom, the boy is a monster because he killed the poacher without guilt; he transgresses what is "possible" and unravels the social bonds of their culture. However, because the monster is also "difference made flesh," it manifests so many kinds of alterity that queer, or dissolve, identity itself; thus, the boy takes on the mantle of monster.[19] He identifies with this liminal status as child inclined toward violence. As a "person not yet a person," he is a "kind of monster" (20), before he is "remade into another kind" (90). Monstrousness for Vann's narrator is inherent to both childhood and adolescence, before and after puberty; growth is an ongoing form of aberrance. That aberrance in his mind is also tied to an innate human need to kill. For Tom, it is the boy's capacity to kill a human without remorse. Killing other humans produces the nonhuman monster; put another way, the nonhuman emerges out of the human's violence against other humans. The boundary between human and nonhuman is first breached by murder.

Even in their calling the boy monstrous, the men have different opinions about how different it is for the boy to kill a man versus killing an elk or another nonhuman. Here, the novel starts to pull apart questions of species difference and the morality of killing. The boy sees the man akin to a dead buck and wonders: What if they "had never been told that killing a man was bad?" (24), and would they slice open the carcass just the same as a buck? As they drag the body into the camp, though, Tom says, "He's not a piece of meat" (37), which the father rebuts by hanging the body from the tree. Later, the buck and the man are suspended next to each other, as if to draw out comparisons between the forms. Tom is insistent that they are "not the same" (188), but their parallel hanging leads the grandfather to ask, "What rule says you eat the buck and not the man?" (189). That question—how are species lines drawn and maintained?—is notable coming from the grandfather, who is the patriarch of the family and the person so intent on following hunting rules. Yet he is also the one that, like the boy, starts to query what it means to be human in the first place.

The apex of the novel's interest in species blurring and the queer entanglement of non/human bodies is when the boy kills his first buck. Out in the heat, the boy shoots the buck but does not kill it immediately (we saw this in Jones's novel too). In vivid detail, Vann depicts the horror of a slow death: the "back half" of the animal collapses, the rest of the body "screaming" in a way "no different from a human voice" (137). Where the boy feels no guilt about killing the poacher, here he "felt that end" of a life (141), as the buck writhes in agony in front of him. Again, the narrator muddies non/human distinctions. The roar of the buck, as he tries to escape, is—echoing the monster/hybrid discussion above—both "mythic and brutal" like a "half giant" (147). The buck then is both animal and not, specific yet far more than itself, much like the boy himself. The ritual of killing the buck and gutting it ends with the boy eating the heart ("slick and rubbery" [156]) which "confirms" his new manhood. That consumption, though, becomes messier when the men leave the boy alone to dismember the animal and drag it back to camp miles away. Such a job seems both part of the masculinist protocol and a punishment for the boy's earlier transgressions.

Vann's description of the dissection focuses on the sexed creature in ways that begin to queer the boy's relation to it. He flays the "sheath off" the penis, leaving its "inner stump," and cuts "around the anus" before pulling "everything out through the hole" (160). Such detail on the penis and anus root this non/human unraveling at the sites of sexing that might be linked to a normative gay male sexuality in ways beyond simply seeing the carcass as just flesh. After searching the buck's most intimate parts, the boy can only carry the carcass back to camp by entwining their bodies. He makes a "backpack" of the carcass, with the forelegs braided through the back ones (164). As he is engulfed, the boy and buck become "a new kind of beast fused with man, walking together and sharing the same breath and blood" (164). This hybrid amalgamation is a form of what scholars like Stacy Alaimo call "trans-corporeality," where the human is "always intermeshed with the more-than-human world," so that the human cannot be separate from what we might call "the environment." Indeed, this framework means the environment is "a world of fleshy beings with their own needs, claims, and actions," rather than a simple blank canvas.[20] (The landscape around the boy too, at this point, has a kind of agency, as it is a "malevolence, watching and waiting" [163]). Chapuis sees this moment as a defensive retreat into "the animal world" to find "shelter" from the exclusionary moral human one, but I would suggest slightly differently that the hybridity depicted is a more radical evocation of non/human life.[21]

The transcorporeal fusion in this scene—in which the human and nonhuman are intermeshed so as to reveal their de facto inseparability—also makes the boy imagine he might transform into something monstrously non/human. He wonders if he "would . . . gain hooves" (164), and "believed this animal would become" him because, as a child, "none of the boundaries of this existence were set" (165). So, even though his kill(s) have, for his family, proven his manhood, the boy is aware that his age (his liminality) might easily enable a transformation into the buck he carries. He references back, too, to "stories of transformation" like "Pan," "mermaids," and "Medusa," all of which have been "erased" in part by Christianity (177). The novel urges both toward a patriarchal Christian authority as well as a pre-Christian cosmology of figures that break apart the human/nonhuman binary. The novel's ending queers the human's boundaries and upends the normative model of the kill in which the buck is easily brought back to camp, strung up, and consumed. Instead, the boy inhabits the buck's body, becomes one with it, and imagines his own non/human transformation from within the flesh. Cohen theorizes the "monster" as a kind of "becoming," because they are "our children": our projections and creations.[22] Vann literalizes the monster as the child who the older men cannot quite fathom because he is both their creation and their queer nightmare.

Goat Mountain is an extension of the mythic imagination in which the non/human is everywhere. In its emphasis on the complications of hunting, in which everything and anything can suddenly become prey (regardless of species distinction), Vann's novel shows how the human and nonhuman are never separable, entangled at the level of the body, and always open to corporeal shifts. When any human can be hunted like a buck—not simply an animalized human but an animal like any other—the dynamics of species differentiation and hierarchy are skewered. When the hunt is gendered such that masculinity comes apart at the seams when the hunt goes "awry" (is queered, in a way), then hunting is as much about the kill as it is defending and reinforcing patriarchal norms. *Goat Mountain*, in its dark confrontation of family, species, and gender, teases out some of the ways that hunting is central to normative models of life and death.

V

Before moving to the final example in this chapter, which thinks hunting more queerly, it is worth pressing upon the notion of which animals might be protected and which are not. In the title story of Tom Franklin's collection *Poachers* (1999), three young poor white brothers, living in rural Alabama, are brought into contact with game wardens, who maintain the boundaries of un/killable life in the sweltering waterways. The Gates brothers are left orphans after their parents die and are partially raised by others in the community, including Kirxy, who owns the local store. He teaches them "fishing, tracking, hunting, killing," but the boys spend their lives, as the title suggests, *poaching*.[23] The difference being, of course, the killing of nonhuman animals "unlawfully."

Not only do the brothers trespass certain killing codes, but they themselves are figured animalistically, minimized in a species hierarchy of this landscape. To the local Black community, they are the kind of white person "not seen often": "nocturnal and dangerous" (130). As threatening predators, the boys slink in the darkness, much like the creatures they try to kill. Their world is inundated by death too. The floor of their truck, for instance, is saturated by nonhuman detritus: It is "tarry black from the blood of all the animals they'd killed," with bits of "teeth, feathers, and fur" sticking out (150). Over the oldest brother's shoulders are a skinned faun and a skinned dog, which are "difficult to tell apart" (129). Here, Franklin begins to show the ways that bodies, beneath the fur, are potentially indistinguishable: Lives blur together. As the story develops, a game warden finds the boys where they should not be, and they end up killing him. This is the first death where poaching and killing crosses species lines. From there, the brothers are picked off one by one—possibly by another warden or perhaps locals—and their deaths stack up.[24] The youngest boy remains alive but blind as someone sprays him with water moccasin venom. The brothers are hunted under the cover of night, just as they had illegally hunted wild animals.

The story ultimately asks what kinds of lives are worth living, which are protected (either by official law or by the invisible laws of sociality). Kirxy, reflecting on the boys' deaths and the possibility that the new warden might be responsible, thinks about how this man's job was "to protect the wild things the law had deemed worthy. Deer and turkeys. Alligators" (168). But given the way that the Gates brothers are so easily cast away, he wonders if the boys fell "into the category of trash animal—wildcats or possums or armadillos, snapping turtles, snakes?" Trash animals are those you can "kill any time, run over in your truck and not even look at it in your mirror to see [it] dying behind you." Franklin's character acknowledges a species hierarchy (those nonhumans that might be protected and those that remain throwaway) but folds the boys into it too. Kirxy notes that the new warden "was exactly the same as them" (169), as disposable as a possum.

Though hunting has produced questions for us about the kinds of animals that might be tracked and killed—human or otherwise—poaching has revealed other tensions within the kill/be killed dichotomy. If some kills are licensed and even encouraged, and some are prohibited, which social powers make and enforce such distinctions? What happens, Franklin's story suggests, when the humans doing the poaching are no more valued or acknowledged by society as the carcasses that line the bed of their truck? The final section of this chapter picks up some of these questions in a queerer framework.

VI

Because Ocean Vuong's *On Earth We're Briefly Gorgeous*—which appears often in this bestiary—is so suffused with non/human connections, it inevitably thinks about hunting in a number of ways. In the novel, hunting is linked to ideas of freedom and captivity, which are enmeshed with gender, race, and sexuality. The book opens, as explored in the "Taxidermy" chapter, with a spectacle of death. The protagonist Little Dog and his mother look at a taxidermized buck and consider its abject interruption into daily life. Little Dog reflects, too, on the letter he is writing (the novel we read) and thinks about how he could possibly "break free" from all that has curtailed him: memory, homophobia, anti-Asian racism, family. Yet freedom, he says, "is nothing but the distance between the hunter and its prey," a dark acknowledgment that liberty and independence are merely transitory and bounded concepts, for the prey is always captured.[25] We see this non/human bind between the hunted and the hunter throughout the book—first, in relation to the Vietnam War memories of Lan (Little Dog's grandmother), and the intertwined story of a macaque being eaten; then in relation to the refusal of Trevor (Little Dog's love interest) to eat veal; and, linked to that, Little Dog's sexual submission. In each, hunter and hunted are understood across species lines especially as those lines are freighted with questions of gender, sexuality, and race.

In an early scene, we witness a tangle of two memories from the Vietnam War: of a woman and girl (who we take to be Lan holding Rose) standing in the rain at a guarded checkpoint, trying to get back to their village; and, "as legend has it," a scene where a group of soldiers drink in a dingy garage, somewhere in the countryside (36).[26] That notion of "legend" only serves to underscore how detached Lan is from her memories, which are then in turn filtered through Little Dog—the past is multiply estranged through both trauma and the act of secondary witnessing/narrating. As Jennifer Cho writes, Lan's PTSD "ignite[s] both spatial and temporal disorientation," where past and present, Vietnam and the United States, "either muddle or collapse," but these memories also become, in a way, Little Dog's, as he narrates them in a third-person voice. The Vietnam War, Cho suggests, is released "from temporal and narrative fixity" in this novel,[27] because, as Little Dog notes, "We travel through time in a circular trajectory" (27). Lan's memorative blurring of two events—which are subsequently retied by Little Dog's narration—connects her return home with the violent consumption of a macaque by the soldiers in the garage. The precarity of both is heightened by their enmeshment.

A macaque "the size of a dog" is brought into the garage "with collar and leash" (38), a description that connotatively ties this abused creature to Little Dog himself. The monkey is strapped beneath a table with his head emerging from a hole in the center. The cross-cutting of this scene with Lan at the checkpoint suggests a relationship between the vulnerable young women during war and the monkeys, both a racialized and gendered link that does not make them equivalent but *relatedly* vulnerable to hunters. As the soldier at the checkpoint intimidates Lan, so too do the soldiers "cut open the macaque's skull . . . like a lid" (41). They eat the macaque's brain while it "kicks beneath them," still alive during the torture. The men do so because they believe it will "rid them of impotence, that the more the monkey rages, the stronger the cure." In consuming the monkey, the men are able to go and "press themselves against their wives and lovers" and have sex (whether consensual or not). The men eat "until the animal is empty, the monkey slowing as they spoon" (43), as if to ensure that all its liveliness is passed on. Lan, in this moment, also pees herself through fear, demonstrating corporeal affinities with the macaque's dissembling body.

By braiding this story of consumption and sexual im/potency with the intimidation of Lan, Vuong links the treatment of humans and nonhumans especially at the site of gendering. The men feel themselves to be emasculated if they cannot impose themselves on women; they work this out *through* the nonhuman animal for its proximity to animacy and vitality. Little Dog tells us that the macaque brain "is the closest, of any animal, to a human's" (41), as if to underscore both non/human inseparability but also a kind of speciesist logic in which if it is possible to torture and consume a monkey, it is also easy to devalue humans. As Vuong notes in an interview with the *LA Times*, "No wonder we would bomb children, because we are a species that would torture an animal like that."[28] Hunters will not stop with nonhumans, Vuong's novel suggests, because to hunt is to dominate, and the domination of one species enables or licenses the domination of another, especially when distilled in the fragilities of male (hetero)sexuality.

Such vulnerability is picked up elsewhere in the novel as Trevor, Little Dog's lover, refuses to eat veal. Little Dog refers to Trevor as his "all-American beef but no veal" (158), both in reference to Trevor's aversion to the meat, but also an acknowledgment of Trevor's transition into manhood. As all-American beef—a heteronormative imagining of white, cis, blue-collar straight masculinity—Trevor is mythologized and nationalized against Little Dog's queer Vietnamese American otherness. Trevor is a kind of purebred. In Vuong's fragmented chapter, where lines and paragraphs run on as if in enjambment (it is almost poetry), Trevor's inner world is made vivid through Little Dog's language. After they have sex (which I will come to) Trevor must, as all-American beef, deny queerness: "*I am not // a faggot. Am I? Am I? Are you?*" Little Dog casts him as "Trevor the hunter," "carnivore," and "redneck," not a "fruit or fairy." Trevor is a "meateater," as though the consumption of nonhuman animals is a sign of straightness and masculinity, or a denial of "faggotry" (155).[29] Notable here, though, is that Trevor is ambiguously both hunter and hunted, meat and meat eater.

Trevor's refusal to consume veal comes to the fore when he finds out they are "the children" (155). That humanized word, children, links calves to human children, perhaps like himself, as things to be hunted and consumed. As he is pressured into a masculine form by his father—like the boy in *Goat Mountain*—so Trevor sees the killing of calves as a symbolic and literal violence against perceived innocence. The calves are "locked in boxes the size of themselves. A body-box, like a coffin, but alive, like a home." Veal, in this imaginary, is curtailed by the kind of death-in-life that we see in taxidermy. Moreover, the narration goes on, the calves "stand very still because tenderness depends on how little the world touches you. To stay tender, the weight of your life cannot lean on your bones" (156). If Trevor and the veal are twinned in this scene it is because he cannot face identification with the calf, with the possibility of being made vulnerable to killing. Yet the calf is also protected from life's cruelties—something that Trevor is not—to keep it *tender*. This entanglement of life and death, child and adult, hunter and hunted, is such that Vuong wants us to see vulnerability as mutually informing across species lines. Trevor (and, by extension, Little Dog) is positioned as veal, ripe for death, while also refused the limited and temporary protections that the veal status brings. The young men are rendered fleshy but are not immune to the "weight of [their] life." Vuong's enlacing of species and species *positions*—physical, social, political—is part of the book's project of ensuring that the slash in *non/human* is ever fungible.

The third hunter-hunted dynamic I want to explore here is how the novel extends the veal analogy into Little Dog and Trevor's sexual relationship as a way of figuring questions of species and queerness. The first time that they engage bodily, Trevor thrusts into Little Dog's hand from behind, as a proxy for anal sex. We will return to the second of these hand-sex scenes in which the power roles are amplified. But for now, it is worth noting that in most of their sexual experiences, Little Dog bottoms and Trevor tops. When they try the hand-sex again, Trevor tries to be in the "bottom" position, but he panics because he does not "wanna feel like a girl. Like a bitch. . . . It's not for me. . . . It's for you. Right?" (120). Trevor conforms to the idea that bottoming in a white patriarchal culture is marked, in Nguyen Tan Hoang's words, "by feminization and emasculation," where emasculation occurs because to bottom is in this mind-frame to be dominated, and to be dominated is a feminine position, and to be feminine is to be weaker.[30] Being a "girl" and a "bitch"—the latter, as we see in the "Dog" chapter, linking bitch-ness to feminine diminishment—is forced onto Little Dog, as it is "for [him]" and not Trevor.[31] *For you* suggests that Trevor can "disidentify the 'faggot' he perceives himself to be, instead projecting those failures onto Little Dog," as Cho explains.[32]

Little Dog's bottoming is caught up in a nest of associations that in turn become linked to the veal: He first inhabits the bottom position, then becomes more submissive, then feels bodily shame when they have anal sex. Let us walk slowly through these associations and how they are weaved into questions of the hunter/hunted at the site of queer sexuality. When Trevor and Little Dog have their hand-sex the second time, Trevor suddenly and without precedent pulls Little Dog's hair (117). While shocked, Little Dog encourages Trevor to pull harder: "He lifted me nearly off the bed by the roots of my follicles. With each light slam, a light turned off and on inside me" (118). Turning off and on is sexually coded and points to the simultaneous enhancement and negation of the self in this masochistic position. Little Dog's role is then described to us in nonhuman (and hunting) terms: "What do you call the animal that, finding the hunter, offers itself to be eaten? A martyr? A weakling? No, a beast gaining the rare agency to stop" (118). In one sense, then, to be a bottom, to be submissive, to withstand pain, is to be a hunted animal with power. It is to inhabit a non/human position with a kind of "agency" unlike many other hunted creatures.

This view of bottoming and submission accords with queer and queer of color theories of sex/uality. For Leo Bersani, reading Freud and Jean Laplanche, "sexuality . . . may be a tautology for masochism" because sexuality "shatters" the self beyond a "threshold of endurance."[33] In other words, sex/uality is always masochistic in its relationship to power and pain, and the queer sex Little Dog embraces exemplifies that. We might tie such corporeal dissolution to the novel's critique and undoing of human exceptionalism. For Ariane Cruz, Black women's engagement with BDSM (submission in particular) can be critical for understanding those women's agency and pleasure in part through interrogating historical racialized and gendered scripts of violence, passivity, and the body, from slavery onwards.[34] In Cruz's view, unpacking BDSM's relationship to race and gender can reveal some of the *binds* of power that can be rethought and reimagined through its practice. For Little Dog, submission is "also a kind of power," where he can be "fucked up, at last, by choice" (119). As he is "fucked up" in all other areas of life, in this domination/submission dynamic with Trevor, he can explore it on his own terms. He refigures the hunter/hunted dynamic through an embrace of sexual undoing.

A later scene finds Trevor and Little Dog having anal sex on the dirt floor of a barn. The tableaux, already animalized, sees Little Dog bear further the pain of bottoming and its associated position: "a strange ache, a weightless numbness" (202), in which the self is subsumed or traversed. Little Dog quotes Simone Weil: "*Perfect joy excludes even the very feeling of joy, for in the soul filled by the object, no corner is left for saying 'I'*" (202). With the "I" disintegrated, as in Bersani's psychoanalytically inflected version of anal sex, Little Dog intellectually and emotionally explores what Avgi Saketopoulou calls "limit consent," which, far from the usual paradigms of consent as maintaining control, is more about "surrendering *to* an other [during sex] or, more precisely, with surrendering to the opacity in the other [and] . . . in ourselves." Such opacity appears in the top/bottom dynamic because with limit consent "power is not dichotomously apportioned" but rather "power, vulnerability, and responsibility are more complexly distributed" between people and "in the texture of their encounter."[35] Little Dog and Trevor's play of power—hunter/hunted, top/bottom, white/Asian American, large/small, active/passive—is about surrendering to the other and to the self.

Little Dog's taking of Trevor, in all its pain, is also what Hoang calls "bottomhood." Bottomhood for Asian American men, Hoang writes, "complicates the links between the bottom position and Oriental passivity," which is a long-standing set of problematic associations, and helps to critique and refigure subjectivity that ties together race, gender, and sexuality within certain positions. Bottomhood's position—literal and figurative—can scramble such identity binds and "rewrites abject masculinity without writing off femininity and the feminine" (by theorizing bottomhood as somehow more "manly," in its withstanding of "pain," as various queer critics have done). Little Dog's bottomhood both engages and resists Trevor's figuration of him as the weaker, feminized part of the couple; it "reveals an inescapable exposure, vulnerability, and receptiveness" of being with another, especially as that exposure is figured across non/human lines;[36] and it gives Little Dog a complicated kind of power (the power to relinquish) that is intimately connected to his race, gender, and sexuality.

Yet the sex scene is complicated further, in a few more imaginative twists, when Little Dog realizes that, because he did not know that he should prepare for the sex act, he can smell his own feces. The scent, "strong and deep, like soil, but sharp with flaw" (203), links this bodily occurrence to the soil as both an earthly, natural substance and the soiling of one's body. Little Dog experiences his body as being "inside out" (203), as more naked than simply being unclothed. Where bottomhood "requires not only conscious control but also a letting go," Little Dog's body literally does that.[37] Though this site of intense vulnerability is common to bottoming, it can also be marked by shame, by a fear that the loss of control reaches apotheosis in this sense of bodily fluids. Worried about what happened, Little Dog thinks that Trevor will be violent toward him, and he even mishears Trevor's sensitivity as an attack. Inhabiting the queerly marked bottom position—"I had tainted him with my faggotry, the filthiness of our act exposed by my body's failure to contain itself" (203)—Little Dog reaffirms his assumed less-than and dehumanized position.[38] Yet, surrounded by the countryside at night (they hear crickets and see moths, are part of the nonhuman world), the two bathe in the river, and rather than lash out at Little Dog (as he expects), Trevor is tender and comforting. The story Little Dog spins about his shame is not met by Trevor's ostensible rough masculinity. Indeed, once "clean," Trevor rims Little Dog, as he has done before, as if this *eating out* is the "hunter's" continued consumption of the hunted, where the hunted wants and desires that self-abnegation.

A final non/human moment in the novel I want to look at that ties hunter and hunted, occurs after the sex, as Little Dog reflects on Trevor's relation to veal. He thinks "of freedom again, how the calf is most free when the cage opens and it's led to the truck for slaughter. All freedom is relative . . . and sometimes it's no freedom at all, but simply the cage widening far away from you, the bars abstracted with distance but still there, as when they 'free' wild animals into nature preserves only to contain them yet again by larger borders" (216).

Little Dog theorizes freedom as always provisional and "relative," not a fixed state but a situation in flux. Freedom for the calf is a mirage: What looks like freedom is the precursor to its violent and deathly opposite. Similarly, when nonhuman animals are released into wildlife preserves, they are made free but within certain strictures. Human curtailment is ever-present when it comes to potential nonhuman freedom.

It is telling that Little Dog reflects in this way just after his and Trevor's transformative sex acts. He thinks, "For a few delirious moments in the barn . . . the cage around me became invisible, even if I knew it was never gone" (216), an acknowledgment of Little Dog's confinement (in history, in family, in racism and heteronormativity) and possible liberation from it enabled by sex. As he loses a sense of himself—self-shattering that becomes bodily evacuation—he is momentarily freed from the bindings of identity and its historical trappings. Little Dog even links that moment of corporeal shame during anal sex to the calf's final moment: "When the calves are finally butchered, surrendering their insides is often their final act, their bowels shocked from the sudden velocity of endings" (216). As the calf's life ends because they are killed for food, so they actively surrender their insides as if in a kind of offering. In this way, Little Dog is twinned with the calf up for slaughter, free inasmuch as they are no longer held captive. If, as Hoang writes, identifying with bottomhood is simultaneously a disidentification with it (in José Esteban Muñoz's formulation), here Little Dog enters the space of the hunted, the captured, the killed in his position as bottom with Trevor.[39]

Vuong braids non/human positions of hunter and hunted, powerful and powerless, so that the binaries begin to warp. When Saketopoulou describes limit consent as an uneven and oscillating distribution of power between parties within sexual scenes, she also sheds light on the hunter/hunted paradigm as depicted in Vuong's novel. As queerly entangled, the novel's depiction of hunting is not simply about power's unidirectional force but also about the "velocity of endings" brought about in its wake. Little Dog's hunger to be captured is not the same kind of capture we saw with the macaque or even the calves: It is a space of desire in which to be captured is to be undone, relinquished from the self that is *itself* an entrapment. Identity's strictures are for a moment held open by the hunter/hunted dynamic that does not end in literal death but does end in the death of something like sovereignty. I am not suggesting that Vuong is *equating* queer bottomhood with the position of the nonhuman animal (the veal, the macaque) as if that positioning is something to be reclaimed or celebrated. The nonhumans in this book are not just metaphors for understanding human life. Rather, by enfolding the hunter/hunted dynamic into the story of queer desire, transgenerational haunting, and transnational memory, Vuong shows how enlaced the violence done to all kinds of non/humans is. That violence is differentially distributed and potentially reworked, but it is nonetheless enlaced.

VII

Hunting narratives in contemporary U.S. fiction, then, reveal not only the precariousness of the hunter's world (they are not as powerful as they think, they can easily be made the hunted themselves) but also the deep entwinement of hunter and hunted. Rather than a one-way power dynamic, the hunter-hunted duo is an enmeshed set of positions and orientations, undoing and destabilizing the definitions of human/nonhuman. To tie this chapter together, it is worth turning back to Franklin's *Poachers* for the way he imagines poaching not simply in the content of his stories but in their form too. In the preface to the book, he writes, "I've never lost the need to tell of my Alabama, to reveal it, lush and green and full of death. So I return, knowing what I've learned. I come back, where life is slow dying, and I poach for stories. I poach because I want to recover the paths while there's still time, before the last logging trucks rumble through and the old, dark ways are at last forever hewn" (16).

There is much to note here, from the "death"-saturated state of Franklin's mind ("*my* Alabama"); the "return" to this landscape (akin to Vann and Jones's hunters); and the "poaching" of stories, where to hunt the world for narrative is of pressing concern while there's "still time." As the logging trucks disappear—the roads, the industry, and the attendant jobs—so too do the stories that emerge from them. Similarly, as Tom in *Goat Mountain* notes early on, as they try to drive across the mountain amid falling scree, in a "few years, won't be a road here anymore" (9). The landscapes these narratives chart are changing or vanishing, an (old) world of hunting and poaching that will be no longer. Such stories are melancholic for a kind of traditional order—both rooted, as we have seen, in heteropatriarchy—and gesture toward a world coming apart, without quite naming climate change or global warming, or the human causes of environmental collapse. (The final chapter of this book, "Extinction," takes this argument further.)

In this way, Vann's narrator, and Franklin as author, both *look back* at the past, at a time of ostensible hunting prolificacy, and *poach* from that past. They hunt a world now gone, however problematically invested in species hierarchy it is. Conversely, in Jones's novel, hunting becomes a ghostly revenge plot. The elk head woman speaks not only to nonhuman revenge against the men that killed her and her unborn baby but also other kinds of violences against Indigenous women and girls. Hunting stories exceed the simple expected binary that the act sets up. Similarly, Vuong's novel, in its queer imagining of sex, memory, history, and non/human entanglement, suggests that seeing the hunt as not simply a human act but a cross-species one that we are all susceptible to, might enliven and enlarge our scope to imagine corporeality anew. Figuring the messy interrelations of non/human hunting as queer—as disrupting identities, bodies, temporalities, forms—Vuong points to a planetary imaginary in which care for different species is at the bedrock of an environmental and queer politics.

NOTES

1. Burton and Mawani, "Introduction," 1.

2. Burton and Mawani, 8.

3. Go back to "Taxidermy" if you haven't already.

4. Traisnel, *Capture*, 7.

5. See, for instance: Potts, *Meat Culture* (2017), or McCorry and Miller's *Literature and Meat Since 1900* (2019), which both look at the ways that meat consumption and industry circulate in Western cultures.

6. We might think here about the wiping-out of bison by settlers throughout the period of westward expansion; something picked up in "Extinction."

7. Traisnel, *Capture*, 9, 8.

8. Traisnel, 10, 12, 13–14.

9. Burton and Mawani, "Introduction," 8.

10. Arnett, *Mostly*, 6.

11. Pexa, "Sovereign," 250, 248.

12. Jones, *The Only*, 349. Cited hereafter in text.

13. The prose is largely terse and plain, often stripped-back and colloquial.

14. Pexa, "Sovereign," 249.

15. Vann, *Goat*, 11. Cited hereafter in text.

16. At a book event I attended, Vann explained that he wrote the novel with the grammatical cadences and sentence structure of ancient Greek, as if to signal the novel's temporal strangeness and indebtedness to ideas of war, morality, family, gender, and so on.

17. Groes, "I love Alaska," 981.

18. Chapuis, "You Will Kill," 193.

19. Cohen, "Monster Culture," 45, 46, 41.

20. Alaimo, *Bodily Natures*, 2.

21. Chapuis, "You Will Kill," 200.

22. Cohen, "Monster Culture," 52

23. Franklin, "Poachers," 142. Cited hereafter in text.

24. Here we see another link to Jones' novel and Vann's. Hunting breeds more and more violence.

25. Vuong, *On Earth*, 4. Cited hereafter in text.

26. There are ways of seeing the memories of war here in light of Marita Sturken's formative *Tangled Memories* (1997). That book looks at the production of cultural memory—remembrance via cultural objects and texts—as entangled with historical discourse. Her examples are the AIDS crisis and the Vietnam War, a set of American and global phenomena that surely haunt Vuong's novel too.

27. Cho, "We Were Born," 138, 134.

28. Wolk, "When Everything," n.p.

29. Being a "faggot"—as we will shortly see—is part of "gay male bottomhood's social and historical adjacency with various techniques of gender dissidence." Hoang, *A View*, 194.

30. Hoang, *A View*, 4.

31. We might compare this version of faggotry with that offered by Danez Smith in their poem "on faggotness" from *Homie* (2020), a collection looked at briefly in the "Dog" chapter. In this prose poem, the speaker suggest that faggot "means different" (25); and is "not the sex. the being filled. but the emptiness. void you didn't know was" (27); and, later, is defined by specificity, "particular walk. particular wrist. particular speech," and so on (28). For Smith's speaker, the faggot is defined as much by an embodied difference or alterity as they are the absence of an identity. Where Little Dog is made a faggot through his sexual position—and attendant gendering and racialization—Smith's faggot is also positional but not because of any act.

32. Cho, "We Were Born," 143.

33. Bersani, "Is the Rectum," 24.

34. Cruz, *The Color*, 3.
35. Saketopoulou, *Sexuality*, 3, 65.
36. Hoang, *A View*, 2, 19.
37. Hoang, 15.
38. Cho, "We Were Born," 145.
39. Hoang, *A View*, 19.

EX TI NC TI ON

Extinction

what comes after the end(?)

I

Our escalating environmental crisis is having a direct effect on the rate and scope of species extinction, and the decline of biodiversity is clearly impacted by climate change. As Rebecca Solnit writes, "Biologists estimate that about 1.7 million species are known, but that there are between 10 and 100 million on earth. Our discovery and categorization of species increases at a manic rate, but so does the disappearance of both known and unknown species. More is known; there is less to know; we lose both what we know and what we don't. It is certain that species are vanishing without ever have been known to science."[1] In other words, species are becoming extinct before humans even know what those species are. Of course, we might ask whether a human's not knowing about a species means that said species' disappearance is more devastating than if we did. Why does it matter that we *know* all species before they potentially disappear? Is this not more anthropocentrism?

In this final part of the bestiary, I think extinction through a short series of fragments, theoretical interventions, and brief textual analyses. Given the extremities of extinction before us (those already passed, those ongoing, those to come), this chapter takes a few sideways looks at it in a mode more elliptical than the chapters preceding. The strangeness of medieval bestiaries—their idiosyncrasies, the particularities of their creators, the contexts in which they were made and read—should not be forgotten, and I want to gesture to some of that quirkiness here. As we have seen, the urge to taxonomize always falls apart; nonhuman after nonhuman has resisted (or tried to resist) the human grasp, whether through simple understanding and description or through captivity. Of course, we have seen caged animals and dead animals, but the human desire to trap and define is an endlessly slippery enterprise. With that impulse in mind, we will move through a series of short queries into the ends of things.

II

In Dominic O'Key's words, the "sixth mass extinction" is, unlike others in the planet's history, "attributed to the agency of humans, or more accurately to the agency of nonhuman processes set in motion by humans, particularly the technologies of industrial capitalism and globalization."[2] The sixth mass extinction is a "widespread and rapid decline in biological and cultural diversity, a dramatic drop-off in relation to the earth's geological time." And while "planetary life has . . . never not been in a time of extinctions," we are now facing a sixth ongoing event that is unlike the others.[3] There are extinctions of other human forms too, like languages, institutions, customs, practices, cultures, and so on, that require our attentions.[4]

III

The wealth of material in extinction studies—a braided set of disciplines and approaches—is too vast to summarize here, yet a few strands are notable.

As the Extinction Studies Working Group argues, an interdisciplinary approach to extinction is vital. Extinction studies says that there is "no singular phenomenon of extinction," as it is seen, felt, lived, and narrated in so many ways.[5] These scholars look to the "storytelling" mode because narrative—unlike in other disciplinary frames—can "allow multiple meanings to travel alongside one another."

Yet, O'Key argues, extinction studies renders extinction a "polysemous if not overdetermined concept." It sees extinction as both "biocultural" (its "causes and impacts are at once natural and social"), and "natural-historical" ("a social and economic articulation of a previously organic process"). As such, the multiplicity of readings of extinction—indeed their proliferations—require us to be "vigilant about not sliding into the reductivism of flat ontology (humans are just an agent among other agents) nor Anthropocene chauvinism (humans are the only agent)." The kinds of stories told about extinction are central to the way we figure it both in scientific and popular discourse.[6]

Ursula K. Heise, for instance, thinks about how "biodiversity, endangered species, and extinction are primarily cultural issues, questions of what we value and what stories we tell, and only secondarily issues of science." Thus, while environmentalists might invest much in nonhuman longevity, "their engagements with these species gain sociocultural traction to the extent that they become part of the stories that human communities tell about themselves."[7]

Hannah Stark similarly argues that an attention to the memorial cultures of extinction reveal the general public's attitudes toward species (and other) loss.[8]

Thom van Dooren looks to the entanglements of human and avian extinction stories to ask what is "lost when a species, an evolutionary lineage, a way of life, passes from the world? What does this loss mean within the particular multispecies community in which it occurs: a community of humans and nonhumans, of the living and the dead?"[9]

Literary responses to climate change (in the form of "cli-fi") are, for Jonathan Elmore, symptoms of the "human need to speculatively imagine ways to survive the changes we see around us every day."[10]

Yet, as Sarah E. McFarland notes, we need fiction that imagines "the potential of human species extinction" so that the "impulse of human exceptionalism" does not dominate the extinction imaginary.[11]

IV

Yet, of course, the sixth mass extinction is not new to some humans on the planet. As Indigenous scholars Daryl Baldwin, Margaret Noodin, and Bernard C. Perley argue, they have each had to "deal with human activities that contribute to the extinction, endangerment, and misrepresentation of their languages, cultures, and communities. The 'sixth extinction' has a start date for native North America: October 12, 1492," when Columbus initiated a series of genocidal acts.[12] (The authors similarly take the language and terminology of "extinction" to task, for its invasion into Native worlds).

Put another way, Nicholas Mirzoeff asks what kind of "man" is inferred in the Anthropocene. Which humans are central to that new geological age? In his words, it's more accurately called the "white supremacy scene," rather than what might more abstractly be called the Capitalocene.[13] If the Anthropocene "began with a massive colonial genocide," the roots of this mass extinction are not solely the webs of power and profit at the heart of capitalism's mechanics. Rather, extinction is imbricated—as seen elsewhere in this bestiary—in the tangled webs of making certain lives and forces valuable, livable, or seen as lives in the first place.

V

O'Key, in writing about how extinction is approached, offers a critique of this very bestiary's method and form. In asking what researchers can do in the face of species extinction, he asks whether the writer's "lively encounters with particular creatures, vividly described in a deliberately engaging academic prose" is enough. The "multispecies ethics" that many extinction studies scholars reach for, O'Key argues, hinges upon "a situated encounter with the other," but a major problem with this approach is that it will "miss out on all those species that cannot be encountered." Indeed, if the stance of nonhuman witnessing—rooted in a Levinasian mode of seeing the Other—"requires a spatial or even epistemic proximity between the human and the nonhuman," there is a problem when that proximity is foreclosed. More particularly, O'Key argues that the mode I could be accused of trafficking in—"knowing more about other critters' lives by 'thickening' our sense of their presence and vitality through description"—is a failure of cross-species ethics because it individualizes the human-nonhuman encounter and thus "elides the important material conditions that must change if we are to stymie biocultural losses."[14]

While I have tried to attend to the "thickening" of nonhuman lives in literary texts, I do not see that move as limiting one's approach to understanding them and their material conditions. Admittedly, the purpose of this book is not to offer the same kind of ethical injunctions as other extinction studies scholars, but O'Key's critique is a useful one to linger on at the end of this bestiary. What does an individual process of "knowing" nonhumans and their environments through description do for the planet? What systemic and material change can be accomplished through careful attention to nonhumans?

VI

As explored in "Mountain Lion," Henry Hoke's *Open Throat* figures the interrelations of human and nonhuman in Los Angeles. The queer mountain lion at its heart is enmeshed in the world of humans (sex, identity, power) against the backdrop of environmental destabilization. From the start, the lion notes, "things are changing" (9): Their habitat (and the planet) are altering for the worse. As their perilous journey down from the Hollywood Hills into the city reaches its conclusion, the lion reflects briefly on a world without humans. When the night was quiet, in their cave they "could almost imagine that all the people were gone," that the canyons were "cleared" and the freeways would be "standing still." The mountain lion imagines "original smells" returning, and "returning what's needed" (149).

This scene stages the world after humans and after rewilding has taken place; it configures the city back to a pre-human (or at least pre–white Western human) time. The lion's final image is of all the animals walking off together into a new Los Angeles, one that matches what Claire Colebrook and Jami Weinstein posit as a radically posthuman imaginary: "*post*human time, a world without and after humans."[15] This is one mountain lion's romantic vision of the planet that groups all humans together (under the sign of Man) as a singular force for trouble. The novel snaps us out of this reverie, however, as the mountain lion attempts to kill a human and the book abruptly ends. A future just for the nonhuman animals remains a dream.

VII

Perhaps there are parts of American culture that could or should go extinct? Not animals of all kinds, or natural forms, or ecologies, but some of the human-made (Man-made) structures that cause, exacerbate, and sustain extinctive processes. Could we lose heterosexism, cissexism, racism, transphobia, ableism, classism? What would the dissolution and extinction of these violent forms look like? Could they ever go extinct, while humans remain fixed on their stable categories? As Marquis Bey argues, "we must let go, yes, of the things we hold so dearly—of our 'race,' of our 'gender,' of our 'humanity'—because those things were imposed, violently, nonconsensually, and in fact impede our ability to come together."[16] Bey's argument, rooted in Black and trans and feminist theorizing, suggests that identitarian categories are the groupings that stand in the way of any truly liberatory politic. It is identity's fixity, rigidity, essentialism, that stands in our way because it was not made by "us." I can hear so many responses to Bey's argument, which argues for the necessity and power of identity formation—of a politics and aesthetics rooted in shared, or at least overlapping, areas of our lives (race, gender, sexuality) and the social positionality that follows—but at the same time, Bey's point is that some of the things that offer us assurances about our humanness are the things that we might most readily slough off.

What other human-made structures, forms, institutions, imaginaries, spaces, violences, and world-making habits might a queer vision want to see go extinct?

VIII

In C. Pam Zhang's *Land of Milk and Honey* (2023), climate change is ravaging the planet, and in this near-future an unnamed narrator is whisked from a smog-filled city (where she is a chef) to a mountaintop resort, high above the clouds. In this protected world of the mega-rich, the narrator cooks all kinds of animals that have ceased to exist in the normal world. Down there, agriculture and farming are dwindling. The queer mixed-race narrator is tangled up with her employer's sexually ambiguous daughter and the family's strange power plays. But the book asks various questions about life after the "end of the world" (if only for some people).

In the mountain resort's laboratories, the narrator witnesses a "de-extinction, . . . life streaming back to its source." Rather than the depopulated world below her, the wealthy live in a haven where Tasmanian tigers, for instance, are birthed by scientists. Similarly, golden chimps are brought back from the brink of extinction. But it is here that the novel stages further questions about the viability of life (at the end of the world). While the scientists and the narrator's employer want to move from this location, the chimps are "deemed insufficiently hardy, useful, or nutritious enough."[17] The scientists set dogs on the chimps (holding "them down with soft mouths") until they are wiped out. When the narrator confronts her overseers with this catastrophe—"*You hunted a species to extinction,*" she says—the answer is that they were "*poised for extinction before we bred them*" anyway.[18] The narrator is accused of piousness and of selective care for nonhumans (after all, she is a chef who has cooked and eaten meat): "*As if you never ate tuna, or used plastics, or flew on planes. . . . Every person on this planet had a hand in killing the chimps. . . . At least I gave the chimps a chance. I gave them the grandest of exits.*"[19] While this point of view is not entirely incorrect, the grandiosity of this enforced extinction seems, for Zhang, to point to a broader point about human exceptionalism. In this novel, the fates of all species—non/human—are in the hands of the wealthy few.

Climate change, extinction, the Anthropocene—while each of these are attributed to *humans,* they might be more pertinently attributed to certain humans. Indigenous populations the world over, and in the Americas particularly, have lived carefully in relation to the land and its inhabitants. With a view to the future, to other generations and to other living (and non-living things), Indigenous communities are far from the drivers human-made climate change. Zhang's novel dramatizes the end of the planet and the ways it will be differentially felt and experienced, depending on one's social position. As a queer mixed-race woman "allowed" into this mountaintop haven, the narrator gets to see the workings of species normativity up close. By the novel's end, though, she is cast out of this warped world. A vision of the future will be striated, as our world is now, by markers of social inclusion and exclusion: Man and his others.

IX

It seems inevitable at this point that a queer bestiary entry about extinction should reckon with queer theory's near endless debates about temporality. I do not want to risk falling into these theoretical floodwaters with you, reader, especially at this late stage. If queerness can be located in the past, present, and future—as various parts of the queer canon will tell you—where does that leave us in terms of thinking extinction, catastrophe, and questions of a non/human future?

In *Strange Natures* (2013), Nicole Seymour parses out this dialogue between queer studies (in its most "anti-social" mask) and environmental studies, especially at the site of futurity. The antisocial thesis of queer studies rejects the teleology of respectable queerness, of homonormativity, of the social fabric as such. Embracing shame, failure, interruption, and negativity, the antisocial move rejects the terms of the social as always already figured in advance. Though, as Seymour puts it, "anti-sociality is central to many if not most forms of environmentalism, including ecocriticism," thus could align precisely with this turn.[20] Could we imagine the antisocial of queer studies as the antisocial turn of radical environmentalism that seeks to shatter, rearrange, and interrupt the present order of carbon capitalism?

Yet one key element of the antisocial thesis in queer studies is the critique and rejection of futurity, which Seymour sees as a key part of environmentalism's vision and politics. Epitomized by Lee Edelman's argument in *No Future* (2004), this refusal of futurity comes in the form of the Child, who is made into the figure of the future around whom politics and culture orient. For Edelman, the Child is the emblem of reproductive futurism because it is the "perpetual horizon for every political intervention"; there is no political position outside of "fighting for the children." If the Child is "the emblem of futurity's unquestioned value," then queerness—as structural negativity—is "the bar to every realization of futurity, the resistance, internal to the social, to every social structure or form." If the Child prescribes "what will *count* as political discourse" altogether, then the future is decided in advance.[21]

But for Seymour, *the future* is a key part of environmentalism, and Edelman's thesis "leaves no room for any consideration of futurity qua the planet and its resources." In other words, if queerness always rejects futurity because that futurity is bound up in the heteronormative Child, then how can queerness be on the side of environmentalism that needs to fight for a future planet? While Seymour says that "many queer theorists have reached a point at which they cannot imagine a queer futurity and, by extension, where they cannot imagine environmentalism, much less a queer one," there are some to whom I will turn shortly. Seymour argues that the antisocial vein of queer studies (perhaps not *the* form of queer theorizing now that it once was) fails to consider the ways that antiracist and environmentalist movements have embraced the future in the face of, and against, the reproductive logics of heterosexist capital. She cites Indigenous activists like Winona LaDuke, who sees "futurity as a necessary mindset," as "future-thinking and optimism are the means of changing" the systems of white heteropatriarchal energy cultures.[22] There are many ways, Seymour argues, that we can unhook the future and futurity from the normative Child and remake an environmental politics for a collective, non-hierarchical future that remains open.

Such an imagining of the future chimes with the work of José Esteban Muñoz, who argues in *Cruising Utopia* (2009) that the future is queerness's domain because queerness "is not yet here." As an "ideality," queerness is a "structuring and educated mode of desiring that allows us to see and feel beyond the quagmire of the present." In the present's delimiting of what is possible—the political that is already shaped for us, casting queers out—it is the future, contra Edelman, where "potentiality" and "possibility" for other worlds might be figured.[23] Put another way, at this bestiary's end, queer studies gestures both forward and back, to history and futurity. Depending on your critical orientation, queerness is the negativity that interrupts the future, or it is the future's domain entirely.

Whether the present or the future is the horizon for which an environmentalism fights, literary figurations of the non/human demand a nonnormative and queerer vision of species interrelation. Contemporary U.S. fiction does not offer a glance in any one direction, but in many directions at once. Queering our sense of species hierarchy, of human exceptionalism, of heteronormativity's prefiguring of "the human," and any sense of a strict boundary between humans and nonhumans is the only route out of our current quagmire. Fictions of non/human relation gestures to some of those journeys.

X

To close this bestiary is oxymoronic: One cannot close an open form. The non/human entanglements that precede this chapter have shown that lives and worlds and imaginaries and possibilities are flourishing in contemporary U.S. fiction. There are literary depictions of non/humans that point to generative and curtailed visions of multispecies life. This bestiary cannot and does not offer a singular view of twenty-first-century U.S. literature; rather it shows the proliferations of queerness—disorientations, remakings, destabilizations, negativities, nonnormativities—at the site of non/human mingling. At the end of the world, or with the extinction of species like our own, the future looks both known and unknown, imaginable and far outside our epistemological grasp. This bestiary, this temporary and particularized and limited archive, must necessarily be left open and unfinished. While we end on "Extinction," we are not confined to that future (or that past and present), but we do well to keep it in our sights.

NOTES

1. Solnit, *A Field Guide*, 187.
2. Grusin, "Introduction," viii.
3. O'Key, "Extinction," 169, 170.
4. Grusin, "Introduction," viii.
5. Bird Rose et al., "Introduction," 2–3.
6. O'Key, "Extinction," 168, 171, 172.
7. Heise, *Imagining*, 5.
8. Stark, "Reckoning."
9. van Dooren, *Flight Ways*, 4–5.
10. Elmore, "Introduction," 2–3.
11. McFarland, *Ecocollapse Fiction*, 3.
12. Baldwin et al., "Surviving," 203–4.
13. Mirzoeff, "It's Not the Anthropocene," 123; Moore, "The Capitalocene."
14. O'Key, "Extinction," 179, 180.
15. Colebrook and Weinstein, "Preface," x.
16. Bey, *Black*, 147.
17. Zhang, *Land of Milk*, 116, 157.
18. All quotes in italics in original.
19. Zhang, *Land of Milk*, 161.
20. Seymour, *Strange*, 6.
21. Edelman, *No Future*, 3, 4, 11.
22. Seymour, *Strange*, 7, 8, 9.
23. Muñoz, *Cruising Utopia*, 1.

Bibliography

Abdur-Rahman, Aliyyah I. *Against the Closet: Black Political Longing and the Erotics of Race*. Durham, NC: Duke University Press, 2012.

Ahmed, Sara. *Queer Phenomenology: Orientations, Objects, Others*. Durham, NC: Duke University Press, 2006.

Alaimo, Stacy. *Bodily Natures: Science, Environment, and the Material Self*. Bloomington: Indiana University Press, 2010.

———. "Eluding Capture: The Science, Culture, and Pleasure of 'Queer' Animals." In *Queer Ecologies: Sex, Nature, Politics, Desire*, edited by Catriona Mortimer-Sandilands and Bruce Erickson, 51–72. Bloomington : Indiana University Press, 2010.

Aloi, Giovanni. *Speculative Taxidermy: Natural History, Animal Surfaces, and Art in the Anthropocene*. New York: Columbia University Press, 2018.

Amin, Kadji. "Trans*Plasticity and the Ontology of Race and Species." *Social Text* 38, no. 2 (2020): 49–71.

Amin, Kadji, Amber Jamilla Musser, and Roy Pérez. "Queer Form: Aesthetics, Race, and the Violences of the Social." *ASAP/Journal* 2, no. 2 (2017): 227–39.

Anderton, Joseph. "Dogdom: Nonhuman Others and the Othered Self in Kafka, Beckett, and Auster." *Twentieth-Century Literature* 62, no. 3 (2016): 271–88.

Armstrong, Philip. *What Animals Mean in the Fiction of Modernity*. Abingdon: Routledge, 2008.

Arnett, Kristen. *Mostly Dead Things*. London: Corsair, 2020.

Baker, Timothy C. *Writing Animals: Language, Suffering, and Animality in Twenty-First-Century Fiction*. Cham: Palgrave Macmillan, 2019.

Baldwin, Daryl, Margaret Noodin, and Bernard C. Perley. "Surviving the Sixth Extinction: American Indian Strategies for Life in the New World." In *After Extinction*, edited by Richard Grusin, 201–34. Minneapolis: University of Minnesota Press, 2018.

Bennett, Jane. *Vibrant Matter: A Political Ecology of Things*. Durham, NC: Duke University Press, 2010.

Bennett, Joshua. *Being Property Once Myself: Blackness and the End of Man*. Cambridge, MA: Harvard University Press, 2020.

Berlant, Lauren. *On the Inconvenience of Other People*. Durham, NC: Duke University Press, 2022.

Bersani, Leo. "Is the Rectum a Grave?" In *Is the Rectum a Grave? and Other Essays*, 3–30. Chicago: University of Chicago Press, 2010.

Bey, Marquis. *Black Trans Feminism*. Durham, NC: Duke University Press, 2022.

Bezan, Sarah, and Susan McHugh. "Introduction: Taxidermic Forms and Fictions." *Configurations* 27, no. 2 (2019): 131–38.

Bhabha, Homi K. *The Location of Culture*. Abingdon: Routledge, 2004.

Bird Rose, Deborah, Thom van Dooren, and Matthew Chrulew. "Introduction: Telling Extinction Stories." In *Extinction Studies: Stories of Time, Death, and Generations*, edited by Deborah Bird Rose, Thom van Dooren, and Matthew Chrulew, 1–18. New York: Columbia University Press, 2017.

Boast, Hannah. "Theorizing the Gay Frog." *Environmental Humanities* 14, no. 3 (2022): 661–79.

Boast, Hannah, and Nicole Seymour. "Quarantining with *Tiger King*." In *Tiger King: Murder, Mayhem and Madness, A Docalogue*, edited by Jaimie Baron and Kristen Fuhs. Abingdon: Routledge, 2022.

Boggs, Colleen Glenney. *Animalia Americana: Animal Representations and Biopolitical Subjectivity*. New York: Columbia University Press, 2013.

Boisseron, Bénédicte. *Afro-Dog: Blackness and the Animal Question*. New York: Columbia University Press, 2018.

Booth, Allyson. "Thank You for Your Service: Negotiating the Civilian-Military Divide in Phil Klay's *Redeployment*." *Texas Studies in Literature and Language* 61, no. 2 (2019): 168–92.

Braidotti, Rosi. *The Posthuman*. Cambridge: Polity Press, 2013.

Burford, Benjamin P., and Bruce H. Robinson. "Bioluminescent Backlighting Illuminates the Complex Visual Signals of a Social Squid in the Deep Sea." *PNAS* 117, no. 5 (2020): 8524–31.

Burton, Antoinette, and Renisa Mawani. "Introduction: Animals, Disruptive Imperial Histories, and the Bestiary Form." In *Animalia: An Anti-Imperial Bestiary for Our Times*, edited by Antoinette Burton and Renisa Mawani, 1–16. Durham, NC: Duke University Press, 2020.

Butler, Judith. *Bodies That Matter: On the Discursive Limits of "Sex."* New York: Routledge, 1993.

———. *The Force of Nonviolence: An Ethico-Political Bind*. London: Verso, 2020.

———. *Frames of War: When is Life Grievable?* London: Verso, 2009.

———. *Notes Toward a Performative Theory of Assembly*. Cambridge, MA: Harvard University Press, 2015.

———. *Precarious Life: The Power of Mourning and Violence*. London: Verso, 2003.

Byrd, Jodi A. "Beast of America: Sovereignty and the Wildness of Objects." *South Atlantic Quarterly* 117, no. 3 (2018): 599–615.

Campbell, Neil. *Post-Westerns: Cinema, Region, West*. Lincoln: University of Nebraska Press, 2013.

———. *The Rhizomatic West: Representing the American West in a Transnational, Global, Media Age*. Lincoln: University of Nebraska Press, 2008.

Chang, K-Ming. *Bestiary*. London: Vintage, 2021.

Chapman, Chris, Allison C. Carey, and Liat Ben-Moshe. "Reconsidering Confinement: Interlocking Locations and Logics of Incarceration." In *Disability Incarcerated: Imprisonment and Disability in the United States and Canada*, edited by Liat Ben-Moshe, Chris Chapman, and Allison C. Carey, 3–24. New York: Palgrave Macmillan, 2014.

Chapuis, Sophie. "'You Will Kill': The Law of the Family in *Goat Mountain* by David Vann." In *Representing the Contemporary North American Family: Family Portraits*, edited by Sophie Chapuis and Marie Moreau, 190–203. Newcastle Upon Tyne: Cambridge Scholars, 2021.

Chen, Mel Y. *Animacies: Biopolitics, Racial Mattering, and Queer Affect*. Durham, NC: Duke University Press, 2012.

Cho, Jennifer. "'We Were Born from Beauty': Dis/Inheriting Genealogies of Refugee and Queer Shame in Ocean Vuong's *On Earth We're Briefly Gorgeous*." *MELUS: Multi-Ethnic Literature of the United States* 47, no. 1 (2022): 130–53.

Choi, Franny. "Turing Test_Boundaries." In *Soft Science*, 37. Farmington: Alice James, 2019.

———. "Turing Test_Love." In *Soft Science*, 69. Farmington: Alice James, 2019.

Clark, Will. "Tommy Pico's Fugitive Forms and the Poetics of Queer Indigenous Life." *ASAP/Journal* 7, no. 3 (2022): 523–49.

Clark, Willene B., and Meradith T. McMunn. "Introduction." In *Beasts and Birds of the Middle Ages: The Bestiary and Its Legacy*, edited by Willene B. Clark and Meradith T. McMunn, 1–11. Philadelphia: University of Pennsylvania Press, 1989.

Cohen, Cathy J. "Punks, Bulldaggers, and Welfare Queens: The Radical Potential of Queer Politics?" *GLQ: A Journal of Lesbian and Gay Studies* 3, no. 4 (1997): 437–65.

———. "The Radical Potential of Queer: Twenty Years Later." *GLQ: A Journal of Lesbian and Gay Studies* 25, no. 1 (2019): 140–44.

Cohen, Jeffrey Jerome. "Monster Culture (Seven Theses)." In *The Monster Theory Reader*, edited by Jeffrey Andrew Weinstock, 37–56. Minneapolis: University of Minneapolis Press, 2020.

Colebrook, Claire. "What Is It Like to Be a Human?" *TSQ: Transgender Studies Quarterly* 2, no. 2 (2015): 227–43.

Colebrook, Claire, and Jami Weinstein. "Preface: Postscript on the Posthuman." In *Posthumous Life: Theorizing Beyond the Posthuman*, edited by Jami Weinstein and Claire Colebrook, ix–xxix. New York: Columbia University Press, 2017.

Coole, Diana, and Samantha Frost, eds. *New Materialisms: Ontology, Agency, and Politics*. Durham, NC: Duke University Press, 2010.

Cruz, Ariane. *The Color of Kink: Black Women, BDSM, and Pornography*. New York: New York University Press, 2016.

Curry, Andrew. "Horse Nations." *Science* 379, no. 6639 (2023): 1288–93.

Cvetkovich, Ann. *An Archive of Feelings: Trauma, Sexuality, and Lesbian Public Cultures*. Durham, NC: Duke University Press, 2003.

Daulatzai, Sohail, and Junaid Rana. "Writing the Muslim Left: An Introduction to Throwing Stones." In *With Stones in Our Hands: Writings on Muslims, Racism, and Empire*, edited by Sohail Daulatzai and Junaid Rana, ix–xxiii. Minneapolis: University of Minnesota Press, 2018.

Dayan, Colin. *With Dogs at the Edge of Life*. New York: Columbia University Press, 2016.

Dean, Tim. *Unlimited Intimacy: Reflections on the Subculture of Barebacking*. Chicago: University of Chicago Press, 2009.

DeLaughrey, Elizabeth. "Submarine Futures of the Anthropocene." *Comparative Literature* 69, no. 1 (2017): 32–44.

Derrida, Jacques. *The Animal That Therefore I Am*. Edited by Marie-Louise Mallet, translated by David Wills. New York: Fordham University Press, 2008.

———. *Archive Fever: A Freudian Impression*. Translated by Eric Prenowitz. Chicago: University of Chicago Press, 1998.

DeVun, Leah. "Animal Appetites." *GLQ: A Journal of Lesbian and Gay Studies* 20, no. 4 (2014): 461–90.

———. *The Shape of Sex: Nonbinary Gender from Genesis to the Renaissance*. New York: Columbia University Press, 2020.

Dickel, Simon. *Embodying Difference: Critical Phenomenology and Narratives of Disability, Race, and Sexuality*. Cham: Palgrave Macmillan, 2022.

Dillon, Stephen. *Fugitive Life: The Queer Politics of the Prison State*. Durham: Duke University Press, 2018.

"DNA: Comparing Humans and Chimps." *American Museum of Natural History*, https://www.amnh.org/exhibitions/permanent/human-origins/understanding-our-past/dna-comparing-humans-and-chimps.

Doty, Mark. *Dog Years: A Memoir*. New York: HarperCollins, 2007.

Duck, Leigh Anne. *The Nation's Region: Southern Modernism, Segregation, and U.S. Nationalism*. Athens: University of Georgia Press, 2006.

Edelman, Lee. *No Future: Queer Theory and the Death Drive*. Durham, NC: Duke University Press, 2004.

Eils, Colleen G. "Deborah Miranda, Natalie Diaz, Tommy Pico, and Metaphors of Representation." *Studies in Indian American Literatures* 33, nos. 1–2 (2021): 82–100.

Ellis, Cristin. *Antebellum Posthuman: Race and Materiality in the Mid-Nineteenth Century*. New York: Fordham University Press, 2018.

Ellmann, Lucy. *Ducks, Newburyport*. Norwich: Galley Beggar Press, 2019.

Elmore, Jonathan. "Introduction: The Urgency of Story during the Sixth Mass Extinction." In *Fiction and the Sixth Mass Extinction: Narrative in an Era of Loss*, edited by Jonathan Elmore, 1–12. Lanham: Lexington, 2020.

Eng, David L. *Racial Castration: Managing Masculinity in Asian America*. Durham, NC: Duke University Press, 2001.

Eng, David L., Jack Halberstam, and José Estaban Muñoz. "What's Queer About Queer Studies Now?" *Social Text* 84–5, nos. 3–4 (2005): 1–17.

Eng, David L., and Jasbir K. Puar. "Introduction: Left of Queer." *Social Text* 38, no. 4 (2020): 1–24.

Everett, Percival. *The Book of Training by Colonel Hap Thompson of Roanoke, VA, 1843*. Pasadena: Red Hen Press, 2018.

———. "Little Faith." In *Half an Inch of Water*, 3–27. Minneapolis: Graywolf, 2015.

———. *Wounded*. London: Faber and Faber, 2008.

Fara, Patricia. *Sex, Botany, and Empire*. New York: Columbia University Press, 2004.

Feith, Michel. "Philosophy Embedded in Space: Rethinking the Frontier in Percival Everett's Western Novels." *African American Review* 52, no. 1 (2019): 87–100.

Ferguson, Donna. "Horses Can Plan Ahead and Think Strategically, Scientists Find."

Guardian, August 12, 2024. https://www.theguardian.com/science/article/2024/aug/12/horses-can-plan-ahead-and-think-strategically-scientists-find.

Finney, Nikky. "Introduction." In *Bestiary: Poems*, ix–xii. Minneapolis: Graywolf Press, 2016.

Flores, Nona C. "Introduction." In *Animals in the Middle Ages: A Book of Essays*, edited by Nona C. Flores, ix–xvi. New York: Garland, 1996.

Foucault, Michel. *The Will to Knowledge: The History of Sexuality, Volume 1*. Translated by Robert Hurley. London: Penguin, 1998.

Fraiman, Susan. "Pussy Panic Versus Liking Animals: Tracking Gender in Animal Studies." *Critical Inquiry* 39, no. 1 (2012): 89–115.

Frank, Erik T., Marten Wehrhahn, and K. Eduard Linsenmair. "Wound Treatment and Selective Help in a Termite-Hunting Ant." *Proceedings of the Royal Society B* 285, no. 1872 (2018). https://doi.org/10.1098/rspb.2017.2457.

Franklin, Tom. *Poachers*. London: Flamingo, 2000.

Freccero, Carla. "Death Do Us Part." In *Long Term: Essays on Queer Commitment*, edited by Scott Herring and Lee Wallace, 117–33. Durham, NC: Duke University Press, 2021.

Gaitskill, Mary. *Lost Cat*. London: Daunt Books, 2020.

———. *The Mare*. London: Serpent's Tail, 2017.

Giffney, Noreen, and Myra J. Hird. "Introduction: Queering the Non/Human." In *Queering the Non/Human*, edited by Noreen Giffney and Myra J. Hird, 1–16. Aldershot: Ashgate, 2008.

Gilbert, Sophie. "The Most-Watched Show in America is a Moral Failure." *The Atlantic*, April 7, 2020. https://www.theatlantic.com/culture/archive/2020/04/netflix-tiger-king-is-an-ethical-trainwreck/609568/.

Goldenberg, Shifra Z., and George Wittemyer. "Elephant Behavior Toward the Dead: A Review and Insights from Field Observations." *Primates* 61 (2020): 119–28.

Gopinath, Gayatri. *Unruly Visions: The Aesthetic Practices of Queer Diaspora*. Durham, NC: Duke University Press, 2018.

Greenwell, Garth. *Cleanness*. London: Picador, 2020.

Griffin, Matthew. *Hide*. London: Bloomsbury, 2017.

Groes, Sebastian. "'I Love Alaska': Posthuman Subjectivity and Memory on the Final Frontier of Our Ecological Crisis." *Textual Practice* 31, no. 5 (2017): 973–93.

Gruen, Lori. "Introduction." In *The Ethics of Captivity*, edited by Lori Gruen, 1–4. Oxford: Oxford University Press, 2014.

Grusin, Richard. "Introduction." In *After Extinction*, edited by Richard Grusin, vii–xix. Minneapolis: University of Minnesota Press, 2018.

Gumbs, Alexis Pauline. *Undrowned: Black Feminist Lessons from Marine Mammals*. Chico: AK Press, 2020.

Halberstam, Jack. *In a Queer Time and Place: Transgender Bodies, Subcultural Lives*. New York: New York University Press, 2005.

———. *Wild Things: The Disorder of Desire*. Durham, NC: Duke University Press, 2020.

Halberstam, Jack, and Tavia Nyong'o. "Introduction: Theory in the Wild." *South Atlantic Quarterly* 117, no. 3 (2018): 453–64.

Haraway, Donna J. "A Cyborg Manifesto: Science, Technology, and Socialist-Feminism in the Late Twentieth Century." In *Manifestly Haraway*, edited by Donna Haraway, 3–90. Minneapolis: University of Minnesota Press, 2016.

———. *When Species Meet*. Minneapolis: University of Minnesota Press, 2008.

Harris, Will. *Mixed-Race Superman*. London: Peninsula, 2018.

Hausman, Gerald. *Meditations with Animals: A Native American Bestiary*. Santa Fe: Bear and Company, 1986.

Hayles, N. Katherine. *How We Became Posthuman: Virtual Bodies, Cybernetics, Literature and Informatics*. Chicago: University of Chicago Press, 1999.

Hayward, Eva, and Che Gossett. "Impossibility of That." *Angelaki* 22, no. 2 (2017): 15–24.

Hayward, Eva, and Jami Weinstein. "Introduction: Tranimalities in the Age of Trans* Life." *TSQ: Transgender Studies Quarterly* 2, no. 2 (2015): 195–208.

Hearne, Vicki. *Adam's Task: Calling Animals by Name*. New York: SkyHorse, 2007.

Heise, Ursula K. *Imagining Extinction: The Cultural Meanings of Endangered Species*. Chicago: University of Chicago Press, 2016.

Henwood, Daisy. "Does Something Terrible Happen to the Dog?" *The Mechanics' Institute Review*, May 18, 2021. http://mironline.org/cnfthedog/.

Hird, Myra J. "Animal Transex." *Australian Feminist Studies* 21, no. 49 (2006): 35–50.

Hoang, Nguyen Tan. *A View from the Bottom: Asian American Masculinity and Sexual Representation*. Durham, NC: Duke University Press, 2014.

Hoke, Henry. *Open Throat*. London: Picador, 2023.

Holland, Sharon P. *An Other: A Black Feminist Consideration of Animal Life*. Durham, NC: Duke University Press, 2023.

———. "Vocabularies of Vulnerability." *Journal for Cultural Research* 22, no. 2 (2018): 204–8.

Houser, Heather. "Knowledge Work and the Commons in Barbara Kingsolver's and Ann Pancake's Appalachia." *MFS: Modern Fiction Studies* 63, no. 1 (2017): 95–115.

Imbler, Sabrina. *My Life in Sea Creatures*. London: Chatto & Windus, 2022.

Irr, Caren. "The Multispecies We: Democracy and Pronouns in the Environmental Novel." *American Literary History* 35, no. 1 (2023): 276–89.
Jackson, Zakiyyah Iman. *Becoming Human: Matter and Meaning in an Antiblack World*. New York: New York University Press, 2020.
———. "Outer Worlds: The Persistence of Race in Movement 'Beyond the Human.'" *GLQ: A Journal of Lesbian and Gay Studies* 21, no. 2–3 (2015): 215–18.
Jama-Everett, Ayize. "I'm Looking to Jump Ship Sooner Than I Should: A Conversation with Percival Everett." *LA Review of Books*, February 4, 2003. https://lareviewofbooks.org/article/im-looking-to-jump-ship-sooner-than-i-should-a-conversation-with-percival-everett/.
Johnson, Michael K. "Looking at the Big Picture: Percival Everett's Western Fiction." *Western American Literature* 42, no. 1 (2007): 26–53.
Jones, Stephen Graham. *The Only Good Indians*. London: Titan, 2020.
Julien, Claude. "The Real and the Unreal, or the Endogenous and the Exogenous: The Case of *Walk Me to the Distance* and *Wounded*." *Canadian Review of American Studies* 43, no. 2 (2013): 243–56.
Kahakauwila, Kristiana. *This Is Paradise*. London: Hogarth, 2013.
Kalof, Linda, ed. *The Oxford Handbook of Animal Studies*. Oxford: Oxford University Press, 2017.
Kapadia, Ronak K. *Insurgent Aesthetics: Security and the Queer Life of the Forever War*. Durham, NC: Duke University Press, 2019.
Keegan, Cáel M. "Getting Disciplined: What's Trans* About Queer Studies Now?" *Journal of Homosexuality* 67, no. 3 (2020): 384–97.
Kelly, Donika. "Love Letter." In *Bestiary: Poems*, 47. Minneapolis: Graywolf Press, 2016.
———. "Love Poem." In *Bestiary: Poems*, 64. Minneapolis: Graywolf Press, 2016.
———. "Love Poem: Chimera." In *Bestiary: Poems*, 10. Minneapolis: Graywolf Press, 2016.
———. "Out West." In *Bestiary: Poems*, 3. Minneapolis: Graywolf Press, 2016.
———. "Self-Portrait as a Block of Ice." In *Bestiary: Poems*, 14. Minneapolis: Graywolf Press, 2016.
———. "Where She Is Opened. Where She Is Closed." In *Bestiary: Poems*, 9. Minneapolis: Graywolf Press, 2016.
Klay, Phil. "Redeployment." In *Redeployment*, 1–16. Edinburgh: Canongate, 2015.
Kohn, Eduardo. *How Forests Think: Toward an Anthropology Beyond the Human*. Berkeley: University of California Press, 2013.
Kuzniar, Alice A. *Melancholia's Dog: Reflections on Our Animal Kinship*. Chicago: University of Chicago Press, 2006.

La Berge, Leigh Claire. *Marx for Cats: A Radical Bestiary*. Durham, NC: Duke University Press, 2023.

Lawlor, Andrea. *Paul Takes the Form of a Mortal Girl*. London: Picador, 2018.

Leach, Amy. *Things That Are: Encounters with Plants, Stars and Animals*. Edinburgh: Canongate, 2013.

Leong, Diana. "The Mattering of Black Lives: Octavia Butler's Hyperempathy and the Promise of the New Materialisms." *Catalyst: Feminism, Theory, Technoscience* 2, no. 2 (2016): 1–35.

Levine, Caroline. *Forms: Whole, Rhythm, Hierarchy, Network*. Princeton, NJ: Princeton University Press, 2015.

Lillvis, Kristen. *Posthuman Blackness and the Black Female Imagination*. Athens: University of Georgia Press, 2017.

Limón, Ada. "Full Gallop." In *The Carrying*, 70. London: Corsair, 2019.

———. "How to Triumph Like a Girl." In *Bright Dead Things*, 3. Minneapolis: Milkweed Editions, 2015.

Lloyd, Christopher. *Corporeal Legacies in the US South: Memory and Embodiment in Contemporary Culture*. Cham: Palgave Macmillan, 2018.

Lloyd, Christopher, and Jessica Rapson. "'Family Territory' to the 'Circumference of the Earth': Local and Planetary Memories of Climate Change in Barbara Kingsolver's *Flight Behavior*." *Textual Practice* 31, no. 5 (2017): 911–31.

Lucas, Julian. "Danzy Senna Is Amused by Your Mixed Feelings." *The New Yorker*, September 3, 2024. https://www.newyorker.com/culture/persons-of-interest/danzy-senna-is-amused-by-your-mixed-feelings.

Luciano, Dana, and Mel Y. Chen. "Has the Queer Ever Been Human?" *GLQ: A Journal of Lesbian and Gay Studies* 21, no. 2–3 (2015): 183–207.

McBean, Sam. "Bent Out of Shape." *The White Review*, May 2020. https://www.thewhitereview.org/reviews/bent-out-of-shape/.

McCorry, Seán, and John Mills, eds. *Literature and Meat Since 1900*. Cham: Palgrave Macmillan, 2019.

McCulloch, Florence. *Medieval Latin and French Bestiaries*. Chapel Hill: University of North Carolina Pres, 1962.

McFarland, Sarah E. *Ecocollapse Fiction and Cultures of Human Extinction*. London: Bloomsbury, 2021.

McHugh, Susan. *Dog*. London: Reaktion, 2004.

———. "Queer (and) Animal Theories." *GLQ: A Journal of Lesbian and Gay Studies* 15, no. 1 (2009): 153–69.

McKittrick, Katherine. *Dear Science and Other Stories*. Durham, NC: Duke University Press, 2021.

Mirzoeff, Nicholas. "It's Not the Anthropocene, It's the White Supremacy Scene; or, The Geological Color Line." In *After Extinction*, edited by Richard Grusin, 123–49. Minneapolis: University of Minnesota Press, 2018.

Mock, Janet. *Redefining Realness: My Path to Womanhood, Identity, Love, and So Much More*. New York: Atria, 2014.

Moore, Jason W. "The Capitalocene, Part I: On the Nature and Origins of Our Ecological Crisis." *Journal of Peasant Studies* 44, no. 3 (2017): 594–630.

Morrison, Toni. *A Mercy*. London: Chatto & Windus, 2008.

Morton, Timothy. *Ecology Without Nature*. Cambridge, MA: Harvard University Press, 2007.

Müller, Corsin A., Kira Schmitt, Anjuli L. A. Barber, and Ludwig Huber. "Dogs Can Discriminate Emotional Expressions of Human Faces." *Current Biology* 25, no. 5 (2015): 601–5.

Mullins, Matthew. "Counter-Counterstorytelling: Rereading Critical Race Theory in Percival Everett's *Assumption*." *Callaloo* 39, no. 2 (2016): 457–72.

Muñoz, José Esteban. *Cruising Utopia: The Then and There of Queer Futurity*. New York: New York University Press, 2009.

———. *Disidentifications: Queers of Color and the Performance of Politics*. Minneapolis: University of Minnesota Press, 1999.

———. *The Sense of Brown*, edited by Joshua Chambers-Letson and Tavia Nyong'o. Durham, NC: Duke University Press, 2020.

Nagel, Thomas. "What Is It Like to Be a Bat?" *Philosophical Review* 83, no. 4 (1974): 435–50.

Nawroth, Christian, Natalia Albuquerque, Carine Savalli, Marie-Sophie Single, and Alan G. McElligott. "Goats Prefer Positive Human Emotional Facial Expressions." *Royal Society Open Science* 5 (2018): np. http://dx.doi.org/10.1098/rsos.180491.

Neimanis, Astrida. *Bodies of Water: Posthuman Feminist Phenomenology*. London: Bloomsbury, 2017.

Ngai, Sianne. *Ugly Feelings*. Cambridge, MA: Harvard University Press, 2005.

Niittynen, Miranda. "Animal Magic: Sculpting Queer Encounters Through Rogue Taxidermy Art." *Gender Forum: An Internet Journal for Gender Studies* 55 (2015): 14–38.

Nunez, Sigrid. *The Friend*. London: Virago, 2019.

———. *The Vulnerables*. London: Virago, 2024.

Nyman, Jopi. "Horsescapes: Space, Nation, and Human-Horse Relations in Jane Smiley's *Horse Heaven*." In *Creatural Fictions: Human-Animal Relationships in*

Twentieth- and Twenty-First-Century Literature, edited by David Herman, 217–39. Basingstoke: Palgrave Macmillan, 2016.
Nyong'o, Tavia. "Little Monsters: Race, Sovereignty, and Queer Inhumanism in *Beasts of the Southern Wild*." *GLQ: A Journal of Lesbian and Gay Studies* 21, no. 2–3 (2015): 249–72.
O'Key, Dominic. "Extinction in Public: Thinking through the Sixth Mass Extinction, Environmental Humanities, and Extinction Studies." *Environmental Humanities* 15, no. 1 (2023): 168–86.
Orange, Tommy. *There There*. London: Harvill Secker, 2018.
Ortiz, Ricardo. "Queer Latinx Studies and Queer Latinx Literature 'After' Queer Theory, or Thought and Art and Sex After Pulse." In *After Queer Studies: Literature, Theory and Sexuality in the 21st Century*, edited by Teagan Bradway and E. L. McCallum, 52–68. Cambridge: Cambridge University Press, 2019.
Parry, Catherine. *Other Animals in Twenty-First-Century Fiction*. Cham: Palgrave Macmillan, 2017.
Pérez, Hiram. *A Taste for Brown Bodies: Gay Modernity and Cosmopolitan Desire*. New York: New York University Press, 2015.
Peters, Torrey. *Detransition, Baby*. London: Serpent's Tail, 2021.
Pettman, Dominic. *Creaturely Love: How Desire Makes Us More and Less Than Human*. Minneapolis: University of Minnesota Press, 2017.
Pexa, Christopher. "Sovereign Flows and the Obligation of Repayment." *American Literary History* 35, no. 1 (2023): 246–58.
Pico, Tommy. *Nature Poem*. Portland, OR: Tin House, 2017.
Poliquin, Rachel. *The Breathless Zoo: Taxidermy and the Cultures of Longing*. University Park: Pennsylvania State University Press, 2012.
Potts, Annie, ed. *Meat Culture*. Leiden: Brill, 2016.
Puar, Jasbir K. "'I Would Rather Be a Cyborg Than a Goddess': Becoming-Intersectional in Assemblage Theory." *philoSOPHIA* 2, no. 1 (2012): 49–66.
Pugliese, Joseph. *Biopolitics of the More-Than-Human: Forensic Ecologies of Violence*. Durham, NC: Duke University Press, 2020.
Quong, Spencer. "Queerness, Cyborgs, and Cephalopods: An Interview with Franny Choi." *Paris Review*, May 21, 2019, https://www.theparisreview.org/blog/2019/05/21/queerness-cyborgs-and-cephalopods-an-interview-with-franny-choi/.
Reid-Pharr, Robert. *Archives of Flesh: African America, Spain, and Post-Humanist Critique*. New York: New York University Press, 2016.
Roberts, Brian Russell, and Michelle Ann Stephens. "Introduction. Archipelagic American Studies: Decontinentalizing the Study of American Culture." In

Archipelagic American Studies, edited by Brian Russell Roberts and Michelle Ann Stephens, 1–54. Durham, NC: Duke University Press, 2017.
Rodríguez, Juana María. *Sexual Futures, Queer Gestures, and Other Latina Longings*. New York: New York University Press, 2014.
Rohrleitner, Marion Christina. "Refusing the Referendum: Queer Latino Masculinities and Utopian Citizenship in Justin Torres' *We the Animals*." *European Journal of American Studies* 11, no. 3 (2017): 1–13.
Roorda, Eric Paul. "Introduction." In *The Ocean Reader: History, Culture, Politics*, 1–4. Durham, NC: Duke University Press, 2020.
Roughgarden, Joan. *Evolution's Rainbow: Diversity, Gender, and Sexuality in Nature and People*. Berkeley: University of California Press, 2004.
Rudy, Kathy. "LGBTQ . . . Z?" *Hypatia* 27, no. 3 (2012): 601–15.
Ryan, Derek. "Introduction." In *The Cambridge Companion to Literature and Animals*, edited by Derek Ryan, 1–20. Cambridge: Cambridge University Press, 2023.
Saketopoulou, Avgi. *Sexuality Beyond Consent: Risk, Race, Traumatophilia*. New York: New York University Press, 2023.
Saussure, Ferdinand de. *Course in General Linguistics*. Translated by Perry Meisel and Haun Saussy. New York: Columbia University Press, 1983.
Segal, Naomi. *Consensuality: Didier Anzieu, Gender and the Sense of Touch*. Amsterdam: Rodopi, 2009.
Senna, Danzy. "The Land of Beulah." In *You Are Free: Stories*, 35–66. New York: Riverhead, 2011.
Seymour, Nicole. *Strange Natures: Futurity, Empathy, and the Queer Ecological Imagination*. Urbana: University of Illinois Press, 2013.
Sharpe, Christina. *In the Wake: On Blackness and Being*. Durham, NC: Duke University Press, 2016.
Singh, Julietta. *Unthinking Mastery: Dehumanism and Decolonial Entanglements*. Durham, NC: Duke University Press, 2018.
Slicer, Deborah. "Joy." In *Ecofeminism: Feminist Intersections with Other Animals and the Earth*, edited by Carol J. Adams and Lori Gruen, n.p. New York: Bloomsbury, 2014.
Slotkin, Richard. *Regeneration Through Violence: The Mythology of the American Frontier, 1600–1860*. Norman: University of Oklahoma Press, 1973.
Smith, Amy Victoria, Leanne Proops, Kate Grounds, Jennifer Wathan, and Karen McComb. "Functionally Relevant Responses to Human Facial Expressions of Emotion in the Domestic Horse." *Biology Letters* 12 (2016). http://dx.doi.org/10.1098/rsbl.2015.0907
Smith, Danez. "Dogs!" In *Homie*, 18–22. Minneapolis: Graywolf, 2020.

———. "On Faggotness." In *Homie*, 25–29. Minneapolis: Graywolf, 2020.
Smith, J. David, Justin J. Couchman, and Michael J. Beran. "The Highs and Lows of Theoretical Interpretation in Animal-Metacognition Research." *Philosophical Transactions of the Royal Society B* 367, no. 1594 (2012): 1297–1309.
Smith, Zadie. "The *Harper's* Columns." In *Feel Free: Essays*, 251–332. London: Penguin, 2019.
Solnit, Rebecca. *A Field Guide to Getting Lost*. Edinburgh: Canongate, 2006.
Solnit, Rebecca, and Mona Caron. *A California Bestiary*. Berkeley: Heyday, 2010.
Stark, Hannah. "Reckoning with Species Loss in the Anthropocene." In *Extinction and Memorial Culture: Reckoning with Species Loss in the Anthropocene*, edited by Hannah Stark, 1–10. Abingdon: Routledge, 2023.
Steinbock, Eliza, Marianna Szczygielska, and Anthony Wagner. "Thinking Linking." *Angelaki* 22, no. 2 (2017): 1–10.
Stockton, Kathryn Bond. *The Queer Child, or Growing Sideways in the Twentieth Century*. Durham, NC: Duke University Press, 2009.
Stoler, Ann Laura. *Carnal Knowledge and Imperial Power: Race and the Intimate in Colonial Rule*. Berkeley: University of California Press, 2002.
———. "Intimidations of Empire: Predicaments of the Tactile and Unseen." In *Haunted by Empire: Geographies of Intimacy in North American History*, edited by Ann Laura Stoler, 1–22. Durham, NC: Duke University Press, 2006.
Strassberg, Richard E., ed. and trans. *A Chinese Bestiary: Strange Creatures from the Guideways Through Mountains and Seas*. Berkeley: University of California Press, 2002.
Stryker, Susan. "My Words to Victor Frankenstein Above the Village of Chamounix: Performing Transgender Rage." *GLQ: A Journal of Lesbian and Gay Studies* 1, no. 3 (1994): 237–54.
———. "More Words About 'My Words to Victor Frankenstein.'" *GLQ: A Journal of Lesbian and Gay Studies* 25, no. 1 (2019): 39–44.
Sturken, Marita. *Tangled Memories: The Vietnam War, the* AIDS *Epidemic, and the Politics of Remembering*. Berkeley: University of California Press, 1997.
TallBear, Kim. "An Indigenous Reflection on Working Beyond the Human/Not Human." In "Dossier: Theorizing Queer Inhumanisms." *GLQ: A Journal of Lesbian and Gay Studies* 21, nos. 2–3 (2015): 230–35.
Tarver, Erin C. "The Dangerous Individual(s) Dog: Criminality and the 'Pit Bull.'" *Culture, Theory, and Critique* 55, no. 3 (2014): 273–85.
Taylor, Sunaura. *Beasts of Burden: Animal and Disability Liberation*. New York: The New Press, 2017.
Taylor, William Timothy Treal, Pablo Librado, Mila Hunska Tašunke Icu (Chief

Joseph American Horse), et al. "Early Dispersal of Domestic Horses into the Great Plains and Northern Rockies." *Science* 379, no. 6639 (2023): 1316–23.

Tompkins, Jane. *West of Everything: The Inner Life of Westerns*. Oxford: Oxford University Press, 1992.

Torres, Justin. *We the Animals*. London: Granta, 2011.

Traisnel, Antoine. *Capture: American Pursuits and the Making of a New Animal Condition*. Minneapolis: University of Minnesota Press, 2020.

Turner, Alexis. *Taxidermy*. London: Thames and Hudson, 2013.

Turner, Lynn, Undine Sellbach, and Ron Broglio, eds. *The Edinburgh Companion to Animal Studies*. Edinburgh: Edinburgh University Press, 2019.

Tyler, Tom. *Ciferae: A Bestiary in Five Fingers*. Minneapolis: University of Minnesota Press, 2012.

van Dooren, Thom. *Flight Ways: Life and Loss at the Edge of Extinction*. New York: Columbia University Press, 2014.

VanderMeer, Jeff. *Hummingbird Salamander*. London: 4th Estate, 2022.

Vann, David. *Goat Mountain*. London: Windmill, 2014.

Voigt, Ellen Bryant. "Groundhog." *The New Yorker*, February 14, 2011. https://www.newyorker.com/magazine/2011/02/14/groundhog.

Vuong, Ocean. "My Father Writes from Prison." In *Night Sky with Exit Wounds*, 18. London: Jonathan Cape, 2017.

———. *On Earth We're Briefly Gorgeous*. London: Jonathan Cape, 2019.

Wakeham, Pauline. *Taxidermic Signs: Reconstructing Aboriginality*. Minneapolis: University of Minnesota Press, 2008.

Walker, Elaine. *Horse*. London: Reaktion, 2008.

Weheliye, Alexander G. *Habeas Viscus: Racializing Assemblages, Biopolitics, and Black Feminist Theories of the Human*. Durham, NC: Duke University Press, 2014.

Weil, Kari. *Thinking Animals: Why Animal Studies Now*. New York: Columbia University Press, 2012.

Weinstein, Jami, and Claire Colebrook. "Introduction: Critical Life Studies and the Problems of Inhuman Rites and Posthumous Life." In *Posthumous Life: Theorizing Beyond the Posthuman*, edited by Jami Weinstein and Claire Colebrook, 1–14. New York: Columbia University Press, 2017.

Weston, Kath. *Families We Choose: Lesbians, Gays, Kinship*. New York: Columbia University Press, 1991.

Wiegman, Robyn, and Elizabeth A. Wilson. "Introduction: Antinormativity's Queer Conventions." *differences: A Journal of Feminist Cultural Studies* 26, no. 1 (2015): 1–25.

Wohlleben, Peter. *The Hidden Life of Trees: What They Feel, How They Communicate.* Glasgow: William Collins, 2017.

Wolk, Martin. "When Everything Changed: Novelist Ocean Vuong Reflets on a Year of Intense Highs and Lows." *Los Angeles Times*, January 8, 2020. https://www.latimes.com/entertainment-arts/books/story/2020-01-08/ocean-vuong-on-earth-were-briefly-gorgeous.

Wolfe, Cary. *Animal Rites: American Culture, the Discourse of Species, and Posthumanist Theory.* Chicago: University of Chicago Press, 2002.

———. *What Is Posthumanism?* Minneapolis: University of Minnesota Press, 2009.

Wortham, J., and Wesley Morris, hosts. "Frosted Flakes." *Still Processing* (podcast). April 9, 2020. https://www.nytimes.com/2020/04/09/podcasts/still-processing-tiger-king.html.

Wynter, Sylvia. "Unsettling the Coloniality of Being/Power/Truth/Freedom: Towards the Human, After Man, Its Overrepresentation—An Argument." *CR: The New Centennial Review* 2, no. 3 (2003): 257–337.

Young, Kevin, and Kaveh Akbar. "Kaveh Akbar Reads Ellen Bryant Voigt." *The New Yorker Poetry Podcast*, October 17, 2018. https://www.newyorker.com/podcast/poetry/kaveh-akbar-reads-ellen-bryant-voigt.

Zhang, C. Pam. *Land of Milk and Honey*. London: Hutchinson Heinemann, 2023.

Index

www.ingramcontent.com/pod-product-compliance
Lightning Source LLC
LaVergne TN
LVHW090722291026
851245LV00035B/319

* 9 7 8 0 8 2 0 3 8 0 5 1 3 *